Pragmatic Idealism
Canadian Foreign Policy, 1945–1995

Providing an overview of Canada's role in international affairs in the post-war era, *Pragmatic Idealism* dispels some of the myths surrounding Canadian foreign policy and celebrates the distinctiveness and distinction of Canada's place in world politics. Costas Melakopides finds an impressive continuity underlying Canadian foreign policy since 1945 and argues that it stems from the sustained pursuit of a coherent set of foreign policy ends and means.

Melakopides defines Canadian internationalism as "pragmatic idealism," a balanced synthesis of idealism and pragmatism, and demonstrates concretely how it reflects the principles, interests, and values of the country's mainstream political culture. Focusing on Canada's record in the areas of peacekeeping and peacemaking, arms control and disarmament, foreign development assistance, human rights, and ecological concerns, Melakopides reveals that at the heart of Canadian foreign policy are the concepts and the practice of moderation, communication, mediation, cooperation, caring, and sharing.

Pragmatic Idealism is an inspiring challenge to the assumption that all foreign policy is premised on *realpolitik*. Students, scholars, and practitioners of Canadian foreign policy as well as historians, Canadianists, members of NGOs, and interested members of the general public will find it an engaging and enlightening experience.

COSTAS MELAKOPIDES taught in Canada for many years and is now assistant professor of social and political studies, University of Cyprus.

Pragmatic Idealism

Canadian Foreign Policy, 1945–1995

COSTAS MELAKOPIDES

McGill-Queen's University Press
Montreal & Kingston · London · Buffalo

© McGill-Queen's University Press 1998
ISBN 0-7735-1722-7
Legal deposit second quarter 1998
Bibliothèque nationale du Québec

Printed in Canada on acid-free paper

McGill-Queen's University Press acknowledges the support of the Canada
Council of the Arts for its publishing program.

Canadian Cataloguing in Publication Data

Melakopides, Costas
   Pragmatic idealism: Canadian foreign policy, 1945–1995
   Includes bibliographical references and index.
   ISBN 0-7735-1722-7
   1. Canada – Foreign relations – 1945–   I. Title.
   FC602.M44 1998   971.064   C98-900157-1
   F1034.2.M44 1998

This book was typeset by Typo Litho Composition Inc.
in 10/12 Baskerville.

Contents

Preface   vii

PART ONE

1 Introduction   3

2 Analysing Foreign Policy   19

PART TWO

3 The Golden Age, 1945–1957   37

4 Diefenbaker's Internationalism, 1957–1963   52

5 Lester B. Pearson as Prime Minister, 1963–1968   66

6 The Logic and Ethics of Trudeauvian Internationalism, 1968–1984   87

7 Mulroney's Constructive Internationalism, 1984–1993   128

8 The 1993 Liberal Comeback: A Preliminary Sketch   164

PART THREE

9 Conclusion: Retrospect and Prospects   191

Notes   201

Bibliography   225

Index   235

Preface

When I began teaching Canadian foreign policy at the University of Manitoba in 1986, I was dismayed to discover the dearth of studies appreciating the distinctness and distinction of Canada's place in the world. Equally disturbing were the interpretive distortions perpetrated against this foreign policy by many cynical critics' transparent biases. If, then, I could account for their fallacies and also demonstrate the multi-layered grounds for Canada's enormous international prestige, there was a book to be written.

Besides reminding readers of the fifty years of Canada's creative role in the world, this book has some ambitious goals: to rehabilitate a re-defined conception of "idealism" so that it might acquire, once again, a good name; to defuse some mean-spirited mythologies surrounding Canadian foreign policy; to explicate Canadian internationalism as "pragmatic idealism" and articulate its values; to show the impressive continuity of its principled style and substance; and to emphasize the good news about Canada's place in the world. By implication, a two-fold bonus may accrue. By celebrating Canada's stubborn (and civil) pursuit of its internationalist values, it can be demonstrated that the narrowness of "political realism" should be put on the defensive. Moreover, after reliving the story of Canada's sophisticated role in the postwar world, Quebeckers may contemplate anew both their crucial contribution to Canada's outstanding international performance and what they risk losing should the sovereignists succeed in forcing French Canada to start as a foreign policy *tabula rasa*.

During the four-year adventurous writing of the present work, I accumulated rich intellectual and emotional pleasures that can only be intimated here. An earlier version was supported by a generous grant from the Canadian Institute of International Peace and Security, and its gracious research director, Roger Hill, to whom I express my deep appreciation. In a totally different sense, I am still thankful to my former colleagues at the University of Manitoba in Winnipeg, for they stimulated me enormously by their dogged refusal to contemplate that there may be life beyond Cold War militarism and crypto-cynical "realism." Then, at Queen's University and the Royal Military College of Canada between 1994 and 1996, a number of students, colleagues, and friends helped strengthen my "normative interpretation" of Canada's international performance. Most of them nurtured my affection for this country's foreign relations; others succeeded in containing some of my hyphenated-Canadian enthusiasm. For support and advice I wish particularly to thank David Haglund, Phil Goldman, Jack Grove, Charles Pentland, Joel Sokolsky, Phil Wood, and John D. Young. Antonio Francheschet and Roger Martin sustained this project unfailingly. And the two anonymous referees of McGill-Queen's University Press convinced me to produce some more fastidious (if not tedious) conceptual analysis of pragmatic idealism.

While this book is dedicated to my mother and brother in Athens and my other brother in Quebec City, I recognize with deep affection my friends and colleagues of twenty-three years in Winnipeg, Ottawa, and Kingston and acknowledge the new-found stimulation with my first (1996–97) students at the University of Cyprus.

PART ONE

1 Introduction

If, as the great Canadian diplomat and wit, John Holmes, put it, "Canadians are perversely loath to face up to any good news,"[1] this monograph may surprise some Canadians. For, among other things, it aims to show why, from 1945 to 1995, Canada has been an enlightened and distinguished member of the international community, and why its corresponding reputation is, therefore, fully justified.

Chapters 3 to 8 will survey the historical record to demonstrate this ultimate thesis. To this end, it is necessary to offer some conceptual and methodological clarifications. For we must revise and refine some essentially contested and opaque analytic terms, in order to organize and interpret the empirical record anew. Terms such as idealism, internationalism, pragmatism, and multilateralism must be clarified for at least two reasons: to unburden them from obscure denotations and misleading connotations; and to establish the precise meaning of "Canadian internationalism."

As a result of this conceptual unfolding and empirical review, this book will defend a number of principal theses. First, post-Second World War Canadian foreign policy has been marked by impressive consistency, in both style and substance. This consistency resulted from the conscious and sustained pursuit of a coherent set of foreign policy ends and means. This foreign policy is best designated as Canadian internationalism, which should be understood as a balanced synthesis of idealism and pragmatism or as pragmatic idealism.

Second, Canadian internationalism reflects the principles, interests, and values of the country's mainstream political culture. At the heart of this political culture are the concepts and the practice of moderation, communication, mediation, cooperation, caring, and sharing.

Third, these domestic interests and values have been projected on the international scene, beginning with the 1945 San Francisco Conference, in pursuit of the simultaneous betterment of Canada, of the international community, and of Canada's place in the world.

Fourth, Canada's international distinction and prestige have been derived particularly from the pragmatic idealism of what I shall call "the internationalist agenda." This agenda covers primarily the following areas: peacekeeping and peacemaking; arms control and disarmament; human rights; ecological concerns; and foreign development assistance.

Fifth, Canadian foreign policy may, therefore, provide an indirect but compelling answer to the perennial question of Canada's "identity." For if Canada is perceived by non-Canadians as one of the most honourable, enlightened, and civilized international actors, which comes mainly from the record and the motives of Canadian foreign policy, we may indeed endorse this perception as objective and even true.

Finally, this work hopes to demonstrate, if only by implication, that the style and the substance of post-1945 Canadian foreign policy – that is, Canada's pragmatic idealism – constitute a theoretical and a tangible challenge to the monolithic assumption that all foreign policy is exclusively premised on *realpolitik* considerations. In other words, Canada has shown the world that there is a coherent and effective worldview which other states can follow to make the world more civilized.

There is widespread academic consensus that the architects and early practitioners of what is described as the golden age of Canadian foreign policy, from 1945 to 1957, adopted, and often celebrated, a special brand of internationalism. There is even grudging acknowledgment that the internationalism of Louis St Laurent, Lester B. Pearson, John Holmes, Escott Reid, Dana Wilgress, and a host of others often exhibited idealistic premises. What has been resisted to date is that Canadian foreign policy, during the entire postwar period, has been marked by an intriguing continuity. The present book attempts to demonstrate this continuity and to identify its principal reasons and causes. Moreover, it will show that the overall coherence of Canadian internationalism can only be explained by its creative and flexible synthesis of idealism and pragmatism.[2]

THE CENTRAL CONCEPTS

The *idealist* component of post-1945 Canadian foreign policy reflects the endorsement by its makers and practitioners of a set of interests conditioned by humane values. Central among these values are the primacy of justice; the satisfaction of global or human needs; the existence of duties beyond our borders (which follows from the "moral insignificance" of borders); respect for universal human rights; and the importance of moderation, communication, generosity, and cooperation in international affairs. Most of these values are currently designated "cosmopolitan."[3]

The *pragmatic* dimension of Canadian internationalism has also shaped the character of these values and their harmonization with Canada's special interests. A major goal of Canadian foreign policy since 1945 has been to satisfy Canada's interests in the context of broader interests. Thus, the pragmatic – that is, flexible, adaptable, and workable – pursuit of Canada's interests and cosmopolitan values should suffice to show that Canadian internationalism exhibited neither romantic naïveté nor groundless utopianism.[4] By the same token, Canada's pragmatic idealism helps distinguish Canadian foreign policy from that of most states.

Pragmatic idealism, then, captures the normative core of Canada's worldview as it informed the shaping of its post-1945 foreign policy motives, goals, and actions. Canadian *multilateralism*, in turn, represents Ottawa's primary method for the satisfaction of its foreign policy objectives. Our use of multilateralism will transcend the popular formalistic definition as "the practice of co-ordinating national policies in groups of three or more states, through ad hoc arrangements or by means of institutions."[5] The hypothesis to be tested in this book is that Canadian multilateralism has been premised on enlightened self-interest simultaneously pursuing the satisfaction of international and even human interests.[6] This conception, as founded by Louis St Laurent and Lester Pearson, has therefore combined pragmatic and idealistic elements.

Thus Canadian internationalism, with its associated multilateralism, distinguishes the style and substance of Canada's foreign policy from the policies of superpowers and great powers. The latter have generally implemented a "realist" conception of their role in the world. Such a conception typically rests on the notions of power-maximization, state-centricity, ethno-centricity, and military security. Indeed, its implied fixation on the "national interest" arguably results in its "ethical poverty," since realism has certainly allowed hardly any space for cosmopolitan values.[7] Therefore, Canadian internationalism must be distinguished from realism.[8] It also follows that Canadian multilateralism is also distinct from the kind of multilateralism pursued by many states for self-regarding or ethnocentric reasons.

In other words, a decisive goal of the present work is to substantiate empirically the conceptual portrait of Canadian internationalism as pragmatic idealism. Methodologically, this clearly necessitates the identification of its normative content – that is, its explicit and underlying values. Moreover, it is important to demonstrate that these values were not pursued by the makers of Canadian foreign policy in an accidental, impressionistic, or ad hoc manner. To this end, in addition to the rich empirical record of the authentic implementation of Canada's pragmatic idealism, it is crucial to show the nature of the sustained and consistent declaration of these values by the Canadian foreign policymakers. This, then, explains this book's heavy reliance on relevant official statements and declarations. Such "verbal actions" constitute a neglected but integral part of Canadian foreign policy. They form the best criterion whereby the consistency of statements is gauged and the coherence of words and deeds is judged.

EARLY DECLARATIONS OF CANADIAN INTERNATIONALISM

Programmatic declarations of the Canadian internationalist framework and the creation of a corresponding lexicon began by the mid-1940s. During a July 1943 speech in the House of Commons, Prime Minister Mackenzie King described Canada's position as a world power as deriving from more than political or material grounds: "It has arisen, I believe, from our recognition of the needs of humanity."[9] Four years later, External Affairs Minister Louis St Laurent authoritatively established what amounted to Ottawa's pragmatic idealism. In his January 1947 Gray Lecture at the University of Toronto, St Laurent reiterated Canada's preparedness "to fulfill the growing responsibilities in world affairs which we have accepted as a modern state," and referred to the United Nations as the primary multilateral forum where these responsibilities would be fulfilled. He explained: "No foreign policy is consistent nor coherent over a period of years unless it is based upon some conception of human values." In Canada's case,

we are continually influenced by the conceptions of good and evil which emerged from Hebrew and Greek civilization and which have been transformed and transmitted through the Christian traditions of the Western World. These are values which lay emphasis on the importance of the individual, on the place of moral principles in the conduct of human relations, on standards of judgment which transcend mere material well-being.[10]

While Canada was to "protect and nurture" these values in world affairs, the pragmatic interests of Canadian internationalism were also stated explicitly. St Laurent observed that "economic revival is a matter of great importance for us"; that Canada is dependent on external markets and supplies of commodities from abroad; and that it becomes "axiomatic, therefore, that we should give our support to every international organization which contributes to the economic and political stability of the world." He added that Canada's geography, climate, and natural resources have conditioned its economy so that "the continued prosperity and well-being of our own people can best be served by the prosperity and well-being of the whole world." Then, capturing succinctly the idealist dimension of Canadian internationalism, St Laurent concluded: "We have thus a useful part to play in world affairs, useful to ourselves through being useful to others."[11]

That the Gray Lecture was no improvisation on the principles of postwar Canadian foreign policy was demonstrated a year later by Lester Pearson. In his January 1948 speech to the Vancouver branch of the Canadian Institute of International Affairs, Pearson reaffirmed Ottawa's pragmatic-idealist worldview. He noted that Canada's "modesty" or "timidity" should not be confused with isolationism; that this timidity is "a sensible recognition of the fact that middle powers ... can now merely expand their responsibilities and their worries"; that it is also "a recognition of the internationalist view that countries must come closer together inside a United Nations rather than take over areas and responsibilities outside it." Pearson added:

We can most effectively influence international affairs not by aggressive nationalism but by earning the respect of the nations with whom we cooperate, and who will therefore be glad to discuss their international policies with us. This principle is based on both political and economic considerations. We instinctively know that Canada cannot easily secure and maintain prosperity except on the broadest basis of multilateralism – which is another name for internationalism.[12]

It already transpires that the earlier principles of Canadian foreign policy qualify as both idealistic and pragmatic. It will be incumbent on this book to show how these principles were in fact implemented in the real world of international relations from 1945 to 1995. What we may demonstrate now is that similar statements on Canada's interests and values have been articulated consistently by Canadian policymakers and practitioners since the golden age. Such consistency is most remarkable for any country's foreign policy over a fifty-year period. Of course, this consistency also creates the standard whereby the actual implementation of the declared principles will have to be judged.

OTHER AUTHORITATIVE VOICES OF CANADIAN INTERNATIONALISM

Paul Martin, Sr, Lester Pearson's minister of external affairs, spoke on the principles of Canadian foreign policy at the University of Waterloo in May 1967. His formulation was almost indistinguishable from that of St Laurent in 1947. This is because, for Martin, Canada's foreign policy goals comprised national security, national unity, political liberty and social justice, the rule of law in national and international affairs, economic development in Canada and the world, the values of Christian civilization, and "acceptance of international responsibility in accordance with our interest, and our ability to contribute towards the building of peace."[13] Therefore, the internationalist motives and objectives of the golden age were faithfully echoed twenty years after the Gray Lecture by the Liberal government of Lester Pearson.

The 1970 white paper, *Foreign Policy for Canadians*, presented the results of the Trudeau government's 1969–70 foreign policy review. The document's list of six policy themes exhibited a remarkable similarity with those of the golden age and of Paul Martin. They were economic growth, sovereignty and independence, peace and security, social justice, enhancement of the quality of life, and a harmonious natural environment. The pragmatic component was clearly apparent in this formulation of the principal ingredients of Canadian foreign policy, primarily by the acknowledgment of various constraints and availability of resources. The idealist dimension was also demonstrably present. To take some typical illustrations: when it referred to the promotion of social justice, the white paper explained that it meant

focusing attention on two major international issues – race conflict and development assistance. It is also related to international efforts: to develop international law, standards and codes of conduct; and to keep in effective working order a wide variety of international organizations – e.g., the UN Development Programme (UNDP), the UN Conference on Trade and Development (UNCTAD), the International Development Association (IDA), the Development Assistance Committee (DAC).[14]

In discussing foreign aid, the document gave pride of place to Canada's values. Noting that our obligation towards the poor of the world originates in "the Greco-Judeo-Christian ethic," it stated: "It was in large measure an extension of this sense of social obligation and justice to the people in the less-fortunate countries that helped provide public support for the transfer of large amounts of Canadian resources to those countries in the post-war period." The awareness of world poverty could not leave unaffected Canadian society "in which concern for the welfare of others is one of the central values."[15] Moreover, "A society able to ignore poverty abroad will find it much easier to ignore it at home; a society concerned about poverty and development abroad will be concerned about poverty and development at home."

Thus, reiterating the Pearsonian theme that foreign policy "is merely 'domestic policy with its hat on'," [16] *Foreign Policy for Canadians* added: "We could not create a truly just society within Canada if we were not prepared to play our part in the creation of a more just world society. Thus our foreign policy in this field becomes a continuation of our domestic policy." [17]

Finally, as regards enhancing the quality of life, the 1970 review argued that, beyond producing a "richer life and human fulfilment for all Canadians," the relevant policies "are designed to yield a rewarding life for all Canadians and to reflect clearly Canada's bilingual and multicultural character. Part of the reward lies in the satisfaction that Canada in its external activities is making a worthwhile contribution to human betterment." [18]

The sophisticated idealism of Pierre Trudeau's worldview will be demonstrated when we discuss its influence on his governments' policies, especially as they pertained to global environmental issues, arms control and disarmament, peacemaking, nuclear non-proliferation, and foreign development assistance. Here it is certainly noteworthy that Trudeau perceived Canada as a "mentor state," capable of being a model to the world. He repeatedly referred to the need for a "global ethic." [19] And he was perfectly comfortable when uttering such quintessentially idealist propositions, as "we are all brothers," or "we are one on this earth." [20]

Trudeau, however, could also articulate the pragmatic idealism of Canadian foreign policy. In his May 1968 speech in Edmonton, he captured succinctly Canada's principal reasons for helping the Third World: humanitarian considerations, the notion borrowed from Pope Paul VI that "the new name for peace is development," and the tangible benefits to accrue to Canada itself. [21] The pragmatic idealism of this triptych – which I shall call Trudeau's synthesis – will emerge in this book as a key to understanding the central motives and objectives of Canadian foreign policy. These three principles serve to refine the meaning of Canadian internationalism as occupying a clear space distinct from narrow-spirited realism and utopian idealism.

Despite some contrary appearances and a few exceptions, the Mulroney government's own foreign policy review essentially endorsed the established parameters of Canada's pragmatic idealism. In 1986 the Report of the Special Joint Committee of the Senate and House of Commons (*Independence and Internationalism*), and the subsequent response by Joe Clark's Department of External Affairs, concluded that "Canada has a great deal to gain from a posture of confident idealism than from one that is mean-spirited and ungenerous to the world at large." [22]

To be sure, the Mulroney government opted at the outset for a far greater emphasis on the pragmatic component in some of its policies. The progressive harmonization of Ottawa's security and economic thinking with that of the American administrations of Ronald Reagan and George Bush entailed the cultivation of continentalism in these two fields. And yet, fully aware of the demands and expectations of Canadians, and tutored in the traditions of Pearsonian internationalism, Brian Mulroney and Joe Clark demonstrated repeatedly Canada's internationalist distinctness. For instance, to explain the principled and sustained Mulroney–Clark campaign against South Africa's apartheid, Bernard Wood detected, as the key motivators in Ottawa's policy, "the projection of Canadian values rather than the protection of narrow foreign policy interest." Noting the early Mulroney government's "quintessentially Pearsonian approach of 'constructive internationalism'," Wood concluded that "it was clear from the outset that the key members of the new government adopted a Pearsonian approach of problem-solving idealism." For Bernard Wood, this was because they had "grown up under the influence of the golden age of Canadian foreign policy under Pearson and his colleagues."[23]

Similarly, the Canadian government was among the first to welcome the demise of the Cold War. An eloquent statement to this effect was contained in Joe Clark's early endorsement of the concept of "cooperative" or "common" security. As he put it in his speech to the UN General Assembly on 26 September 1990:

Security has ceased to be something to be achieved unilaterally. Security has ceased to be something to be attained through military means alone. Security has become cooperative.

In a world where poverty and underdevelopment plague most of the planet, the developed world cannot pretend to be secure simply because it alone is prosperous. In an era of nuclear and chemical weapons, of ballistic missiles, of terrorism, of interdependent markets and economies, of diseases, the development of prosperity throughout the world is not a question of charity but of security.[24]

Pragmatic idealism was also detectable in the statements of Clark's successor at External Affairs, Barbara McDougall. For instance, her 10 December 1991 speech in Toronto was marked by internationalist enthusiasm: "Has Canada made a difference? Of course we have!" Among the reasons why, Ms McDougall noted that "Canada has always believed that a stable, peaceful world, based on fundamental human values, is in its own best interests. Our efforts to encourage international acceptance of moderation, tolerance, and the rule of law are

rooted in our own domestic traditions." Adopting the distinct language of Canadian internationalism, where "values" happily coexist
with "interests," McDougall added: "Our pursuit of political and economic security through multilateral systems based upon recognized
rules is not simply self-serving. Canadians are convinced that a world
so forged will also be to the advantage of the broader international
community."

After noting that our "skills and success at war made us believers in
peace," McDougall argued that it was the postwar policymakers of the
golden age who "recognized that, in spite of our momentary power, we
were neither by size nor by leaning a great military nation." Hence
Canada adopted "a greater collective commitment" to assure its own
defence and "to help preserve peace elsewhere ... In the postwar
period, we quickly earned an envied reputation as a nation of peacekeepers. In so doing we were extending the values on which we had
built our own country into the international arena."[25]

Once again, therefore, even the committed neo-conservatives of the
Mulroney era – and despite the protracted deep recession of the early
1990s – endorsed the distinct language of post-1945 Canadian internationalism. As we will also show, they implemented in great measure the
corresponding interests and values in the foreign policy domain that I
propose to label "the internationalist agenda." This agenda includes
primarily peacekeeping, arms control and disarmament, human rights,
ecological concerns, and foreign development assistance.[26]

We finally turn to the Chrétien government's 1994–5 foreign policy
review. Although the pragmatic component permeates it, Canada's
cosmopolitan values are also ever-present. As page 1 of the parliamentary committee's report put it:

Foreign policy matters to Canadians. They have deep-rooted values that they
carry over into the role they want Canada to play – nurturing dialogue and
compromise; promoting democracy, human rights, economic and social justice; caring for the environment; safeguarding peace; and easing poverty. And
they can offer corresponding skills – mediating disputes; counselling good
governance in a diverse society; helping the less fortunate; and peacekeeping.

Throughout our hearings we were struck by the moral convictions and idealism of the Canadians who testified ... They want to make the world a better
place.[27]

The February 1995 government statement, *Canada in the World*, was
moderate, cautious, and overly pragmatic. It recognized repeatedly
Canada's values; it referred to its "history as a non-colonizing power,
champion of constructive multilateralism and effective international

mediator"; and it promised the "projection of Canadian values and culture."[28] According to the statement, "The Government has listened carefully to Canadians over the past year for their views on the directions we should collectively pursue." Moreover, the Canadian people's "views and priorities, in all their diversity, inform the directions outlined in this Statement." The first message conveyed to Ottawa was that "they want to remain actively involved in the world." The third message was that "they understand the importance in their daily life of our success in the world." And the second message received by the federal government was that "Canadians are confident in their values and in the contribution these values make to the international community." Overwhelmingly, these Canadian values are the cosmopolitan or idealist ones that have shaped the entire record of post-1945 Canadian foreign policy:

Our principles and values – our culture – are rooted in a commitment to tolerance; to democracy, equity and human rights; to the peaceful resolution of differences; to the opportunities and challenges of the marketplace; to social justice; to sustainable development; and to easing poverty. Canadians wish these values reflected and advanced internationally.[29]

The statement, however, also harped on risks, costs, and financial constraints. Of course, in addition to the profound fluidity characterizing the post-Cold War international environment, one should also keep in mind the domestic Canadian climate at the time. After all, the country was dealing with the legacy of the protracted recession, high unemployment, disconcertingly large deficits and debts, and fears of disunity. In such a context, the pragmatic tone of Ottawa's February 1995 statement may appear understandable.

As regards the declaratory level, then, Canadian decision-makers and practitioners have consistently endorsed Canadian internationalism for the last fifty years. What they have professed will form the framework for our analysis. Moreover, as part two of this book will try to show, there is compelling evidence to confirm the following propositions:

1 Ottawa's official statements have been implemented by Canada's principal foreign policy decisions and actions; indeed, there has been remarkable coherence between Canada's rhetoric and its international deeds.
2 There has been notable harmony between Canadian decisions and intended results. This harmony, then, encouraged the propagation of more of the same.

3 The Canadian public has generally supported the interests and values of Canadian internationalism; in fact, these interests and values have been at the heart of Canada's traditional or mainstream political culture.
4 Successive Canadian governments have seen the need to strengthen the patterns and traditions of Canadian internationalism, given the tangible domestic benefits accruing from the corresponding policies.
5 The evidence is compelling that Canadian internationalism has enjoyed widespread international recognition and respect.

In any event, the officially reiterated worldview of Canadian internationalism deserves to form the standard by which Canada's motives, decisions, actions, and results should be assessed. In other words, the analytic framework used in this book corresponds to the professed self-definition of Canadian foreign policy. Accordingly, by Canadian internationalism we shall understand Canada's post-1945 activist involvement in world affairs, as a self-proclaimed middle power, favouring multilateral forums, advocating communication, cooperation, moderation, mediation, generosity, and justice, and pursuing the broad ends of a more rational, developed, just, ecologically responsible, and peaceful world, in the interests of Canada itself and of the world at large. This style and substance of Canadian internationalism is what I propose to understand as the synthesis of pragmatism and idealism.

As for the policy range where Canada's pragmatic idealism was implemented, it will be shown that it affected profoundly even the hard-nosed areas of security and defence. Thus, Canadian internationalism conditioned Ottawa's conception of, and stance on, the character of the North Atlantic Treaty Organization; the nature and depth of the Soviet threat; the employment of communication, bridge-building, and moderate rhetoric as necessary conditions in the handling of East-West relations during the Cold War; the level of Canada's military expenditures; the paramountcy of detente over mere deterrence; and the need for authentic negotiations on arms control and disarmament.

More familiar, of course, are Canada's goals and results in the following areas: peacekeeping and peacemaking; multilateral cooperation, primarily under United Nations auspices, but also in NATO, the Conference on Security and Cooperation in Europe, the Commonwealth, and la Francophonie; human rights; ecological concerns; opposition to racism and oppression; and foreign development assistance. In all these fields, Canadian foreign policy has clearly exhibited a consistently honourable record. It is certainly true that other countries have exhibited international policies akin to Canada's. But our study will show that the foreign policies of countries such as Denmark, the Netherlands, Norway, Sweden, Australia, and New Zealand have demonstrated neither the range nor the depth of commitment which have distinguished Canadian internationalism. It is therefore intriguing that, whereas the world has recognized and applauded Canada's internationalist performance, Canadian scholars and the public at large have shied away from such an appreciation. This is especially paradoxical because, for a country that appears perennially sensitive about its identity, Canadian foreign policy seems, in fact, to contain the most promising answer. If a country's identity hinges on the perceptions of others, Canada's identity could best be captured by the way it is seen, and the reasons it is so seen, by the world.

CANADIAN REALISTS AND NATIONALISTS

One major cause for many scholars' reticence to acknowledge Canada's internationalism as a form of pragmatic idealism derives from the post-Second World War academic hegemony of "realism." Trained in the axioms, aphorisms, and interests of the realist worldview, such scholars imported to the study of Canadian foreign policy the theoretical biases and methodological preferences present in the analysis of the foreign policies of great powers and superpowers. Kim Nossal's *The Politics of Canadian Foreign Policy* exemplifies this phenomenon. It contains a powerful and sophisticated analysis of Canadian foreign policy-making from a perspective which is decidedly "power"-centred. It also gives primacy to the "external parameters" of decision-making (where US-Canadian relations and security considerations predominate), and minimizes the internationalist agenda. Therefore, although Nossal at times admits an internationalist undercurrent in some aspects of Ottawa's post-1945 foreign policy, his adoption – tacitly, but clearly – of the realist framework explains his ultimate rejection of the internationalist orientation of Canada's interests and values.[30]

A valiant attempt by David Dewitt and John Kirton to avoid treating Canada as an internationalist middle power was made in their 1983 book, *Canada as a Principal Power.* They conceived of Canada in essentially realist terms, as a top-tier nation possessing corresponding capabilities, interests, and status. The authors admitted partial validity and temporal applicability to the competing approaches of internationalism and economic nationalism, but they concluded by advocating a "complex neorealist" perspective. To sustain their interpretation, Dewitt and Kirton stressed Canada's assertive pursuit of its national interest; they argued for the country's power-related leading status in the world; they downplayed Ottawa's multilateral commitments after 1957 (including the United Nations); and they minimized Canada's internationalist agenda, choosing as their case studies Ottawa's policies on immigration, energy, space, and the Middle East.

Different grounds for denying the ends and means of Canadian internationalism have been propounded by the variegated school of Canadian nationalism. Whether economic, cultural, or both, such nationalist analyses have conceived of Canada as a satellite of the United States. For them, what distinguishes Canadian foreign policy is its quasi-servile style and substance which derive from the manifold and suffocating American penetration of Canada's economy, society, and culture. Consequently, Ottawa's defence and foreign policy autonomy is nearly lost. It follows, for them, that Canadian internationalism is essentially stifled, since Ottawa, as Washington's "choreboy," either has little room for independent manoeuvre or executes, in the final analysis, American wishes.[31]

Needless to say, there are valuable insights in the work of both sophisticated realists and subtle economic nationalists. However, as our historical survey will suggest, neither approach is ultimately tenable, since they both fail to do justice to the consistent internationalist motives and the abundant internationalist record of post-1945 Canadian foreign policy. Therefore, it is a major thesis of this book that Canadian internationalism as pragmatic idealism is flexible enough to accommodate moderate suggestions of the other two perspectives, whereas they could not retain both their premises and those of internationalism without risk of self-contradiction.

EARLIER INTERNATIONALIST WORK

Elaborate analyses of Canadian internationalism (generally understood as "liberal internationalism") are few and far between. Michael Tucker's *Canadian Foreign Policy* (1980) is an important study of aspects of Trudeauvian internationalism from 1968 until 1979. However, by not covering the foreign policy of Trudeau's last four years in power, and by not elaborating on the crucial issues of peacekeeping, peacemaking, mediation, ecological concerns, human rights, and foreign aid, Tucker's quasi-anthology of case studies could not provide more holistic answers on the nature and distinctness of the entire post-1945 Canadian international performance.

Peter Dobell's *Canada's Search for New Roles* (1972) was most significant for its insights on Canada's "idealist impulse" and the thesis that Canadian internationalism may be Canada's best road to "independence." But this book, just as Thomson and Swanson's *Canadian Foreign Policy* (1971), was written primarily in order to examine the nature, context, and goals of the 1969–70 Trudeau foreign policy review. Both books, however, have been valuable for their empirical richness and their valid observations on pre-1970 Canadian foreign policy patterns. The same should be said about Peyton Lyon and Brian Tomlin's important work, *Canada as an International Actor*, which was also published before the completion of the Trudeau foreign policy agenda. The present book will frequently draw on and appeal to all these authors.

Another important contribution which endorsed, but did not expand on, the internationalist nature of Trudeau's foreign relations is Tom Axworthy's elegant and persuasive portrait of Trudeau's liberal internationalist worldview in his introduction to *Lifting the Shadow of War*, as well as his chapter on Trudeau's foreign policy record in *Towards a Just Society* (1990).[32] Recently Cranford Pratt has produced sophisticated critiques of Canada's "humane internationalism" and some analysis of the concept itself.[33] Given the importance of Pratt's recent work, we will return to him repeatedly, albeit at times critically. We should also recognize the study of the multilateralist tradition of Canada's post-1945 foreign policy in Tom Keating's *Canada and World Order* (1993) for its sustained empirical demonstration and its critical caution. It does, however, examine exclusively the traditional dimensions of security and political economy, and it does not embark on an investigation of the normative component of Canadian multilateralism. Finally, scattered articles in journals as well as memoirs and biographies have endorsed aspects of Canadian internationalism as traditionally understood.[34]

This book, then, is indebted to some earlier internationalist (and crypto-internationalist) works. For the reasons suggested, however, much remained to be done. The dearth of analytic work on the nature, assumptions, sources, and implications of Canadian internationalism necessitated its conceptual unfolding. Equally important, it was about time to attempt to demonstrate the remarkable historical continuity of fifty years of Canadian internationalism as pragmatic idealism.

By the same token, the present work has benefited from various insights of realists and nationalists. For instance, as both nationalists and realists insist, there are undeniable constraints on Ottawa caused by the Canada-US special bilateral relationship. In some contexts, Canada may be perceived as a major player, and it would be bizarre to deny that Ottawa exhibits on occasion a propensity to stress some perception of the national interest above the idealist impulse. That is why conceptual clarification is of the essence. Our internationalist interpretation retains from realism the concern for a state's special needs, but places them in the cosmopolitan context. And whereas some internationalism is arguably a species of idealism, Canada's pragmatic idealism should not be conceived as self-sacrificial or exclusively altruistic. This therefore may suffice to establish that Canadian internationalism is far more flexible than realism, far more realistic than utopianism, and arguably, a more rational and reasonable worldview.

Conceptual clarity and methodological sophistication are needed for the analysis of the motives, goals, and results of Canadian foreign policy, and it must be said that many students of Canada's international relations embark on their work without a prior exposure to the general methods of foreign policy analysis. Furthermore, the predominance of realism is increasingly being questioned even for the study of other countries' foreign policies and of international relations in general.[35] For all these reasons, the next chapter will survey some concepts and means of analysing foreign policy. Then chapter 3 will begin our survey of the empirical record of fifty years of Canadian internationalism.

CONCLUSION

By now the reader should not be surprised that Canadian internationalism will emerge as this book's favourite framework. Its endorsement seems justified because this internationalism has been the declared pattern and professed goal of Canadian foreign policymakers; because Canada's actions have conformed, to an impressive degree, to the corresponding declarations; because Canadian internationalism has been widely recognized by the world; and in the final analysis, because no other method has emerged as superior.

The conceptual and methodological defence of pragmatic idealism, as the proper meaning of Canadian internationalism, will be completed in the next chapter. Of course, its ultimate credibility hinges on the empirical evidence provided in part two. Here, it can safely be asserted that the term pragmatic should cause no semantic discomfort or substantive anxiety to careful readers. By the end of this book, pragmatic idealism will qualify Canadian internationalism so as to capture both its (redefined) idealist and its *quasi*-realist dimensions. To this end, it is sufficient to keep in mind that Canada's motives, interests, needs, and values have certainly been quite distinct and that Canada's international behaviour has been in part, but clearly, humanitarian. In this manner, it will be possible to dispel two myths: the *realpolitik* one of essentially selfish motives, and the romantic idealist notion that Canada should have been more altruistic towards the world even at sacrificial costs to itself. In sum, by adopting the concept of pragmatic idealism this book situates Canadian foreign policy between the poles of orthodox realism and classical idealism.

Inevitably, some readers may disagree on occasion with interpretations and judgments contained in this work. They must, however, agree that strict objectivity in the social sciences is an elusive ideal. What one can, however, expect was perhaps best expressed by economist Gunnar Myrdal, who advocated that it is wiser to put one's methodological and interpretive cards on the table, right from the outset.[36]

2 Analysing Foreign policy

Given the amorphous flux of data confronting the observer, the study of foreign policy is best conducted by adopting organizing devices known as models, frameworks, or perspectives. They provide the methods, concepts, assumptions, and hypotheses by which we analyse and evaluate the relevant material. It follows that the chosen framework or perspective conditions or determines the interpretation of "the facts." Since different issues are regarded as more important by the various perspectives, a number of distinct questions, research agendas, and, therefore, answers can be expected to flow from them. This is appreciated by looking at the pervasive dichotomy of realism and idealism, which has important implications for the study of Canadian foreign policy.

REALISM AND IDEALISM

Observers of the school of realism believe that the international system and human history are essentially characterized by anarchy, conflict, violence, insecurity, and war. Accordingly, the nation-state must always increase its power, protect itself appropriately, and satisfy its national interest in this antagonistic, violent, and dangerous world. In this conflictual system, realists have concluded, each state is out for itself, and, therefore, international cooperation and ethical behaviour are non-existent or rare and short-lived.[1] Starting from such pessimistic assumptions and premises, realists favour a methodology that employs corresponding concepts, hypotheses, and analytic tools.

Idealists, on the other hand, reach different conclusions, since their assumptions and their premises are quite distinct. Their image of the international scene does accept as obvious the existence of conflict, violence, and war. Instead, it emphasizes the manifest presence of cooperation and peace. Moreover, idealist thinking focuses on ways to enhance peaceful means and to reduce the conditions which encourage violence and conflict. According to idealists, whose views on human nature and history are generally optimistic, the world's manifold malaise can be confronted by new institutions, norms, attitudes and mindsets. Consequently, idealist scholars urge the employment of the principles and means of international law, international organizations, collective security, multilateral cooperation, and international ethics. Justice, most idealists propose, is more important than power (the central concept for realists), and human interests must replace national interests. In this way we can handle the multidimensional problems of the global village, such as poverty, malnutrition, illiteracy, overpopulation, depletion of resources, and environmental catastrophes.[2] For these reasons, idealists opt for analytic means that cultivate their worldview and prescribe or recommend the enhancement of the corresponding agenda.

Realism has been the predominant framework for the analysis of foreign policy. Idealism, after a brief and partial popularity in the interwar years, fell into practical and theoretical disrepute in the aftermath of the Second World War and the eruption of the Cold War. During the last two decades or so, however, idealism has launched a respectable counter-attack, even before the end of the Cold War.

REALISM AND IDEALISM: STRENGTHS AND WEAKNESSES

Allowing for variations in emphasis, the major strengths of realism include the following: (1) some of its claims or general propositions closely approximate such phenomena of human history and international relations as the dramatic manifestation of conflict, violence, and war, the preoccupation with military security, and the fixation on a vaguely defined national interest; (2) order and the avoidance of war are obvious goals for all states under most circumstances; (3) security is a necessary condition if other state goals are to be met; (4) the interests of the nation, if identified, must obviously be served; and (5) many statesmen/stateswomen and decision-makers have, to date, operated with a *realpolitik* worldview.

This is an impressive list of strengths. Yet realism also suffers from serious weaknesses and problems which should render unwise its unqualified endorsement, as theorists of the behaviouralist revolution

Table 1

	Realism	*Idealism*
Assumptions	Human nature is fallen, evil or corrupt. History is the history of war, violence, and conflict. There are no supra-national authorities or institutions that can guarantee international order.	Human nature is neither evil nor static. Human history also contains the story of peace and cooperation among peoples. With improved education, communication, and institutions, further progress can occur.
Major concepts	Power, pursuit of power, anarchy, insecurity, military strength, balance of power, national interest.	Justice, human needs, human rights, global or human interests, security as a means to satisfy human needs.
Means advocated	Military power, balance of power, alliances, deterrence, unilateralism.	Collective security, international cooperation, international law, international morality, multilateralism.

first noted, and as Robert Keohane recently demonstrated.[3] First, vagueness or ambiguity characterize many of realism's key concepts, including power, anarchy, balance of power, order, and national interest. Second, its central assumptions, such as those pertaining to the Hobbesian conception of human nature and human history, are defective by being slanted or oversimplified. Third, the realist agenda is clearly narrow; it has either ostracized from its analysis or severely downplayed a whole array of issues, such as poverty, overpopulation, ecological concerns, North-South problems, human rights, non-military security, and more. Fourth, the positivist-determinist assumptions of realism have severely discouraged the discussion of ethical or normative issues. Therefore, international ethics are rarely found in the body of its work. Finally, while the realist preoccupation with order has usually celebrated the status quo, it has also constituted a theoretical/practical self-fulfilling prophecy. This is because the constant stress on the inevitability of conflict has facilitated its eruption, tolerated the arms race, and did next to nothing to contain the Cold War.

As for idealism, its strengths would appear to include the following: (1) its descriptive scope and prescriptive agenda are far broader than those of realism. This is evident because at the heart of idealism we find the struggle against Third World poverty, malnutrition, disease, overpopulation, energy problems, ecological degradation, racism, violation of human rights, and so on; (2) idealism is premised on change-oriented, optimistic assumptions of human nature and of human history. As opposed to the Machiavellian or Hobbesian conception of human nature endorsed by most realists, the idealist school seems to propagate the benign Lockean view and the perfectibility thesis advocated by John Stuart Mill; (3) the idealist stress on the primacy of justice is an important moral corrective of the narrowness of realism as is its broader conception of security, which goes far beyond the narrow military dimension; (4) as opposed to realism, idealism's far richer agenda proposes new methods for the analysis of foreign policy and new means to transcend the morally unacceptable global status quo; and (5) the idealist emphasis on human needs and human interests combines with proposals for inter-state and international cooperation to confront the truly planetary problems that seem unsolvable in realism's state-centric manner.

But idealism, at least in earlier formulations, also has notable weaknesses. First, it has been accused of sentimentalism, naïveté, and romantic excesses, particularly in some of its extreme or uncautious assumptions of human nature and human history, its optimism about inter-state cooperation, and its emphasis on ethical principles and values. Second, it has been found to exaggerate the role and effectiveness of international law, international organizations, and international morality. Third, idealism has downplayed the importance of defence and security, because of its inherent optimism and anti-militarism. And fourth, it has been slow in proposing effective ways to implement its overly ambitious agenda.

In view of the strengths and weaknesses of both worldviews, the question may arise about a possible synthesis: Could the best elements of each school or perspective be combined and their weaknesses removed? This convoluted issue still awaits a compelling answer in the relevant literature. We may, however, suggest that idealism itself, if properly reconstructed to become freed from unrealizable goals and misleading connotations, could well provide a desirable synthesis. Moreover, Canadian internationalism itself can be shown to constitute both a superior analytic model for the study of Canadian foreign policy and a role model for the conduct of post-Cold War foreign policy. In other words, Canadian internationalism could, *au fond*, contain the enlightened synthesis – away from the narrowness of realism and the utopian dimensions of idealism. As I have already intimated, this conclusion may be reached by conceiving of Canadian internationalism as pragmatic idealism.

MARXISM, BEHAVIOURALISM, PLURALISM, POST-MODERNISM

Whereas realism and idealism are the two principal models, perspectives or worldviews in the analysis of foreign policy and international relations, marxism, behaviouralism, pluralism, and post-modernism have also been employed as alternative ways of seeing and handling the relevant material.

Marxism. In its postwar formulations, marxism was decisive in shaping the official ideology and many declarations (if not the practice) of China and the Soviet-led bloc of countries. But marxism has clearly been influential in conditioning the varieties of western radicalism. Western neo-marxist, new left, and milder radical schools of thought have, among other things, produced challenging critiques of American foreign policy and postwar "western imperialism."[4] In addition, marxist and neo-marxist authors also elaborated a powerful reading of the nature and origins of the Cold War. Some perceptible echoes of such interpretations may be detected in the work of Canadian economic nationalists. Moderate tenets of neo-marxist thought have been incorporated in some liberal thinking on international relations. They include the recognition that powerful economic interests profoundly affect political and strategic decisions and actions; that a better understanding of North-South issues cannot ignore the structures of domination generated by the world capitalist system; that economic and technological developments condition socio-political institutions, ideologies, laws and cultures; and (along with other worldviews) that duties exist to help the underprivileged people of the world.

Some of these insights constitute the legacy of what may be regarded as valid in marxist thought.[5] They must, however, be contrasted to the errors of marxist theorizing such as those on the scientific nature of Marx's system.[6] For instance, an array of unfulfilled predictions and unsubstantiated claims have been made about the course of history, the collapse of capitalism, the growth potential of socialist societies, the sources of nationalism, and the causes of war. Moreover, recent international politics have dramatically falsified the central marxist theses that nationalism and war, as phenomena that would disappear with the fall of capitalism, would be alien to the free and classless world of post-capitalist societies. Therefore, while some moderate neo-marxist insights may enrich descriptive and explanatory accounts of aspects of international politics, orthodox marxism appears now to enjoy few adherents.

Behaviouralism. This perspective operated as both a meta-theory (that is, a theory *about* theorizing in our field) and as a set of guidelines about the so-called scientific study of international relations.[7] Perhaps its most valuable contributions comprised its demands for conceptual clarity, precision, and methodological sophistication and its telling critiques of "traditional" international relations schools. Behaviouralists exposed the sloppiness of realist writings of the early postwar period, regarding such central realist concepts as power, order, the state, and balance of power as oversimplified assumptions as they pertain to human nature. All this, as Michael Banks has emphasized, was salutary.[8]

Behaviouralism itself, however, suffered from obvious weaknesses. They include its fallacy that social science can be value-free and the fact that it was fixated on its own positivistic and determinist assumptions. These assumptions ultimately entailed both a questionable toleration of the status quo and strong opposition to normative or ethical proposals for change. In any event, behaviouralism now belongs to the history of ideas of international relations.

Pluralism. In some respects this perspective occupies a middle ground between realism and idealism. It is broad enough to embrace a variety of approaches known as liberal institutionalism, neorealism, and even the model of interdependence.[9] Robert Keohane and Joseph Nye are credited with launching the most influential work of this fruitful framework, *Power and Interdependence.* Its impetus was well illustrated by a telling admission by Henry Kissinger in 1975: "Now we are entering a new era. Old international patterns are crumbling; old slogans are uninstructive; old solutions are unavailing. The world has become interdependent in economics, in communications, in human aspirations."[10]

The pluralist approach redefined the notions of power, influence, non-state actors, interdependence, and hegemony. Four principal theses or assumptions may distinguish it from the realist worldview.[11] First, the state is not to be conceived as a unitary actor, given that it is composed of, or clearly affected by, numerous and often conflicting bureaucracies, individuals, groups, non-governmental organizations, and special interests. Second, the state cannot be treated as rational, contrary to the realist "rational actor model" of decision-making.[12] Third, non-state actors (international, interstate, and intergovernmental) have emerged as critical players on the international scene. Such actors, which include institutions and organizations of global reach with global consequences – from the United Nations to multinational corporations – have clearly affected, if not dramatically altered, the nature of power, authority, and influence in the contemporary world. Finally, a fourth thesis follows from these three: the agenda for the study of and practice in international relations is by now far richer than traditional realism supposed. These four propositions of pluralism have attempted to revise realism realistically.

By broadening further the conceptual and empirical scope of analysis, this framework has performed an invaluable function. However, operating primarily in the field of global political economy, it has not yet produced important work in other areas, such as those at the centre of the internationalist agenda. Moreover, the application of the Keohane-Nye model to Canadian-US relations in *Power and Interdependence* has yielded partial and hence misleading conclusions. Finally, as our schematic critique of Dewitt-Kirton has implied, this perspective cannot do justice to the rich array of issues at the heart of Canadian internationalism.

Post-Modernism. A lively, provocative, and even subversive constellation of sub-schools is currently developing a manifold challenge to the traditional international relations approaches, under the general heading of post-modernism. Authors such as Richard Ashley, James Der Derian, Michael J. Shapiro, and R.B.J. Walker, accompanied by writers variously designated as post-structuralist, deconstructionist, and associated feminist, have assaulted the epistemological and methodological foundations of modernity, opposing its "logocentric" pursuit of truth, knowledge, explanation, and causality. As Pauline Rosenau has perceptively noted, post-modernists turn their attention "to language, symbols, alternative discourses and meaning rather than goals, choices, behaviour, attitudes and personality"; they focus on "the accidental, the borderline, the disjointed or the forgotten"; the sceptical among them emphasize the era's "radical uncertainty, its overall meaninglessness, its apocalyptic and catastrophic potential"; but post-modernism's "positive identity is yet to be definitely established and may not exist."[13]

For these reasons, the present book is unsympathetic to the post-modernist meta-theoretical project. For what is creative about it (for example, its inherent anti-positivism and its passionate opposition to inequality and oppression) is already covered by our endorsement of a pragmatically refined idealism. The rest, at least to date, is either ill-formed or incomprehensible or nihilistic. It is not, therefore, relevant to the study of Canadian foreign policy, if only because Canadian internationalism demonstrates how cosmopolitan values, when pragmatically pursued, have made a real difference for both Canada and the world.

In view of this brief survey of alternative approaches and methods for the study of international relations and foreign policy, we may now turn to some types of internationalism in general before clarifying further the nature of Canadian internationalism.

INTERNATIONALISM REVISITED

Broadly speaking, internationalism constitutes an activist involvement in the affairs of the world, as opposed to isolationism. When its motives and means are not geared exclusively towards the satisfaction of a state's own interests, it is clearly distinct from both nationalism and imperialism. However, so-called internationalist rationalizations or excuses may be used by a state when it wishes to pursue self-serving interests but is unwilling to acknowledge them as such. For instance, the concept of socialist internationalism was generally employed by the Soviet Union until the rise to power of Mikhail Gorbachev. It was used to refer to the purported solidarity among communist states, when in fact the focus of many of these policies was to antagonize Western states, world capitalism, and primarily the United States. The means and goals of socialist internationalism would suffice to distinguish it from internationalism as pragmatic idealism, because Moscow's policies also entailed the authoritarian control of satellites and even invasions of foreign territories for the purpose of "saving" them (Hungary in 1956, or Czechoslovakia in 1968).

By the same token, revisionist and even post-revisionist historians and political scientists have criticized postwar American foreign policy because of its own thrusts of manifold intervention in other states.[14] The creation of an "American empire" (until the relative US retrenchment of the mid-1970s) has been regarded by many as a consequence of American interventionism since 1945. Others, however, have spoken of the globalism or even internationalism of Washington's foreign policy because, being overtly sympathetic to US motives and goals, they have wished to refer to the country's post-isolationism as America's benign support of allies or assistance to friends.[15]

It follows, then, that the varieties of internationalism must be distinguished at least in terms of means and goals. First, the means favoured by a state provide a powerful criterion to identify its goals and intentions. Thus, the international performance of the two superpowers during the Cold War cannot be perceived as internationalist in the same sense as that of the "ethically motivated" middle powers, if only because the former, with their "sense of mission" and superpower "responsibilities," frequently employed coercive instruments in their narcissistic attempt to shape the world in their own image. It already follows, therefore, that it is rational and even necessary to distinguish internationalism of the *pragmatic idealist* variety (as exhibited by Canada and the "like-minded middle powers") from the *interventionist* kind as manifested in the post-1945 foreign policy of the United States and the Soviet Union.

Second, evidence that self-aggrandizement or self-interest are the primary goals of a realist policy should suffice to contrast it to behaviour that aims cooperatively at broader or human interests. Internationalism, when it exhibits idealist goals and cosmopolitan values stands, of course, in opposition to such realism. As we said in chapter 1, Canada's internationalist foreign policy has typically declared the nation's interests to be harmonized with the broader interests of the international community. Michael Tucker has captured this succinctly. Having defined Canada's internationalism as "an exercise in collaboration on the part of Canadian governments, groups or individuals with like-minded governments or peoples elsewhere," Tucker identified the aim of such internationalist collaboration: "This has been the enhancement of interests or values commonly shared with others outside Canada, with a view to helping create or sustain a better world order."[16]

Finally, a policy's scope and duration must also be considered. To designate a foreign policy as internationalist, in our pragmatic-idealist sense, it should also exhibit breadth and coherence consistently, and over a long period. Merely fragmented or isolated instances of caring, sharing, moderate or cooperative behaviour cannot properly qualify, just as a few isolated acts of goodness are not sufficient to ascribe the term "good" to a person.

Some necessary and sufficient conditions have thus emerged to distinguish the older types of internationalism from the cosmopolitan and pragmatic idealist variety. The latter has been pursued by Canada and like-minded middle powers since the 1945 San Francisco Conference. We shall therefore retain the conception of pragmatic idealism to refer to Canadian internationalism and to the parallel internationalism of Australia, Denmark, the Netherlands, Norway, New Zealand, and Sweden.[17] For it is generally acknowledged that, overall, their foreign policy values, interests, methods, and goals have been distinct in kind from those of the superpowers and even the great powers. As intimated earlier, however, Canada's internationalist record is arguably more impressive than that of most like-minded middle powers, by virtue of its scope, duration, versatility, and depth of commitment.

Scholars such as Michael Tucker, Peyton Lyon, Peter Dobell, Tom Axworthy, and Charles Doran have written as though they might broadly agree with this framework. Arguably, however, only Tom Axworthy, Peter Dobell, and Michael Tucker can be said to have celebrated the idealist impulse behind aspects or moments of Canadian foreign policy.[18] For instance, Charles Doran has identified the "liberal principles" and "liberal bias" of Ottawa's policies. Contrasting Washington's permanent postwar proclivity towards the balance of power with Canada's liberal idealist notion, he dispassionately observed that it "favours reform through supranational institutions, such as the United Nations, and through limitation on force, rather than reliance on efforts to balance force through the deterrence doctrine."[19] Tom Axworthy, on the other hand, presented the Trudeauvian idealism of 1968–84 in a different light; he applauded Trudeau's cosmopolitan values as having emphasized justice, international cooperation, satisfaction of human needs and human rights, a "global ethic," and a richer conception of security that is premised on our common humanity.[20]

Finally, special mention should be reserved for the recent work of Cranford Pratt. Pratt has investigated humane internationalism and Canada's own "eroding internationalism," and has edited studies of the sources and manifestations of this internationalism in a number of middle powers.[21] He distinguishes three forms of humane internationalism, in terms of its favoured goals and methods – liberal, reform, and radical. Pratt's humane internationalism is, in an important sense, akin to what I have labelled pragmatic idealism. This is so because he clearly identifies idealist or cosmopolitan values – such as our duties to persons beyond our borders – as the ethical foundation of some of the policies of Canada and other middle powers in the sphere of North-South issues, such as foreign economic assistance. One major difference, however, is that I apply the concept to a far broader policy range. Beyond North-South concerns, this book will reveal Canada's pragmatic idealism in the areas of peacekeeping, human rights, diplomatic mediation, Cold War moderation, arms control and disarmament, and ecological concerns. Accordingly, my reading of the validity and continued viability of Canadian internationalism will be far more optimistic.

Another difference flows from the fact that Pratt's moral expectations from Canada's international behaviour have been remarkably high. His argument on Canada's eroding internationalism, although insightful in many ways, appears to be premised on purely altruistic expectations. However, the notion that states should absorb sacrificial costs to themselves in order to help others transcends the realm of the ethical. Indeed, this form of self-negation amounts to supererogation.[22] This, although no doubt honourable, is clearly excessive. In any event, altruistic self-negation is unnecessary for the legitimate application of the terms humane or idealist to either human beings or foreign policies.

While the above conceptual distinctions may serve to identify the Canadian variety of internationalism as pragmatic idealism, the nature of this internationalism can be clarified even further by addressing Canada's power status and the relevance of Canadian internationalism for the bilateral Canadian-us relationship.

Canada's Status as a Power

Realist and nationalist scholars, by adopting different conceptions of Canada's power status, inevitably draw conflicting results. For instance, whereas Kim Nossal, like the economic nationalists, infers Ottawa's relative foreign policy impotence (primarily because his explanatory focus is placed on its relationship with Washington), Dewitt and Kirton assert the country's "top-tier" status and predict its unimpeded ascendancy. Nossal correctly points out that "Canada lacks the most important attribute needed for great-power status: the subjective recognition of other states."[23] He therefore rejects the Dewitt-Kirton thesis of Canada as a "principal power," which is, of course, itself anathema to the economic nationalists. Nossal also distances himself from the "power image" approach as inconclusive, and from "the pitfalls of trying to establish middle power by statistical means."[24] However, his own conclusion on Canada's status appears inconclusive. While he denies the "great power" and "weak state" classification, and is uncomfortable with "the fuzzy, if comfortable, notion of Canada as middle power," his ending of the relevant discussion is sybillic: "[Canada] cannot avoid the necessity of showing 'how wit with small means may accomplish wonders where great force availeth not.'"[25]

There is, however, a third way. The meaning of middle power can be retained as suggesting both a ranking and a foreign policy manner or style. The former is bound to be fluid and in permanent need of a comparative context. The latter can be identified and defined. Thus, Canada is a middle power in the broad but safe sense of belonging neither in the group of great powers nor in that amorphous group of the weak and poor states categorized as less developed or Third World. And yet, Canada is a *sui generis* middle power: its resources, capabilities, territory, degree of economic development, and so on all point to its special and idiosyncratic status near but not at the top of the world's hierarchy of the powerful. But Canada's population, its political culture, its military strength, its willingness to use force, and its recurrent domestic anxieties, all point in a different direction. Equally important, subjective recognition has two aspects. It refers both to the perception of the ego or self-perception, and the perception of the alter or that of others.[26] Here, again, the *sui generis* nature of Canada's status in the world is clear: Canadians have a far more modest (and even self-effacing) perception of themselves than the world has of Canada. It is here that the internationalist style of Canadian foreign policy, and its manifestations on the world scene, become decisive.

"Middlepowermanship," as Canada's foreign policy style has been variously perceived,[27] has been seen to embrace functionalism, voluntarism, the avoidance of conflict, respect for international law, and support for international institutions. In this book, we shall demonstrate these defining characteristics of Canada's pragmatic idealism which, jointly, seem to capture its formal identity: moderation, cooperation, communication, mediation, caring and sharing, multilateralism, and support for international law and international morality.

In sum, therefore, the internationalist interpretation recognizes and reflects the modesty of the middle power ranking. It represents the very status that Ottawa decision-makers and Canadian political culture have aimed at. It also recognizes the concomitant style of postwar Canadian foreign policy. Finally, it represents the interests of Canada as more complex and ambitious than those of weak states, as distinct from the principles and interests of the superpowers and top-tier states, and as akin to those of the like-minded middle powers.

Internationalism and Canada–United States Relations

It may appear at first sight that the application of our approach to the continental bilateral relationship would be limited, since Canada's internationalist worldview has been intended to guide the country's postwar behaviour in the world at large. However, central elements of the internationalist philosophy have been either inspired by or applied to the special Canada-US relationship. Thus, "sandwiched between two superpowers" (in Lester Pearson's phrase) and neighbour to the strongest country in the world, Canada regularly attempted to mediate among world capitals, and frequently between Washington and Moscow. It employed quiet diplomacy and a variety of associated tools to moderate American policies during the Cold War. Canada has used its influence, diplomatic suasion, and moral authority in multilateral forums often in opposition to American wishes. Ottawa contradicted Washington's Cold War perceptions as early as 1948–49, during the negotiations for the formation of NATO. It emphasized a far broader conception of security, at various junctures, again in opposition to the Western superpower's doctrines. And, as Lawrence Martin has admirably documented, Canada has frequently irritated American policymakers on a large number of issues.[28] Arguably, such perceptual and political dissonance between the two capitals can best be explained by the constellation of interests, values, and associated perceptions at the heart of Canadian internationalism. It is this type of internationalism, understood as pragmatic idealism, that has stood in perceptible opposition to the *realpolitik* premises that have typically marked the postwar foreign policy of the United States.

CONCLUSIONS

Besides introducing this book's main argument, central theses, and the associated concepts, these first two chapters have also sketched some broader analytic issues and methodological devices. The latter are employed in the examination and evaluation of foreign policy and international relations and are therefore relevant to the study of Canadian foreign policy. It thus transpired that realism, the hegemonic analytic framework since the 1940s, suffers from conceptual and normative defects, rendered more transparent by the monumental global developments following the end of the Cold War. These developments have witnessed the concomitant rise in importance of the United Nations and other multilateral organizations, such as the Conference on Security and Cooperation in Europe (CSCE, now OSCE) and the General Agreement on Tariffs and Trade/World Trade Organization (GATT/WTO); the reassertion of the need for collective security; the serious re-evaluation of the traditional conception of the principle of sovereignty; and the expansion of opportunities and needs for international cooperation to confront the manifest global malaise. All these emerging realities constitute additional arguments for the validity and viability of pragmatic idealism.

Canadian internationalism has long been an avant garde synthesis of pragmatism (understood as policy adaptable to the country's needs in the real world) and idealism (conceived without the defects of its classical or naïve formulations). It constitutes the self-professed, and consistently articulated, worldview of Canada's post-1945 foreign policymakers. And, as the rest of this book will try to show, it reflects the persistent commitment to implementing this worldview in the real world. It thus follows that Canadian internationalism should determine the manner of analysing Canadian foreign policy. That is why this book has adopted the framework of pragmatic idealism and why the alternative analytic approaches appear to be wanting.

A final methodological clarification seems required to establish why Canadian realism and nationalism are unacceptable as autonomous analytic methods for the study of post-1945 Canadian foreign policy. Given the consistent commitment to Canadian internationalism avowed by all Canadian governments since the San Francisco Conference, it seems incumbent on realists and nationalists to demonstrate how, for exactly fifty years, Ottawa has deceived both the Canadian people and the entire world. In other words, Canadian realists and nationalists ought not only to assert their assumptions and perspectives but also to show explicitly why Canadian internationalism should be rejected. To do the latter it seems necessary to demonstrate either that Ottawa's motives or actions or both were consistently hypocritical, or that the rhetoric of post-1945 Canadian foreign policy has not been implemented in fact. To the best of my knowledge, none of this has been attempted. What is more, it is a fact that both Canadian realists and nationalists (for their own distinct reasons) have refused to address and evaluate Canada's post-1945 internationalist agenda. These reasons, therefore, should suffice to suggest why, taken by themselves, their perspectives were partial and thus defective.

Needless to say, the adoption of Canadian internationalism does not imply that every single action or decision of post-1945 Canadian foreign policy has served religiously every interest and value of the pragmatic idealist worldview. To expect this would be to confuse the framework with its subject matter. Rather, the adoption of the proposed analytic model entails two propositions. First, this framework must provide the criteria or standards whereby both the successes and the flaws of actual policy should be examined and assessed. And second, to confirm the legitimacy of the model it is sufficient to show that Canadian foreign policy, *most of the time and in most respects*, was committed to and consistent with the interests and values of the Canadian internationalist worldview.

Thus, the present analysis will point on occasion to decisions or actions where Ottawa's characteristic pattern of pragmatic idealism was modified, in a manner that could perhaps be described as realist. Such instances include Trudeau's early years' relative passivity towards South Africa or his decision to allow the testing of the cruise missile; the early Mulroney period's "hawkish" defence posture; and the Chrétien government's stance on China's problematic human rights record. Such cases are few and far between. In the good sense of the old cliché, they only serve to prove the rule. In other words, pragmatic idealism can indeed accommodate such realist moments which pure idealism cannot. Given their limited number, context, and surrounding rationale (that is, as marginal to and even explicable by the main body of Canada's solid pragmatic idealism), these occasions are perfectly understandable and cannot possibly cast doubt on the country's defining foreign policy pattern. By the same token, of course, our clarification suggests that this analysis is immune to "Popperian objections."[29]

Finally, it is crucial to stress that the present work can also be seen as a grand case study which, by explicating the foreign policy patterns of one of the like-minded middle powers, serves to undermine empirically the one-dimensional assumptions of realism. Moreover, it can help to demonstrate that the alleged dichotomy of interests and values (taken for granted by the positivism of realism) is conceptually fallacious and empirically false. This will be shown by the fact that Canada's internationalist rhetoric and practice have constantly implemented and persistently celebrated cosmopolitan values as serving simultaneously Canada's own interests and needs and those of the international community at large.

We now turn to an overview of the empirical record to begin testing our major hypothesis: that, in the main, Canadian foreign policymakers from 1945 to 1995 have really meant what they have said.

PART TWO

3 The Golden Age, 1945–1957

Canada's control over its foreign policy could not, by definition, begin before the recognition of the country's sovereignty. This recognition was legally conferred by the Statute of Westminster (1931), which followed the 1926 Balfour Declaration whereby Canada, along with the United Kingdom and the other dominions, became "autonomous communities within the British Empire, equal in status, in no way subordinate to one another in any aspect of their domestic or external affairs, though united by a common allegiance to the Crown."

The Department of External Affairs was established by Ottawa in 1909. Until 1945, however, Canada's external relations were conducted in a semi-autonomous fashion.[1] Thus, the declaration of war against Germany by London in 1914 entailed Canada's automatic involvement in the First World War. When Canada participated in the 1919 Paris peace conference, the country's representatives were part of the imperial delegation. During the inter-war period, Canada opted for an isolationist policy both in an effort to avoid overseas entanglements and in view of the conscription crisis, caused by the First World War, which had divided anglophone and francophone Canadians. At the same time, and until the outbreak of the Second World War, Canada relied on London for the conduct of its external relations, having only five diplomatic legations abroad in addition to the High Commission in London. And in the spirit of isolationism, still favoured by Prime Minister Mackenzie King, Ottawa gave support to British Prime Minister Chamberlain's policy of appeasement towards the Nazis.

When war broke out, however, Mackenzie King submitted to Parliament the government's declaration of war on Nazi Germany, which did not receive approval until a whole week later. The delay was intended to signal that Canada's decision to join the allied effort was taken independently.[2] During the war, Canada's performance was more than honourable. Its contribution involved placing over a million men under arms. Canadians suffered 85,000 casualties: 53,000 wounded and 32,000 dead. In addition, the country trained allied airmen; it supplied war material to the Allies, being a serious source of help to the Soviet armed forces; and its 1941 Defence Production Agreement with the United States allowed Canada to channel American support to Britain at a crucial juncture of the war effort.[3]

Having thus made an important contribution to the victory, and having been called by Winston Churchill in September 1941, "the linchpin of the English-speaking world," Canada emerged in 1945 as one of the world's economic powers, being the second-largest trading nation, while also possessing remarkable military strength.

Canada's former isolationist inclinations were now receding, and the country was poised to play an activist new role in the world. Indeed, already in July 1943, with hostilities still flaring, Prime Minister Mackenzie King expressed Canada's emerging internationalism. In a House of Commons speech, he enunciated the "functional principle." As King put it,

on the one hand, authority in international affairs must not be concentrated exclusively in the largest powers. On the other, authority cannot be divided equally among all the thirty or more sovereign states that comprise the United Nations, or all effective authority will disappear ... Representation should be determined on a functional basis which will admit to full membership these countries, large or small, which have the greatest contribution to make to the particular object in question.[4]

This principle has been captured memorably by Blair Fraser as amounting to the aphorism, "Let those who can, do." Functionalism was energetically and creatively employed by Canada's delegates to the United Nations San Francisco Conference in 1945. After the Bretton Woods Conference of December 1944, which founded the postwar international politico-economic order, this was the country's next major opportunity to help shape the postwar world. The San Francisco Conference ushered in the golden age of Canadian diplomacy.

The 1945–57 period, also known as the St Laurent–Pearson era, crystallized the principles of Canadian foreign policy for subsequent years. It established the major patterns of Canada's international behaviour and its conception of its role in the world. Telling manifestations of these principles and patterns relate to Canada's relations with the United Nations, the North Atlantic Treaty Organization (NATO), Britain and the Commonwealth, and the two superpowers, the United States and the Soviet Union.

CANADA AND THE UNITED NATIONS

At San Francisco, Canada emerged as a committed advocate of the United Nations' role as humankind's best hope to attain and maintain international security, cooperation, and peace. Canada also assumed a leading position among a group of countries that came to be known as middle powers. At the conference Canada aimed to achieve a number of objectives: to contain the great powers' overwhelming weight at the new global organization; to increase the voice and role of the middle powers, on the basis of the functional principle; to limit the veto power of the Security Council's five permanent members; to create a United Nations police force; and finally, to emphasize the importance of economic and social cooperation and development as the best means to consolidate international security and peace.[5]

Canada's energetic pursuit of middle-power functionalism bore impressive fruits. The entire United Nations Charter is marked by the Canadian delegation's influence. For instance, because of Canadian proposals, article 23(1) includes the declaration that, in the election of non-permanent members of the Security Council, "due regard [will also be] specially paid" to the contribution made by members of the United Nations "to the maintenance of international peace and security and to the other purposes of the Organization." Other examples of articles affected, and at times determined, by Canada's views and proposals include: articles 10 and 12 on some functions of the General Assembly; article 23 on the composition of the Security Council; article 24(3) about the Security Council's submitting reports to the General Assembly; article 44 regarding the participation of a member in Security Council deliberations, if that member's armed forces were invited to send contingents under the chapter VII "Action with Respect to Threats to the Peace, Breaches of the Peace, and Acts of Aggression"; and articles 100, 101, and 105 concerning the Secretariat. Finally, many of the proposals submitted by Canada regarding the Economic and Social Council (ECOSOC) were adopted and written into chapter 10 of the charter.[6]

Louis St Laurent, as minister of external affairs, articulated explicitly the interests and principles of Canada's internationalist commitment in the Gray Lecture of January 1947, as we know from chapter 1. That is why, as St Laurent concluded, "We are preparing ourselves to fulfil the growing responsibilities in world affairs which we have accepted as a modern state"; and we have "a useful part to play in world affairs, useful to ourselves through being useful to others."[7]

The United Nations was the primary vehicle chosen by Canada for the fulfilment of these internationalist "responsibilities." In the same spirit, when Canada was elected to the Security Council, St Laurent observed in September 1947: "We in this country continue to believe that the best hope for mankind lies in the establishment of a world organization for the maintenance of peace … [and] if we wish to enjoy the benefits of such a development we must also accept its responsibilities."[8] We must, of course, recall that by September 1947 the Cold War was in full swing. East and West, under the leadership of Stalin in Moscow and Harry Truman in Washington, were poised for confrontation. Mutual suspicions and mistrust had elevated the antagonism to the point where military conflict between the former Second World War allies could not be precluded. To recall this dramatic context (six months after the enunciation of the March 1947 Truman Doctrine) helps one appreciate the significance of St Laurent's view of the United Nations as "the best hope for mankind."

Peacekeeping under United Nations' auspices was a major avenue that Canada employed to fulfil its internationalist vocation. It began participating in all UN peacekeeping activities although, strictly speaking, the term came into use only with the 1956 Suez mission. Thus, Canada's first observer missions began in 1948 in Palestine, with the setting up of the United Nations Truce Supervision Organization (UNTSO), and in 1949, with the UN Military Observer Group in India and Pakistan (UNMOGIP).

Quite clearly, the Suez crisis of October 1956 is properly regarded as having provided the opportunity for Canada's, and Lester Pearson's, most successful diplomatic intervention. Pearson's immediate goals seem to have been, first, to defuse the Suez crisis which was threatening regional and global security, given Nikita Khrushchev's vociferous threats that he would "shower" the West with nuclear rockets. Second, Pearson aimed to help Britain and France save face once their governments had been widely condemned as aggressors and abandoned at the Security Council even by the administration of President Eisenhower. The third goal was to save the Commonwealth from the nearly fatal blow to its integrity caused by the widespread perception that London's Suez action was an "imperialist adventure." And fourth, Lester Pearson wished to demonstrate the United Nations' capability to handle regional or global crises by diplomatic means.[9] Pearson's masterful 1956 initiative at the United Nations was rewarded, a year later, by the Nobel Peace Prize.

Meanwhile, however, the Korean War of 1950–3 had seriously threatened world peace. Here, too, Canada's skills of communication, moderation, and mediation were instrumental in ending the conflict. By the summer of 1952, it looked as though the Soviet Union might enter the war, thus widening the conflict and causing a new global conflagration. Canada, with Lester Pearson holding the presidency of the UN General Assembly, initiated a series of diplomatic contacts and behind-the-scenes negotiations which produced a resolution agreed to by the conflicting sides.

As former Canadian high commissioner to India, Chester Ronning, wrote in 1966, Pearson's historic success was due to a number of factors: to his cooperation with India and other member states which shared Canada's views; to persistent consultations with all UN members which secured support for the armistice resolution; and to "friendly behind-the-scene negotiations" with the United States and other participants in the UN-sponsored action in Korea. As a consequence, Canada's achievement, according to Chester Ronning, was "fully as important as the Suez success to which greater importance was attached because Korea was away off in Asia."[10]

Beyond these peacekeeping and peacemaking triumphs, Canada's role in the United Nations – which has been called "the cornerstone of the country's external relations" during this period[11] – included sustained contributions that spanned the entire spectrum of the UN's agenda and mandate. Thus, Canada's own representatives, and Canadians as international civil servants, dealt energetically and creatively with social, economic, educational, and technical issues, including those of disarmament and arms control. The success of Canada in the various committees, commissions, and councils of the UN's specialized agencies can be illustrated through the list of Canadians who held crucial posts. Dr Brock Chisholm was elected as the first director of the World Health Organization (WHO). He had already helped prepare the International Health Conference of June 1946 and the draft constitution of WHO. Before accepting the post of WHO's director general in June 1948, he had been executive secretary of its Interim Commission for two years. When he retired from his WHO post in 1953 he had been offered a three-year extension. He declined arguing that "a permanent organization should not have the same head for too long, particularly at the beginning of its history."[12] Dr George Davidson served as high commissioner for refugees, while Major-General Howard Kennedy was first director general of the United Nations Relief and Works Agency for Palestine Refugees in the Near East (UNRWA), an agency created in 1949. Dr Hugh Keenleyside was the first director general of the UN Technical Assistance Administration. Escott Reid, among other activities, occupied an important position at the World Bank, while numerous Canadians served with the other international economic organizations created under the auspices of the Bretton Woods system. Finally, this list must recall that General E.L.M. Burns served both as chief of staff of UNTSO in Palestine (from 1954 to 1956) and as commander of the United Nations Expeditionary Force.[13]

A major ground for Canada's success story at the United Nations is associated with the superb diplomatic skills, the engaging personality, and the internationalist credentials of Lester B. Pearson. The great Canadian diplomat and statesman had attracted the respect of the international community even before receiving the Nobel Prize. Having already served as president of the General Assembly, he had played important roles in establishing the United Nations Relief and Rehabilitation Administration (UNRRA) and the Food and Agriculture Organization of the United Nations (FAO). Lester Pearson was also nominated twice for the post of secretary general – a nomination vetoed by Moscow. In a review of his book, *Diplomacy in the Nuclear Age,* John F. Kennedy wrote, in 1959, that "already 'Mike' Pearson has been the chief architect of the Canadian foreign service, probably unequalled by any nation; he has been a brilliant ambassador and foreign secretary; he has been a central figure in the growth of the Atlantic Community and NATO, even while taking a leading role in the shaping of the United Nations."[14]

"Clearly," wrote Peyton Lyon, "there is substance in the conventional judgment that Pearson's personal commitment and talent contributed greatly to Canada's internationalist image." Yet Pearson was not alone, neither was he "the most profound thinker within the Ottawa mandarinate." The period of the golden decade (as Peyton Lyon more modestly calls it) also witnessed the outstanding contributions of many more inspired Canadian internationalists than we have already mentioned. Thus, Peyton Lyon could hardly contain his enthusiasm about them. Hume Wrong "earned an awesome reputation for being right about global trends," being also "exceptionally influential in Washington." Norman Robertson "displayed comparable knowledge and a strikingly fertile imagination." Wynne Plumptre and Louis Rasminsky "made outstanding contributions" in the founding of the International Monetary Fund and the International Bank for Reconstruction and Development (World Bank). And Escott Reid, distinguished by "his faith in grand designs" (as recorded in his autobiography, *Radical Mandarin*) "proved extraordinarily effective as a drafter of international constitutions."[15]

The list of the internationalists reserves a special place for two other contributors to the shaping of the postwar world through the UN and Canada's role therein. The first is Paul Martin, who successfully negotiated with Moscow – over strong opposition from Washington – the expansion of UN membership in 1955. The other is John Holmes, the distinguished diplomat, scholar, and teacher about whom Margaret Doxey has written:

A firm believer in multilateralism, and in the United Nations as an important framework for diplomatic and peacekeeping initiatives, John ... never tilted at windmills, but looked for practical ways to achieve progress towards a more peaceful and equitable world. And he was, of course, particularly concerned that Canada as a "middle power" should play its full part in this process.[16]

Behind-the-scenes bridge-building and informal but effective mediation became hallmarks of Ottawa's golden age middlepowermanship. The Canadians' talent for such mediation, as Peyton Lyon has stressed, is "a fact widely appreciated by foreign diplomats." In particular, Pearson's success in achieving the Korean armistice under United Nations auspices "did much to intensify the Canadian elite's conviction that as moderators of US behaviour, they were performing a service vital to mankind."[17]

It has already transpired, therefore, why the familiar appellations "honest broker" and "helpful fixer" became entrenched during the golden age of Canadian diplomacy. But these terms also derived from Canada's consistent pursuit of functionalist principles and internationalist values in a variety of other forums, including the North Atlantic Treaty Organization.

CANADA AND NATO

Idealist optimism fuelled the creation of the United Nations and sustained Canada's committed support for its mandate. This optimism, however, was dramatically undermined by the eruption of the Cold War between 1946 and 1947. Whatever one views as the precise locus of responsibility for the antagonism of the two camps or blocs, Ottawa was profoundly concerned with the ominous changes in the international climate. These changes followed Stalin's threatening conduct in the Middle East and Eastern Europe; Winston Churchill's March 1946 "Iron Curtain" speech at Fulton, Missouri; and President Harry Truman's March 1947 speech to the joint session of the US Congress which enunciated his historic doctrine.[18] From Ottawa, St Laurent was among the first to call for the creation of an instrument of collective Atlantic defence, to parallel the UN's role as an institution of collective security.[19]

During the negotiations for the creation of NATO, from 22 March 1948 to 15 March 1949, Canada distinguished itself in at least two ways: by being an ardent supporter of the emerging Atlantic alliance, which would involve the United States in the defence of Europe and thus help "contain" Stalin's perceived expansionist designs; and by insisting that NATO would have to be more than a mere military bloc.

As Escott Reid has shown, Canada's principal objectives during the multilateral negotiations for NATO were: to produce a treaty, and not just a relevant declaration by the American president; to attain an article guaranteeing the collectiveness of the common defence; to include a strong article on non-military cooperation among the members; and to oppose Italy's membership and the treaty's extension to cover Algeria (then a French territory).[20]

Canadian negotiators succeeded fully in their first goal, but were not successful in keeping Italy out. And while Washington opposed a stress on non-military cooperation, Canada succeeded in inserting article 2 in the NATO Charter. This article has been known ever since as "the Canadian Article."[21]

Canada's contribution to the formation of NATO demonstrated the country's penchant for moderation, exemplified by less bellicose stands and less threatening options than other allied capitals would favour. Ottawa consistently advocated moderation in the handling of Moscow, attempting to dissuade the allies from rhetoric or tactics that might be perceived by the Soviet Union as provocative and thus fuelling the vicious circle of East-West mistrust and insecurity. In addition, Canadian statesmen (St Laurent and Pearson in particular) tended to believe that the manifest superiority of Western political principles and values would suffice, ultimately, to win the Cold War:

Perhaps naïvely – certainly naïvely in the opinion of some American leaders at the time – men like St. Laurent and Pearson never lost hope of piercing the Iron Curtain, of re-building confidence among the leaders of the two blocs, and of hammering out at the Conference table the conditions for peaceful coexistence. Even at the height of the Cold War, the view prevailed in Ottawa that as the West demonstrated its superior ability to meet human needs and aspirations, Communist Society would become more liberal.[22]

Be that as it may, from 1950 to 1957 Canada's defence expenditures averaged 6.3 per cent of the country's GNP. More than half of this was Canada's contribution to NATO. During this period, Canada deployed ground forces to Germany and air forces to France, thereby demonstrating its pragmatic endorsement of the concept that security for the Atlantic allies began at the central front in Europe. Canada's motives regarding NATO, however, also involved the persistent effort to attain an effective "counterweight." Now that Britain's power as Canada's traditional protector had clearly receded, NATO Europe could be expected to counterbalance the overwhelming power and influence of the United States. In other words, while Canada's Western interests and credentials were being cultivated and enhanced through membership in NATO, Canada's consuming need for distinctness was also ever-present. The Atlantic alliance, therefore, being an organization for collective defence, could, among other things, meet Canada's need to contain the influence and raw power of the Western superpower.

BRITAIN AND THE COMMONWEALTH

During its golden age, Canadian diplomacy used the Commonwealth as another vehicle or forum for special contacts and relations with a large part of the Third World and the advanced industrial democracies of the United Kingdom, Australia, and New Zealand. Indeed, just as Canada was instrumental in the adoption of the Balfour Declaration by the 1926 Imperial Conference (which recognized the autonomy of the dominions), Canadians helped decisively in the expansion of the Commonwealth to cover the millions of people of the Indian subcontinent in the 1940s. Thus, the assurances of Mackenzie King to Prime Minister Jawaharlal Nehru convinced India to remain a member. Nehru's fears that the Commonwealth was just another name for the British Empire and membership would contradict India's status as a republic were assuaged. Nehru decided on Indian membership when Canada proposed, and had it adopted, that by also calling the British sovereign "Head of the Commonwealth" some states would not have to accept him/her as their monarch. In this connection, Thomson and Swanson have observed: "Nehru was touched by the Canadian attitude, and decided ... that if a country like Canada could be a member without sacrificing its principles, then India, too, could perhaps do so."[23] When Nehru convinced his country's political elite to remain in the Commonwealth, Pakistan and Ceylon followed the Indian lead.

At the Commonwealth meeting in Colombo, Ceylon, in January 1950, Lester Pearson was the main protagonist in negotiations which resulted in the Colombo Plan for Cooperative Economic Development in South and Southeastern Asia. As Indian Ambassador Rajeshwar Dayal has written, "Lester Pearson's participation in the opening meeting ... helped to endow the plan with body and substance ... Pearson was instrumental in assuring the Canadian government's generous financial contribution towards the plan's objectives."[24]

The Colombo Plan was the first multinational aid program of the postwar era. Lester Pearson's pledge of $25 million a year as Canada's contribution established the honourable, and later distinguished,

Canadian record in the field of development assistance to the Third World. If India was the top recipient of Canada's aid among the Commonwealth nations, this was both because of that country's genuine development needs and the emergence of the "Indo-Canadian love affair." Fruits of this relationship included a number of common initiatives and diplomatic projects, such as collaboration during the crises of Korea and Suez as well as in peacekeeping.

At the same time, Britain remained a focal point of Canadian foreign policy, given the deep roots of historical, linguistic, cultural, and political commonality of interests and values. In addition to the sentimental ties developed by these interests and by Canada's support of Britain during and after the Second World War, there was also the sharing of many politico-strategic perceptions surrounding the Cold War and the need to ensure the continued American presence in Europe. Finally, if the Suez crisis caused a certain schism within Canada (the Conservative party argued that Ottawa had "betrayed" London), it is certainly the case that Pearson's performance in the United Nations served the best interests of both the Commonwealth and Britain itself.

Thus, the Commonwealth emerged as a major forum for the exercise of Canadian middlepowermanship. Canada's longer-term goals here included the strengthening of political, commercial, and cultural links with a host of Third World members. In addition, the Commonwealth offered Canada numerous opportunities for North-South mediation and for enhanced credibility and prestige. Finally, of course, the multi-ethnic and multi-racial organization could provide Canada with another counterweight to the indisputable power of its southern neighbour.

CANADA AND THE SUPERPOWERS

If the facts of geography had resulted in Canada's being "sandwiched between two superpowers," the presence of the United States at Canada's southern border and the manifest asymmetry of their power resulted in the Canada–United States connection becoming one of the most convoluted, variegated, intimate, and at times intense postwar bilateral relationships. One inescapable by-product was Canada's perennial sensitivity to the retention of its normative autonomy and its treasured distinct identity.

That this special relationship also contained the potential for friction did not follow only from the two countries' differences in political culture, size, power and capabilities, security perceptions, and strategic interests. Their interdependence inevitably involved Canada's profound fear of economic dependence on the United States. Whereas British capital had supported Canadian growth until the First World

War, American capital began flowing massively to Canada after 1946.
While this capital sustained Canadian growth, it also produced a disconcerting indebtedness. Canada's total indebtedness during 1945–70
reached $40 billion, and of this sum, 80 per cent was owed to the
United States. The spectre of American economic domination thus
developed, reaching peaks by the late 1950s and the late 1960s. Canadians became concerned that American capital was being attracted by
crucial sectors of the country's economy. These sectors included mining, and the manufacturing of transport equipment, machinery, petro-
leum and coal products, and rubber and chemical products. Walter
Gordon, a former Liberal finance minister, put the issue dramatically
in his 1966 book, *A Choice for Canada: Imperialism or Colonial Status*.
He wondered whether "Canada had become free of Britain's colonial
influence only to fall under the spell of the United States' economic
imperialism."

As it developed, therefore, Canada's policy towards the superpowers
amounted to a sensitive synthesis. Ottawa policymakers on the one
hand aimed at close collaboration with the United States and the Western alliance. On the other hand, they were committed to moderation
in both Cold War rhetoric and in corresponding actions. The former
dimension stemmed from Canada's anti-communist attitudes and the
need to establish unambiguous Western credentials. The latter dimension, deriving from Canada's political-cultural distinctness, permitted
Canada to perform a mediating and moderating role, even at the
height of the Cold War.

More specifically, a certain independence in Ottawa's relations with
Moscow began as early as the immediate postwar years. This relative
Canadian autonomy – to be demonstrated repeatedly in subsequent
chapters – seemed anchored on the following principles: reduction of
international tensions through East-West bridge-building; increased
communication through diplomatic contacts, moderate pronouncements, and exchange of official visits; persistent stress on detente;
emphasis on a broader conception of security; de-ideologization of
Canadian trade; and finally, cultivation of Canada's sense of independence and distinctness. In sum, Ottawa's post-1945 policy towards
Moscow was an eloquent and tangible reflection of Canadian internationalism in action.

In Ottawa, St Laurent and Pearson were convinced that the West
was bound, ultimately, to win the Cold War, given its moral and material superiority. In Moscow, Ottawa's ambassador, Dana Wilgress, was
producing explanatory and predictive accounts of Soviet foreign policy designs which endorsed Washington's perceptions that led to the
policy of containment. It was, however, an endorsement with a clear

Canadian difference. As shown in his cable to Ottawa of 27 September 1945, Wilgress was also aware of the Kremlin's own alarmism vis-à-vis the West: "The Western World is living in dread that the Soviet Union is out to spread Communism throughout the world. Do they ever stop to think that the Soviet Union is also living in dread that the Western World is out to restore capitalism to the Soviet Union?" Wilgress's prescription was entailed in his reply to his own question: "If we would succeed in removing these two obsessions, cooperation between the Soviet Union and the Western World would become operative without the friction now so obvious."[25]

Similarly, Escott Reid channelled the policy analysis of the Department of External Affairs along the lines of what we now call "post-revisionism." In other words, both superpowers were expanding powers; the Americans were not bereft of all the blame; but, for the next decade, the possibility of war appeared to be "remote," since the balance favoured the United States and the Kremlin policymakers abhorred "adventurism."[26] Given, therefore, Canada's interests in seeing Cold War tensions reduced, two policy prescriptions followed. First, Canada should moderate the extremist proclivities of some Washington circles: "If Canada can follow a policy which is consistent in purpose, though variegated and resourceful in application, it can exert a very considerable influence upon United States policy." And second, presaging Ottawa's philosophy that led to the insistence on article 2 of the NATO Charter, Escott Reid noted that the West's "firmness need not be accompanied by rudeness." He added: "We should endeavour to follow a course which is neither that of excessive flattery nor of excessive ostracism."[27]

Thus, Ottawa's Cold War premises amounted to what Larry Collins labelled "containment without ostracism" and "containment with a 'human face'." Canada's concomitant attitudes were manifested during the negotiations for the formation of NATO. And, along with the principle of Canadian distinctness, these attitudes help explain the Liberal cabinet's repeated refusals to join Washington and London in confronting the Soviets' Berlin blockade of 1948–9.

Prudential internationalism continued to distinguish Ottawa's decisions at the beginning of the 1950s. While the Korean War was under way, the Department of External Affairs produced another document that kept endorsing a policy of caution and non-provocation. Entitled *General Limitations on Canadian Foreign Policy,* the November 1951 study advised: "Canadian foreign policy has to aim at promoting conditions most favourable for the achievement of an understanding with the Soviet Union which will provide reasonable relief from fear of imminent war or subversion."

Canada's Cold War role, then, was identified as follows: "Canada must ensure the Atlantic alliance does not infringe on vital Soviet interests which would provoke the very Russian response the alliance was set up to discourage. In sum, Canada must work in the alliance to protect the West's security without threatening the Soviets."[28]

Then, in September 1955, another External Affairs study capitalized on "the spirit of Geneva" and on the rising hopes for an easing of East-West tensions in a post-Stalinist world. The study, *Canadian Policy in the Light of Soviet Tactical Changes Since Geneva*, noted the risks to Canadian sovereignty from any escalation of the Cold War, since Washington could then pressure Canada to accept US bases and troops. It concluded that Canada's twin aims of security and national independence converged on one policy: namely, to attempt "to exploit the present Soviet willingness to establish more peaceful and normal relations between the two power blocs."[29]

Solidly in the internationalist forefront of pragmatic optimism, such thinking was soon translated into diplomatic action. Lester Pearson became the first NATO foreign minister to visit the Soviet Union in October 1955. His visit to Moscow, Leningrad, and the Crimea implied Ottawa's determination to employ palpable communication and a preparedness to negotiate as the vehicles for the normalization of Canadian-Soviet relations. Pearson's trip was certainly successful. Besides repeatedly assuring Nikita Khrushchev and his entourage of NATO's "peaceful intentions," the visit marked the start of Canadian-Soviet cooperation in the economic, technical, and cultural fields.[30] The January 1956 trade agreement between the two "northern neighbours" established a new pattern of lucrative Canadian exports of wheat to the Soviet Union and extended each other most favoured nation (MFN) status. Moscow agreed to buy annually between $60 and $75 million worth of wheat. Notable also was the shift in Soviet attitudes towards Canada, which seems to have began with *Pravda's* October 1955 piece, "For Good Neighbourly Relations Between the USSR and Canada."[31]

During the next year, however, when Moscow-led Warsaw Pact troops invaded Hungary, Canada joined in condemnation of the bloody aggression. Nevertheless, St Laurent's telegram to Moscow exhibited traditional Canadian moderation: it employed the vocabulary and tone that were to become the hallmarks of a distinct style of Canadian internationalism. Assuring Moscow that Canada did not intend to influence the type of government chosen by the Eastern Europeans, St Laurent appealed "in the name of humanity" for the minimization of suffering. After all, the Suez crisis, perpetrated by Canada's own allies, was taking place simultaneously.

It thus transpires that Ottawa's attitudes and policies towards Moscow were a faithful reflection of its entrenched decision to exercise middle-powermanship at the height of the Cold War. Similarly, Ottawa's attitudes towards Washington sprung from Canada's decision to strike a sensitive balance between the genuine commitment to its Western obligations and values and the parallel need to protect its distinctness. Ottawa's relevant attitudes towards American foreign and security policies were a function of two clear decisions: to cultivate as harmonious and cooperative relations as possible with Canada's NATO allies and with Washington itself; and to assert Canada's special perceptions, interests, and values whenever the situation warranted. As we have seen, the latter implied that Ottawa would express subtly its disagreements with Washington. The most notable such cases arose during the negotiations for the formation of NATO; during the Berlin blockade of 1948–9; during the Korean War; and during the 1956 Soviet invasion of Hungary. As for Ottawa's manner of expressing its occasional disagreements, it was only natural that quiet diplomacy would emerge as Canada's favourite policy option.

CONCLUSIONS

This overview of the golden age may suffice to establish the set of clearly defined Canadian foreign policy goals. Central among them were the following: to contain the role of great powers and the explosive potential of the superpowers; to increase the rightful room for action by the middle powers; to expand the role and the significance of multilateral institutions; to be ready and willing to defuse major crises and to enhance simultaneously the long-term prospects for stability and peace; to forge manifold links with individual states and groups of states; to establish solid credentials as a moderating influence and mediating force in the world; and to contribute to the advancement of world prosperity by assisting in economic, technical, and educational programs under bilateral and multilateral auspices.

The interests and values on which these goals were premised constitute the essence of Canadian internationalism. Arguably, Ottawa's actual international performance during the golden age transcended the expectations of the optimists. Certainly, Canada's diplomatic energy, imagination, and at times brilliance established its superb internationalist prestige. Simultaneously, of course, Canadian foreign policy served a broad set of domestic interests and needs.

We can now appreciate far better both Lester Pearson's own role in implementing the pragmatic idealism of Canada's foreign policy and the predictive wisdom of his 1948 speech in Vancouver: "We instinctively know that Canada cannot easily secure and maintain prosperity except on the broadest basis of multilateralism – which is another name for internationalism ... We also know, or should know, that there can be no political security except on the widest possible basis of co-operation."[32]

4 Diefenbaker's Internationalism, 1957–1963

The post-golden age decade may not deserve the laudatory epithets attached to the pragmatic idealism of Canada's early postwar period. The foreign policy of the Conservative government of John Diefenbaker exhibited numerous positive results but was also marked by inconsistencies, controversies, and some serious conflicts with Washington. As for the years of Lester Pearson's prime ministership (1963–8), it turned out that the brilliant architect of Canadian internationalism was not encouraged, either by the domestic climate or by the international landscape, to repeat Canada's earlier diplomatic feats.

Yet it seems incontrovertible that the patterns of Canadian foreign policy goals, interests, and values – solidly established during the golden age – were amply confirmed during the succeeding decade. It is therefore noteworthy that, in spite of domestic difficulties, major international shifts, and changes in government, the Diefenbaker and Pearson years entrenched the essential continuity of Canadian internationalism. This conclusion need not be surprising. After all, Canada's foreign policy is essentially conditioned by its political culture which remained constant, and the accumulated Canadian distinction and prestige were too good to be either ignored or resisted. Therefore, any variations on the Canadian internationalist themes during the 1957–68 period may best be interpreted in terms of the flexibility of Canada's pragmatic idealism – that is, its capacity to adapt itself to the changing world.

THE INTRIGUING RECORD
OF DIEFENBAKER'S RELATIONS
WITH WASHINGTON

The Conservatives, led by John Diefenbaker, came to power in June 1957. Domestically a populist, Diefenbaker soon emerged in the area of foreign policy as pro-UN, pro-Commonwealth, pro-British, anti-communist, and attached to the country's internationalist image. His preparedness to distinguish Canada's stance from that of Washington, whenever Canada's special needs or worldview deemed it appropriate, proved to be Diefenbaker's Achilles heel. This propensity to antagonize American policy developed especially after Howard Green, a religious man and a "peacemonger," assumed the portfolio of External Affairs in June 1959.

Diefenbaker's critics have assaulted him with charges of incoherence, incompetence, and the effective disintegration of Canada's diplomacy. One critic entitled his discussion of the Diefenbaker period, "How not to have a foreign policy."[1] The major cause of such antipathy was the prime minister's *volte-face* on a couple of security-related decisions, tinged by behaviour that bordered on "anti-American."

A more sympathetic interpretation, however, may well recognize Diefenbaker's stylistic idiosyncrasies but also acknowledge his efforts to maintain Canada's established internationalist credentials. Despite his complaints that the Department of External Affairs was full of "Pearsonalities," Diefenbaker was clearly sensitive about Canada's image and role in the world. The relevant record (1957–63) could well be interpreted as an (occasionally clumsy) implementation of the following traditional Canadian premises: strong support for the goals of the United Nations; simultaneous opposition to communism and to militarism; consistent commitment to the Commonwealth; de-ideologization of trade, in spite of vociferous American objections; support for human rights; anti-racist and anti-apartheid policies; and a penchant to distinguish Canada's principles and values from those of its superpower neighbour. Our discussion will support this internationalist interpretation.

It is unfortunate that Diefenbaker's critics have concentrated on his 1962–3 fight with Washington, for they were bound to distort the larger picture, which was captured succinctly by Peyton Lyon: "For four of his six years in office, Diefenbaker's foreign policy was generally sensible, confident and consistent with both his long held views and well established Canadian positions."[2] To be sure, Ottawa's conflicts with the administration of John F. Kennedy were serious. Arguably, their accumulated effect was to undermine Diefenbaker's credibility in Washington and, ultimately, his hold on power. The two major bilateral crises arose with respect to the Cuban missile crisis of October 1962 and the Bomarc episode of early 1963.

In one sense, both crises had their roots in the North American Air Defence agreement (NORAD). This Canada–United States arrangement for the defence of North American airspace was intended to confront the threat posed by Soviet bombers. According to the 1957 agreement, the air defence of the continent was undertaken jointly: the United States would cover most of the costs; a USAF general would be the commander, with a Canadian deputy; and Washington had the right to station American personnel on Canadian territory and to use Canadian airspace. Canada had wished to subsume NORAD under NATO, rendering multilateral what the Americans insisted should be a bilateral arrangement. Washington won.[3]

When the Cuban missile crisis erupted in October 1962, President Kennedy expected Canada to go on full alert, in unison with the United States and in view of NORAD. Diefenbaker, however, procrastinated. Canada's part of the NORAD system was put on alert status "Defcon 3" only forty-two hours after the American request. Needless to say, Washington officials were not impressed.

Conflicting hypotheses on Diefenbaker's procrastination abound. Among them the following seem plausible. First, Diefenbaker was deeply frustrated by the lack of American consultation before Kennedy's perilous decision to threaten the Soviets; second, the Canadian prime minister was convinced that Kennedy had acted in haste thus endangering world peace; third, Diefenbaker harboured a personal pique at Kennedy ever since their 1961 Ottawa encounter which was marked by behaviour insulting to the Canadian prime minister; and finally, confusion characterized Ottawa decision-making.

In his autobiography, Diefenbaker seems to have opted for a combination of the following explanatory reasons: Canada needed to contain the crisis; the United Nations had to be given a central role in the crisis; fear and panic would have resulted in the Canadian public; and the Canadian dignity had to be protected, since Ottawa was not consulted by Washington but was just told what it was expected to do.[4] On reflection, Diefenbaker's own account does not seem hyperbolic or blatantly self-serving. It also appears to agree with the internationalist interpretation which is confirmed by the rest of his foreign policy's style and substance, as we shall see.

The second crisis erupted in early 1963. Under the NORAD arrangement, Ottawa had agreed to contribute the Canadian-designed Arrow interceptor fighter plane. This advanced weapons system had been hailed as proof of Canada's high-tech sophistication in the defence sector and as demonstration of the potential autonomy of the Canadian air force. However, after ordering five hundred Arrows in 1953, the DND order was reduced to one hundred in 1958, and in February 1959 Diefenbaker cancelled the order. The official grounds for the cancellation were high costs and obsolescence. Instead of the interceptor planes, Canada offered to construct two Bomarc anti-aircraft missile sites in Ontario and Quebec. These missiles were capable of carrying only nuclear warheads. When the construction of the Bomarc sites was completed, Diefenbaker hesitated to accept the warheads, opposing the two-key (Canadian-American) nuclear weapons arrangement. Washington decision-makers, inimical to Diefenbaker's anti-nuclearism, were furious with Ottawa's backsliding. Serious political undermining of John Diefenbaker allegedly ensued.

Intriguing hypotheses have been advanced regarding Diefenbaker's post-Eisenhower relationship with Washington. A major one elaborates on the prime minister's anti-Americanism and his perception of a strong anti-American undercurrent in the country. As Lawrence Martin reported in *The Presidents and the Prime Ministers*, Diefenbaker's mail in the fall of 1960 had thoroughly convinced him of the unflattering views of Washington entertained by Canadians. A flood of letters contained proverbial anti-American conceptions. Canadians were expressing profound unease concerning the Pentagon's militarism and the American economic penetration of Canada. The Canadian ambassador to Washington, Arnold Heeney, noted in his diary that, in Diefenbaker's view, "anti-American sentiment was now worse than at any time in his lifetime or mine ... This was causing him the greatest concerns."[5] When Heeney inquired about the grounds for Canadians' bad feelings, Diefenbaker offered four: "the widespread impression that the U.S. was 'pushing other people around', distrust of the U.S. military and anxiety over the Pentagon's real intentions, the economic aggressiveness of U.S. interests, and the adverse trading position."[6]

This was still the Eisenhower period. John F. Kennedy was inaugurated as president a few months later. In May 1961 he visited Ottawa. His meetings with the Canadian prime minister were marked by controversy and tension. While Diefenbaker had tended to perceive Kennedy as "the young pup" or "an arrogant upstart," Kennedy had referred to the Canadian leader as "Mr. Diefenbawker" and had spent far more time at receptions with the leader of the opposition, Lester Pearson. Moreover, there was "the missing-memo affair." A one-page memo, prepared by US Assistant Secretary of State Walt Rostow, was entitled, "What We Want from Ottawa Trip." What the Americans wanted was "to push the Canadians" on a number of issues. Diefenbaker found the memo, left behind by the Americans, and used it as a weapon, twice, until his 1963 demise. The memo also contained a marginal note by John Kennedy allegedly calling the Canadian prime minister "an s.o.b."[7]

Arguably, therefore, there are grounds for supposing that Diefenbaker's pique at Kennedy might have coloured his 1962–3 attitudes towards Washington. By the same token, it seems highly unwise to personalize Diefenbaker's stance. Convoluted issues, such as Ottawa's response to the Cuban missile crisis and the Bomarc episode, require multi-causal explanations. It therefore seems far more rational to seek other reasons: for example, the numerous internationalist grounds provided by Diefenbaker in his memoirs;[8] the backdrop of perceived anti-Americanism in Canada; the evidence that Canada's overall foreign policy patterns had remained typically internationalist; and the fact that Diefenbaker was not the single decision-maker in Ottawa. After all, while Sidney Smith, Diefenbaker's first external affairs minister, had been actively engaged in attempts to moderate the Cold War, it was Howard Green who, in the words of Peyton Lyon, emerged "as the boldest and most dedicated advocate of disarmament within the NATO community."[9] It follows that the Diefenbaker government could not simultaneously sustain Canadian middlepowermanship and Washington's nuclear brinkmanship without blatant self-contradiction. Therefore, it had to choose middlepowermanship.

BEYOND THE BILATERAL CONUNDRUM: THE INTERNATIONALIST AGENDA

A principal goal of this chapter is to explore the continuity thesis – namely, that Canadian foreign policy during the Diefenbaker years remained staunchly internationalist. We have argued that the thesis receives substantial support even from Ottawa's response to the Cuban and Bomarc crises. This interpretation is amply supported by the Diefenbaker government's attitudes and policies towards what I have called the internationalist agenda. To this agenda we may now turn, paying particular attention to arms control and disarmament, peacekeeping, foreign aid, human rights, and Canada's relations with the Third World.

Arms Control and Disarmament

Writing in 1968, Peyton Lyon observed that "disarmament and related issues deserve a large and honourable place in any study of Canadian foreign policy during the years Mr. Howard Green was Secretary of

State for External Affairs … Mr. Green was the most ardent crusader for disarmament among the foreign ministers of the world."[10]

The authenticity of Howard Green's idealism has never been doubted. What was questioned, by some, was the effectiveness of his disarmament campaign. However, in the nature of the case, it is hard to demonstrate effectiveness if only because authentic disarmament hinges on the perception and behaviour of others. To be sure, Howard Green appeared to "overestimate the degree of influence which Canada could exert in negotiations"; this, as General E.L.M. Burns noted, "sometimes put Canadian diplomats in the position of being asked to make bricks without straw."[11] In addition, Green irritated some NATO allies with his passionate rhetoric and actions. In one sense, therefore, it becomes easier to demonstrate that the Diefenbaker minister meant what he said.

Howard Green's "magnificent obsession" with disarmament was implemented in a variety of ways. "He put some of the best minds in his department to work on the problem, directed all of his subordinates to give it top priority, and missed no opportunity to prod other governments into taking it seriously."[12] Furthermore, Green employed traditional Canadian functionalism, by mobilizing what Canadians were capable of doing best: taking legal and diplomatic initiatives, encouraging other parties to conduct negotiations, formulating proposals, identifying areas of agreement, and participating in the formulation of draft treaties.

During this period, as John Barrett has concluded, "Canada's role was to encourage the United States and the Soviet Union to agree on a common language in their discussions and to eliminate differences between the two sides in the areas of complete deadlock. This meant persuading the Americans through private diplomacy while seeking clarification from the Soviet Union publicly."[13] The activism of these years allowed a Department of External Affairs document to generalize: "In the disarmament field, Canada has been one of the most prominent and active non-nuclear-weapon powers in initiating new proposals and in responding to the proposals of other countries. Canada has been a member of every United Nations disarmament body, including those otherwise confined to the major powers."[14]

Among other decisions and actions, Ottawa pressed for the application of international law to outer space. In 1962 Canada submitted to the Eighteen-Nation Disarmament Committee (ENDC) a draft declaration to ensure the use of outer space solely for peaceful purposes. Canada supported the proposal for a partial test ban during the first meeting of the ENDC in March 1962. When agreement was reached in Moscow in 1963 during consultations among the United States, Britain, and the Soviet Union, Canada adhered to the test ban treaty three days after its signature.[15] Already in 1959–60 Canadian delegates to the Ten-Nation Committee on Disarmament "devoted particular attention to the possibility of checking development of the new class of nuclear weapons vehicles, the intercontinental and other long-range nuclear-headed rockets."[16] In any event, by 1962 Howard Green had "his attention turned more to ending nuclear testing."[17]

"Even if one believes that nothing of substance was accomplished by Mr. Green's activity," wrote Peyton Lyon, "most of his countrymen seemed to be pleased that their foreign minister was labouring for a worthy cause."[18] Evidence from the editorials of Canadian newspapers supports this claim. In March 1962 the *Montreal Star* called Green "that incorrigibly cheerful believer in miracles." Assessing his April 1962 performance at Geneva, the Toronto *Telegram* was inspired to suggest "that there is room once again, in international diplomacy, for the old eternal virtues of honesty, truth, sincerity of purpose, steadfast purpose and firm resolution, based on a deep faith in providence and a genuine belief in the desire of all men for peace on earth." And while the *Fredericton Gleaner* (26 July 1962) wrote that "Mr. Green speaks to the world as Canada's conscience," the *Financial Post* observed in April 1962 that "Mr. Green has been doing a job for all humanity of which Canada can be proud."[19]

Such editorial voices echoed the idealism embedded in Canada's political culture. They suggested that, when Canadian foreign policy focused on difficult internationalist goals, the celebration of idealist optimism could win over the fixation on "effectiveness."

Peacekeeping and Foreign Aid

In his 23 September 1957 statement in the United Nations General Assembly, Prime Minister Diefenbaker declared that the recent change of government in Canada "does not mean that there has been any change whatsoever in fundamental international principles or attitudes." He then added: "So far as Canada is concerned, support of the United Nations is the cornerstone of its foreign policy."[20] Diefenbaker's statement was hardly hyperbolic. Besides Canada's recognized activism in the arena of arms control and disarmament, genuine commitment was also demonstrated, among other fields, in peacekeeping and in UN-sponsored foreign aid. In addition, Canadian internationalism was energetically pursued in the Commonwealth, where the emphasis was placed on Canada's relations with the developing countries of the Third World.

The United Nations Emergency Force (UNEF), created after the Suez crisis, was a force of over five thousand men. In 1958 the Canadian contingent had reached about one thousand. The commander of UNEF, which was deployed between Israelis and Egyptians, was the Canadian, General E.L.M. Burns. In addition, Canadian officers were serving with the United Nations Truce Supervisory Organization (UNTSO), an observer group created in the late 1940s to supervise the armistice agreements between Israel and its Arab neighbours, Syria and Jordan. Canadian Lieutenant-Colonel G.A. Flint was killed by a sniper in May 1958 while serving with UNTSO.[21]

Canadian peacekeepers served in three other observer groups during this time. Although for brief periods, these operations helped establish Canada's unparalleled record in this field. Thus, seventy-eight Canadians were sent to Lebanon (UNOGIL) in 1958; a small number participated in the observer group in Yemen (UNYOM) in 1963; and a third force was dispatched to West New Guinea (UNTEA) in 1962.

But by far the largest, most costly, and hardest of all UN peacekeeping operations during the Cold War was ONUC, the Congo operation. It began in July 1960, when the newly independent African country (later known as Zaire) confronted internal disorder and a separatist threat in its province of Katanga. Canada supported the ambitious operation and the bold initiative of the UN Secretary General Dag Hammarskjold. As John Diefenbaker stated in his speech to the General Assembly on 26 September 1960, "the African nations must be permitted to work out their own destinies; when they need help, the best source is through the agencies of the United Nations." The Canadian prime minister also stated that the Congo tragedy had again demonstrated the need "to have military forces readily available for service with the United Nations when required."[22]

Canada responded to the July 1960 request for peacekeepers by sending 280 signals personnel and a small air contingent. As Richard Preston has commented, "The reason for requesting a Canadian contribution was partly Canada's experience in international forces and partly her reputation of anti-imperialism. The other important factor was her ability to provide a substantial number of expert communications personnel who could speak both French and English, the two languages used in running the Congo operation."[23]

Canada's authentic commitment to the principles and goals of the United Nations was being conscientiously pursued by the Diefenbaker government. Canada's diplomatic credit was thereby rising. Heath Macquarrie, Green's parliamentary secretary, said in the House of Commons about the 1962 session of the General Assembly: "There is something extremely humbling to be at an international organization and note on every hand the high respect in which Canadians are held ... The Canadian point of view is constantly sought."

In a similar vein, a British journalist was cited by Canadian journalist Earl Berger as expressing a typical view: "When you come right down to it, the Canadian delegation is the best at the United Nations. Can't understand why." Berger submitted his own explanation in terms of the Canadian delegates' "surprisingly high" personal calibre. He then added: "Deliberately and conscientiously abstaining from propaganda or self-glorification the Canadian delegation has become the 'honest broker', the mediator, the bridge-builder. It only moves when asked to, and then quietly, behind the scenes."[24]

Even Peyton Lyon was obliged to admit: "The sincerity of Mr. Howard Green's enthusiasm for the United Nations cannot be questioned. No man has ever taken the organization more seriously, and he was always prepared to give it more than its due credit for such developments as the containment of the Cuban crisis. Under Mr. Green's direction, the Canadian delegation continued with devotion and considerable success to strengthen the manifold activities of the United Nations."[25]

One of the central pillars of Canada's internationalist commitment concerned the field of foreign development assistance. Even though, as we shall see in chapter 6, it was the Trudeau government that catapulted Canadian Official Development Assistance (ODA) to remarkable heights, the Diefenbaker administration did not betray the internationalist credentials that were established during the golden age. Moreover, it is notable that Canada's ODA performance was maintained despite the economic malaise characterizing the country's economy during this period. As Tom Keating has observed, "Diefenbaker's dollar dilemmas were part and parcel of an economic downturn that hit the Canadian economy in the late 1950s and continued into the 1960s. The post-war boom was coming to an end and competition from Europe and Japan was on the rise. The US economy also moved into a downturn and Canada's close links with it meant that Ottawa could not avoid some of the spillover effects."[26] Be that as it may, John Diefenbaker's Ottawa manifested its genuine concern for the development needs of the Third World in various ways, under the auspices of the United Nations and of the Commonwealth, as the following illustrations will suggest.

Diefenbaker was the first statesman to call for an increase in the contributions to the International Monetary Fund (IMF) and the World Bank by the member nations of these international financial institutions. Linked to the United Nations, both the IMF and the World Bank were created in 1944 by the Bretton Woods system. The Western powers attempted thereby to liberalize the international monetary system and, with the creation in 1947 of the General Agreement on Tariffs and Trade (GATT), the world trade system; the World Bank was conceived in 1944 as a multilateral aid agency.[27] What Diefenbaker proposed in 1958 was a 50 per cent increase in the IMF members' quotas or contributions. The London *Economist* praised the Canadian prime minister for the idea; and Professor Trevor Lloyd attributed even more credit, given the difficulty of the prime minister's task to convince Washington to follow suit. In fact, the proposal was accepted at Delhi in October 1958: there was a 50 per cent increase in IMF quotas and a 100 per cent increase in those of the World Bank for most member states. And because the German, Japanese, and Canadian economies had progressed remarkably since the original assignment of quotas, these three countries agreed to provide additional funds.[28]

The Diefenbaker government proceeded to offer further contributions to those specialized UN agencies which depended on voluntary funding.[29] From 1957 to 1959 Canada was placed third among contributors to the following agencies: Extended Program for Technical Assistance, Special Fund, United Nations Relief and World Agency for Palestine Refugees (UNRWA), and United Nations International Children's Fund (UNICEF). Three of these programs received $2 million each in 1959; UNRWA, which had received a Canadian gift of $500,000 in 1957, was given $2 million in 1958 and in 1959. Some of these figures included Canadian gifts in kind, such as $1.5 million worth of flour given to UNRWA and millions of pounds of dried skim milk given to UNICEF (ten million pounds in 1958 and thirty-three million pounds in 1959). Finally, in the years 1959 to 1961 Ottawa contributed generously to the newly created International Atomic Energy Agency and to the peacekeeping budget of the UN. The latter was quite significant: among other things, by refraining from asking reimbursement for its UNEF airlifts, Canada gave the UN an additional $800,000 in 1958.

By 1960 the proliferation of aid programs, recipients, and funds led John Diefenbaker to set up an External Aid Office under the minister of external affairs. The first director-general of the office was Ambassador Herbert O. Moran. In 1961 he visited India and Pakistan, where he witnessed the opening of the Warsak hydroelectric dam. Moran described his visit as a moving experience; he reported his conviction that "there was an awareness among the people of the place whence the gifts had come"; and he suggested that this was "one of the great advantages of bilateral over multilateral aid."[30]

Canada, however, did not confine its ODA contributions to bilateral projects. The greater part of its aid during this period was provided through the Colombo Plan. This Commonwealth-inspired program combined attributes of both bilateral and multilateral aid: "Projects are arranged on a multilateral basis, with the full participation of the receiving nations in the Colombo Plan Council ... Aid is given directly or bilaterally; however, the recipient has a say in the execution of the project. Canadian aid given under these conditions does not appear to carry heavy political strings."[31]

The Colombo Plan for Cooperative Economic Development in South and South-East Asia celebrated its tenth anniversary in 1960. By then, Canada's contributions had been doubled. They rose "from $25.4 million in 1951–9 to $34 million in 1956–7 and $50 million in 1959–60 and 1960–1"; and they combined technical assistance with capital aid. As Richard Preston noted, Canada's capital assistance had been "largely directed towards helping establish or improve basic facilities upon which the countries of the area can develop their own economies."[32]

Beyond Asia, however, Canadian aid began flowing to new Third World regions by the early 1960s. For instance, in September 1958 Diefenbaker announced the building of two passenger-cargo ships for the West Indies, at a cost of $5.7 million. As regards Africa, Canada's interest in it had primarily been limited to trade relations with South Africa. After 1960, however, Canadian attention to Africa increased: $500,000 was contributed to the Commonwealth Technical Assistance Programme for Africa; the government announced its decision to ask the Canadian parliament to appropriate $10.5 million for aid to Africa over three years, beginning in fiscal 1961–2; and Howard Green announced in 1961 the government's decision to provide $300,000 a year to help francophone African states.[33]

Canadian assistance to Africa continued under the auspices of the Special Commonwealth African Aid Program. Begun in 1961, the program involved teachers and expert advisors. At the same time another program was launched to supply "educational assistance for independent French-speaking countries in Africa."[34]

More generally, Canada spent $70 million for ODA in 1962. Once again, the Colombo Plan absorbed the lion's share. In early 1963, as the federal election was approaching, the debate about Canadian overseas aid intensified. Most of the major newspapers seemed to support an increase in aid, as did "elite" groups. As Peyton Lyon reported, "73 per cent of the members of Parliament who were consulted, 75 per cent of the labour leaders, and 44 per cent of the businessmen, expressed the view that the aid program was 'too little'."[35] A few months earlier, however, even Lester Pearson and Paul Martin had refrained from criticizing the Diefenbaker government's aid-related performance. While admitting that "he personally favoured more aid," Pearson noted: "There is always a relationship between what can be done in Canada for people who need help and what can be done for people in Pakistan who need help … This is not a political matter because more is being done now than was done a few years ago."[36]

As for John Diefenbaker himself, he expressed his pride in the fact that his government was the author of another Canadian initiative in the field of foreign aid – the proposal for a world food bank as early as 1958. The World Food Program was finally launched on 1 January 1963 by the UN's Food and Agriculture Organization (FAO). Canada pledged $5 million worth of aid (one-third of which was in cash) over a three-year period. Diefenbaker could thus argue in January 1962 that "the Canadian plan had 'been altered very little', and its adoption brought 'honour to Canada'."[37]

The Commonwealth Connection

John Diefenbaker's commitment to the Commonwealth was partly a function of his sentimental attachment to the crown and to Britain, although it was premised also on a number of pragmatic interests and idealist considerations. Among other things, the Commonwealth could serve to strengthen Canada's links with Britain; it could act as another multilateral counterweight to the United States' influence and power; it would support Canada's trade interests with Britain, Australia, and New Zealand as well as the Third World or developing member states; and it could be a forum for such Canadian functionalist goals as communication and mediation, foreign aid, and support for human rights.

The manifold Canadian interests and values that could be satisfied by the Commonwealth had, in Diefenbaker's view, been hurt by Lester Pearson's stance on the Suez crisis, and he could be counted on to move to repair relations between Ottawa and London.[38]

Diefenbaker's relations with London were not, however, crowned with unmitigated success, mainly because of Britain's application to join the European Common Market in 1960. Diefenbaker feared that British membership in the ECM would affect Canada's trade interests and Britain's interest in the Commonwealth. The latter would result from London's necessary diplomatic reorientation towards its new European partners. As for Canada's trade interests, they derived from the Commonwealth and British preferential tariff arrangements (whose loss could well be feared) and from Diefenbaker's decision to diversify Canadian trade away from the United States. Thus, in the 1962 Commonwealth Heads of Government meeting in London, Diefenbaker disappointed the British delegates, who concluded that he was "the principal obstacle to UK objectives" despite his "impassioned declaration of faith in the Commonwealth."[39] As it transpired, Paris vetoed London's first application to the EEC, hence Britain would only join in 1973. But Diefenbaker's stance caused a chill in the bilateral relationship without achieving the desired diversification of Canadian exports away from the United States.

In other respects, however, Canada's interests and values were fulfilled in the Commonwealth forum. Diefenbaker's long tour of Commonwealth states in November and December of 1958 seems to have contributed to his policies' success. He was warmly received throughout the official trip, which cultivated Canada's multidimensional relations with India, Pakistan, Ceylon, Malaya, Singapore, Indonesia, Australia, and New Zealand. Canadians were on the whole pleased "to have a prime minister who could make so strenuous and so successful a trip around the world and to the extent that they realized that its success was a tribute to Canada as a nation, they must have felt some personal pride in it all."[40]

While trade and foreign aid were at the centre of Canada's Commonwealth policies, its prestige was also rising because the Third World Commonwealth states started to see Canada as an influential anti-colonial actor marked by generosity and a broad vision. Thus, by the start of the 1960s, Canada "became increasingly regarded as an ally of the New African and Asian countries of the Commonwealth, while Britain lost their sympathy and was driven to turn towards some of the other white members."[41]

A major personal success for the Canadian prime minister resulted from his anti-racist stance against the South African regime. By the 1960 Commonwealth summit a debate was already under way concerning the expulsion from the organization of the racist Pretoria regime. The debate had pitted those who drew on the principle of sovereignty and wished to refrain from condemning a member state's internal affairs,[42] against those who could not tolerate the inhumanity of the South African state. The opportunity for a denouement arose when South Africa became a republic. By asking Pretoria to apply anew for admission, expulsion would be avoided while new admission need not be granted. At the London Commonwealth summit in March 1961 South African Prime Minister Verwoerd applied for readmission. The majority of member states desired expulsion while Britain, Australia, and New Zealand wanted to find some formula for inclusion. The Diefenbaker answer set the tone for subsequent Canadian contributions which saved the Commonwealth from a break-up while siding with its Third World members. Diefenbaker, along with Indian Prime Minister Nehru, did not opt for expulsion. Instead, they insisted on a general Commonwealth resolution against race discrimination. As a result, "Mr. Verwoerd, finding himself

boxed in, announced after a night of consideration that he would with-
draw South Africa's application for membership. It was the Ides of
March, and the Canadian Prime Minister undoubtedly was a leader in
forcing the fateful decision."[43]

CONCLUSION

This survey of the implementation of the internationalist agenda
during 1957–63 can safely be said to verify the continuity thesis. For
it was shown that, in the entire range of concern to Canada's pragmatic idealism – arms control and disarmament, peacekeeping, foreign assistance, human rights, moderation, mediation, cooperation –
John Diefenbaker and his government performed with clear motives
and, overall, achieved successful results. Hence, as Basil Robinson concluded, Diefenbaker "left the foreign policy scene without having significantly altered the values, the priorities, or the continuing threads
which he inherited from his predecessors. His impact on foreign policy
was more in the method and the emphasis than in the substance."[44]
Similarly, Peyton Lyon, from the vantage point of 1989, concluded that
Diefenbaker's foreign policy "was generally sensible, confident and
consistent with both his own long held views and with established
Canadian positions."[45] In fact, even the results of the difficult months
in 1962–3 when the bilateral relationship with the United States deteriorated, could be re-evaluated in light of the following considerations:
first, the Canadian people were certainly exhibiting anti-American and
anti-nuclear sensitivities; second, the Canadian economy was subjected
to a prolonged downturn; and third, as Basil Robinson attested, "the
fact was that with Kennedy in office, the supply of understanding and
goodwill in the White House had quickly dwindled."[46]

   Arguably, therefore, the internationalist interpretation of Canadian
foreign policy from 1957 to 1963 receives its confirmation. After all,
the continuity thesis presented here is not about some blissful state of
unmitigated success by Canadian foreign policy, for success is crucially
a function of expectations and the state of the external environment.
The expectations during Diefenbaker's years were inordinately high, in
view of the triumphs of the golden age; the external environment was
that of a world in dramatic flux. If, therefore, the continuity thesis of
Canadian internationalism is essentially about authenticity and depth
of commitment to the principles, interests, and values of Canada's
pragmatic idealism, then John Diefenbaker, Howard Green, Canada's
UN delegates, and the Pearsonalities of the Department of External
Affairs seem to have amply sustained and served the motives and the
goals of Canadian internationalism.

5 Lester B. Pearson as Prime Minister, 1963–1968

Two interrelated clichés mark most discussions of Canadian foreign policy during Mike Pearson's years as prime minister: that he did not duplicate the diplomatic triumphs of the golden age, and that he could not have done so, given both his domestic preoccupations (primarily vis-à-vis Quebec) and the substantial global changes characterizing the new era. Like many clichés, there is some truth in these propositions. After all, as John English suggests, "the central question for Lester Pearson between 1965 and 1967" was "if France and Quebec were to work together, what part would Ottawa play?"[1] In addition, whereas the first postwar decade presented remarkable opportunities to establish Canada's international prestige, the changed global landscape had narrowed Canada's space to celebrate its vocation as an internationalist actor. For, among other things, decolonization was now almost complete; London was cultivating its special relationship with Washington; a mini-detente between the superpowers was still in effect; and, as Peter Dobell wrote, some "inherent" UN weaknesses had rendered peacekeeping problematic, so that "since 1965 not one new force or observer mission has been approved or even seriously considered."[2]

Emphasis on these facts, however, should not obscure another truth: that Canada continued the coherent and principled pursuit of its pragmatic idealism. If anything, therefore, these new external constraints and domestic anxieties could well justify additional respect for Ottawa's internationalist persistence. And while no doubt could be raised about the credentials of the architect of Canadian internationalism, our discussion of 1963 to 1968 will illustrate both the declarations and the actions of Lester Pearson and Paul Martin as clear examples of Canada's pragmatic-idealist foreign policy commitment.

PEARSON'S CANADA BETWEEN EAST AND WEST

Soon after his April 1963 election victory, Lester Pearson visited John F. Kennedy at Hyannis Port. The recent damage to the crucial relationship had to be repaired, and there were more issues to address beyond the bilateral nuclear débâcle. The atmosphere of the new summit was "almost euphoric"; the two leaders "liked each other thoroughly."[3] While Pearson later referred to the "stimulating experience to be exposed to the charm of Kennedy's personality and to the toughness and clarity of his mind,"[4] the American president had already written about Lester Pearson:

In the diplomatic history of the free world since World War II the name of Lester Pearson has many entries. Still in full vigour as leader of the Opposition in Canada, Mr. Pearson's stature cannot be assessed for another decade. Yet already "Mike" Pearson has been the chief architect of the Canadian foreign service, probably unequalled by any nation; he has been a brilliant ambassador and foreign secretary; he has been a central figure in the growth of the Atlantic Community and NATO, even while taking a leading role in the shaping of the United Nations.[5]

In view of such mutual admiration, and despite the sensitivity of some items on the agenda, the May 1963 summit was highly successful. Among other issues, it covered economic relations, the negotiations on the Columbia River Treaty, industrial unrest on the Great Lakes, disagreement on territorial waters and fishing zones, and, most sensitive of all, the problem of nuclear weapons on Canada's soil. Lester Pearson had argued all along that Canada should accept them to honour its alliance obligations. But, to pre-empt vociferous objections, he now promised a parliamentary debate on the nuclear issue, just as he had promised during the election campaign to renegotiate the agreement.

Early in his term of office, therefore, Pearson had succeeded in placing the bilateral relationship on a pragmatic footing, replacing the recent hysteria by a rational euphoria. To be sure, the fishing zones issue, boldly handled by Paul Martin, annoyed the Americans in the summer of 1964. But when, in June 1963, the nationalist finance minister, Walter Gordon, brought down a budget containing a takeover tax widely seen as anti-American, the controversial proposals were rapidly withdrawn. Canada clearly intended to re-establish a constructive *modus operandi* with the United States. Among other things, the 1959 Defence Production Sharing Arrangements were renewed in 1963. This would allow Canada to compete equally for lucrative American contracts with American firms, while Canada's armed forces would benefit from the lower prices of major US weapons systems.[6] The governments of Canada and British Columbia reached the requisite agreement on the way to finalizing the Canadian-US Treaty on the Columbia River project. *Time* and *Reader's Digest* were exempted from tax measures taken in 1964 to strengthen the publication of periodicals in Canada. And on 31 December 1963 the American nuclear warheads arrived at the Bomarc missile site at North Bay. In short, the Pearsonian approach to the most sensitive bilateral issues seemed to reflect what Lester Pearson believed about Canada's "participatory internationalism" in the early postwar years: "It helped us to escape the dangers of a too exclusively continental relationship with our neighbour without forfeiting the political and economic advantages of that inevitable and vitally important association."[7]

Ottawa, indeed, felt free to cultivate the internationalist grounds of its relative autonomy. In mid-September of 1963 it announced the renewal of the Canada-USSR trade agreement and the sale of over six million tonnes of wheat to the Soviets. The minister of trade and industry, Mitchell Sharp, described the sale, worth about $500 million for 1963, as "the largest in Canadian history." Moreover, some of this wheat was to be shipped directly to Cuba, apparently without Washington's objections. In addition, Canadian wheat was sold to three Warsaw Pact members: Czechoslovakia, Bulgaria, and Poland. Concluded in the second part of 1963, and lasting for a few years, these contracts constituted, according to Charlotte Girard, "a fine achievement."[8] Similarly, wheat sales were extended to the People's Republic of China. On 2 August 1963, Sharp announced the conclusion of a "new long-term wheat agreement" with China under more generous credit arrangements than before. Therefore, the Canadian pattern of de-ideologizing trade – which began with Lester Pearson's 1955 trip to the Soviet Union and continued with Diefenbaker's trade with China and Cuba – was now becoming a tradition.

The Pearsonian principles of moderation, mediation, and bridge-building were working simultaneously with the idea of de-ideologized trade. This is not a mere hypothesis; Pearson explicitly spoke of broad contacts with the Soviets as the best means towards better East-West relations. During his January 1964 visit to Paris he argued that communism could not be defeated by armed force given the danger of a nuclear war. The only reasonable policy in Canada's view was to "maintain as close contact as possible with the Soviet bloc leaders with a view to seeking and exploiting openings for negotiations on major east-west issues." And to reach success, one should be "ready to seize any opportunities presented."9 In November 1966, Paul Martin implemented these principles by visiting the Soviet Union. Among other things, he "sought to engage the Soviet leaders in discussion of the principal international issues of the day such as Vietnam." Martin had already appealed for a better exploitation of the mini-detente by the West during the NATO council meeting of May 1964. In particular, he recommended "the encouragement of contacts and trade with Eastern Europe, which would thus come to feel 'less subservient to Moscow,' a development that 'should be a reasonable NATO objective in this area.'"10

As regards defence policy, it should be noted that the promise to renegotiate with the United States the issue of nuclear weapons on Canadian soil was not fulfilled. Canada, however, attained joint control, whereby the weapons could not be used without Ottawa's authorization. The Liberal government issued the 1964 white paper on defence wherein participation in NATO and NORAD was unquestioned, "sovereignty protection" and peacekeeping were upgraded, and the integration and unification of the armed forces were begun. The reasons offered for this controversial initiative were related to savings and to flexibility and mobility of the forces. In any event, Pearson froze the defence budget in 1964 at an annual $1.5 billion (or 4.5 per cent of GNP) for five years. Personnel levels were being reduced amounting to about 100,000 in 1968 and accounting for some 80 per cent of the defence budget.11

Finally, it is noteworthy that Pearson, who in 1949 achieved "the Canadian article" in the NATO Charter, retained unaltered his conception of security fifteen years later. In his September 1964 speech to a NATO audience Pearson identified three main areas which the organization had to address "if we are to retain our freedom, carry out our international responsibilities and maintain the values common to our Western society." The second area was the relations "between the materially rich and developed countries and those that are poor and underdeveloped."12

PEARSON, JOHNSON, AND VIETNAM

On the tragic death of John Kennedy on 22 November 1963 the vice-president, Lyndon Johnson, became president. Pearson met with Johnson in a January 1964 Washington summit where the Columbia River Treaty was signed. Then, on 12 March, Johnson phoned Pearson from the White House anxious over "the delay in establishing the UN peace-keeping force for Cyprus. The situation was rapidly deteriorating and the UN should act quickly. Could we help?" Pearson replied that the situation was in the hands of the United Nations; that the major difficulty was in securing the participation of additional nations besides Britain and Canada; and that Ottawa would "have our men on the way by air as soon as we got the go ahead." Pearson's account continues: "I said not to worry; we knew our duty to the UN; we knew the danger of war breaking out there very, very quickly between Greece and Turkey (Turkish forces were already on a troop ship ready to leave). The President seemed reassured and very grateful."

After the necessary action by Secretary General U Thant, Canada's troops reached Cyprus within twenty-four hours. The US President "was amazed and filled with admiration at our ability to act so quickly, and I think this may have changed his attitude toward Canada." Indeed, Lyndon Johnson was as impressed as he was relieved. As Pearson relates, he phoned the Canadian prime minister again, at night: " 'You'll never know what this has meant, having those Canadians off to Cyprus and being there tomorrow. You'll never know what this may have prevented.' Having praised us for our action, he concluded: 'Now, what can I do for you?' I replied: 'Nothing at the moment, Mr. President.' But I had some credit in the bank."[13]

Arguably, the credit in question was employed towards the automotive agreement that Pearson and Johnson signed on 16 January 1965. According to one commentator, the Auto Pact "gave much advantage to the Canadian automobile industry and helped to lower Canada's ever large balance-of-payments deficit with the United States." Another analyst, who similarly seems to imply such a link, observed that the agreement "facilitated a rapid growth in the Canadian industry."[14]

This bilateral bliss, however, was not destined to last. America's moral trauma caused by the Vietnam War had also been affecting – and dividing – Canadians. By early February 1965, when the Americans were bombing North Vietnam, Pearson felt obliged to express his opposition and to abandon his treasured principle of quiet diplomacy. During his 10 February address to the Canadian Club of Ottawa, he stated:

We must protect and advance our national interests, but we should never forget that the greatest of these is peace and security. The achievement of this aim … does not depend on our policies so much as it does on those of our neighbour … It does not mean that we must always remain silent if there is strong disagreement on matters of great moment or principle. Not at all.[15]

A few weeks later, Pearson was awarded the Temple University World Peace Award. When he delivered his acceptance speech at Philadelphia in April, he called for a suspension of American air strikes: "I merely suggest that a measured and announced pause in one field of military action *at the right time* might facilitate the development of diplomatic resources which cannot easily be applied to the problem under the existing circumstances. It could, at the least, expose the intransigence of the North Vietnam government."[16]

The American government had requested an advance copy of the text, but Pearson had declined. The next day, Lyndon Johnson invited Pearson for lunch at Camp David. "After lunch the President and I went out on the terrace, cool and sunny with a wonderful view. It was only then that we got down to Vietnam." Pearson's diary relates that Johnson found his speech at Temple bad; that "for an hour … he told me why it was bad, allowing me to get in only a word or two of explanation and justification"; and after expounding "his Vietnam policy at some length," Lyndon Johnson gave Pearson "a frank and revealing exposition of US plans, told with great vehemence, many short and vigorous vulgarities at the expense of his opponents, and a few Texas illustrations."[17]

According to John English, "If the language came from the locker room, the bullying was from the schoolyard." Journalist Lawrence Martin interviewed a number of Canadian and American officials and diplomats who witnessed the meeting, and has thrown further light on Johnson's demeanour, his vulgarities, and his "Texas illustrations":

Inside, the houseguests minced uncomfortably around the dining-room table, not catching all the defamation, but guaranteed a resounding "Horseshit!" from the president every three minutes.

For more than an hour he tore on until ultimately, in a piece of bilateral diplomacy knowing no equal, he moved beyond the realm of words. Having pinned the much smaller Pearson against the railing, the president of the United States grabbed him by the shirt collar, twisted it and lifted the shaken prime minister by the neck. The verbal abuse continued in a venomous torrent. "You pissed on my rug!" he thundered.[18]

Pearson's statesmanship was manifested in the dignity of his subsequent letter to Lyndon Johnson, which aimed at clearing the interpersonal air by articulating his views, and in his diary's entries which showed some understanding for the president's manifold crises. But Pearson's caution not to antagonize the United States overtly was overwhelmed by his principled decision that the Vietnam War had to stop.

He manifested this decision in a variety of ways. In January 1966 he permitted Paul Martin to send Chester Ronning to Hanoi, and perhaps

Beijing, "to put out 'feelers' about the war and about the possibility that Canada would recognize the Communist regime." Paul Martin seemed "enthusiastic about the task" of Canadian mediation. The American ambassador, Walt Butterworth, (who "exploded" when he heard the Canadian plan) claimed in his cable to Washington that Martin also believed "that at some point he should demonstrate to the Canadian people that Canada had not just been a US satellite but had done what it could to bring about a solution." Ronning's visits took place in February-March and then in June. They were not fruitful; but Paul Martin has argued that the Americans "failed to take advantage of an 'opening' that occurred when Ronning met North Vietnamese premier Pham Van Dong in early March 1966."[19]

Canadians were told about Canada's mediation efforts when Paul Martin met with the Standing Committee on External Affairs in June 1966. He stated that Blair Seaborn, the Canadian commissioner serving on the International Commission for Supervision and Control in Vietnam, had visited Hanoi six times in 1964 and 1965. Martin argued that "our role in Vietnam has not been supine and that we have attempted to use the channels available to us by virtue of our Commission membership to establish contact with North Vietnam." He added that Seaborn "had an interview with the Foreign Minister [of North Vietnam] on May 31, in which he expressed Canada's concern, and our willingness to play a helpful role if possible."[20]

Clarifying the role of Blair Seaborn five years later, Mitchell Sharp stated in the House of Commons:

Canada's motive in agreeing to this special mission for the Canadian Commissioner was a try to promote a peaceful settlement to the conflict in Vietnam. Thus the Canadian government considered it entirely consistent with, and indeed reinforcing, our role in the ICC. I should like to emphasize that the Commissioner acted at no time as a direct representative of the United States government or President but only as a part of a Canadian channel of communication.[21]

Lester Pearson met Johnson for the last time in May 1967 at Harrington Lake, the Canadian prime minister's summer cottage. There, Pearson had a few private minutes with the American president:

I then put very frankly to him the proposition that he should stop the bombing, without any conditions regarding time or anything else, and merely announce that he would now meet the other side without delay to discuss a ceasefire, an armistice, and peace. I told him this would put the Communists on the spot and remove their last proclaimed excuse for refusing to begin negotiations.[22]

When Paul Martin spoke at the United Nations General Assembly in September 1967, he called for the unconditional end of the American bombing. The Vietnam War was too serious to be left to quiet diplomacy. As John English commented, Martin's "choice of forum was symbolic and, for Canada, appropriate." After all, "The speech reminded Canadians of how much the institution had meant in the past, and how committed Mike and Martin remained to it."[23]

Finally, on 31 March 1968 Lyndon Johnson announced his twofold decision to halt the bombing and not to seek re-election. Lester Pearson wrote him again to express appreciation of the decision on Vietnam and to say "how deeply grateful I think the whole world should be for the proposals you have made and for the courage and wisdom you have shown in making them." He ended: "I had wanted to telephone you but I know you will be deluged by calls so I hope you will accept this personal message instead which is sent with my most sincere and warmest good wishes."[24]

On 1 May 1968, two days before retiring as prime minister, Lester Pearson stated to the Canadian Press: "The industrial and economic and financial penetration from the south worries me, but less than the penetration of American ideas, of the flow of information about all things American; American thought and entertainment; the American approach to everything."[25]

PEARSONIAN INTERNATIONALISM AT THE UNITED NATIONS

The sophisticated internationalism of Lester Pearson and his government was demonstrated primarily at the United Nations and the Commonwealth. Both remained primary counterweights to American power and influence. But they also provided the most opportune forums for the entrenchment of Canada's synthesis of pragmatism and idealism in the five areas of arms control and disarmament, peacekeeping, human rights, foreign aid, and relations with the Third World.

Arms Control and Disarmament

Canadian delegates to the relevant UN agencies and conferences continued the energetic pursuit of arms control and disarmament which began with the golden age and was sustained by the Diefenbaker-Green team. The clarity of Canada's purpose is demonstrated by Paul Martin's statement in Geneva on 26 March 1964. Speaking to the Eighteen-Nation Disarmament Committee, he presented Canada's proposals for an early agreement on "collateral measures" as a prelude to a treaty on general and complete disarmament:

First, the freeze of strategic nuclear-weapon vehicles proposed by the President of the United States;

Second, the destruction of a number of long-range nuclear bombing aircraft proposed in different forms by the Soviet Union and the United States;

Third, the non-dissemination of nuclear weapons;

Fourth, the cessation of production of fissile material for nuclear weapons and diversion of existing stocks to peaceful uses;

Fifth, the establishment of a system of observation posts to prevent surprise attack;

Sixth, a comprehensive test ban; and

Seventh, the strengthening of the United Nations capacity to keep the peace.[26]

The Disarmament Division of External Affairs was now headed by the leading Canadian peacekeeper, General Burns. Under his direction a set of proposals for non-proliferation of nuclear arms was prepared by May 1965. Numerous aspects of these proposals were endorsed by the Disarmament Committee in Geneva. Hence, Albert Legault has concluded that "General E.L.M. Burns is and will remain one of the key figures connected with disarmament in the history of Canadian diplomacy ... Already in 1965, Canada was beginning to sow the seeds of the Treaty on the Non-proliferation of Nuclear Weapons."[27]

The Canadian delegates actively sought to influence international discussions and negotiations, with notable success, despite the inherent constraints. For as Paul Martin put it in August 1963, Canada's obligations to its allies and friends conditioned its relevant behaviour as much as the fact that "our relations with the Communist world are governed by the general state of East-West relations and particularly by the climate and the relations between the United States and the Soviet Union." Therefore, Canada's relations with the Communist countries could not be "at wide variance with those of our closest friends and allies." But

within these limits there are possibilities open to us which serve our interests and the interests of our allies. There are possibilities for increasing trade in non-strategic goods. There are possibilities for more cultural, scientific and personal contacts which we will also encourage in the firm belief that they will help to break down the barriers of mistrust.[28]

In this explicit internationalist framework, the Canadian representatives continued the Pearsonian application of functionalist skills and talents. They identified areas of agreement, formulated proposals, took diplomatic and legal initiatives, encouraged negotiations, and participated in the formulation of draft treaties. Canada played "a prominent role in encouraging the conclusion of, and often in formulating" a number of treaties on "collateral or partial" disarmament measures. It continued its participation in the Disarmament Committee negotiations for an Outer Space Treaty. After agreement was reached on a draft of the treaty in 1966, the General Assembly approved it by acclamation. Canada was a party to the treaty which entered into force in October 1967. Canada supported in 1967 the conclusion of the Treaty of Tlatelolco, creating a nuclear-weapon-free zone in Latin America.[29] As two French-Canadian experts have written, "The issue of general and complete disarmament was as much a preoccupation for Burns as for Green. Canada expended a good deal of effort in tidying up the proposals under discussion, and was active both in consultations between allies and in discussions within the Eighteen-Nation Committee."[30]

Finally, despite inevitable nuances caused by the complexity of the issues and Canada's allied obligations, the same authors epitomized a major thesis as follows: "Legal and political idealism reached its height with the Green-Burns combination."[31]

Peacekeeping

Canada's intimate association with UN peacekeeping was not confined to the uninterrupted contribution of highly professional and effective personnel to all operations and missions. Lester Pearson, who in 1951 had recommended a standby force for use by the United Nations, suggested in 1957 that member states should "earmark units of their regular forces for peacekeeping service." The same concept of a less ad hoc arrangement was emphasized by Pearson during his speech at the General Assembly on 19 September 1963. A novel dimension was added by proposing "a compact planning team of military experts which would provide the advice and assistance which the Secretary-General should have for organizing emergency peace-keeping operations." Canada, which already possessed forces to be deployed by the UN on short notice, was ready and willing to share its experience and expertise with other interested member states.[32]

Pearson's statement was not rhetorical. It was followed up by an article he wrote for *Maclean's* in early May 1964. There he proposed that, if the General Assembly could not agree to arrange for a standby peace force, the initiative should be taken by concerned states: "There must be leadership to bring this about. Interested governments must be prepared to give it. As a leading middle power, with a well-known record of support for United Nations peace-keeping operations in widely spread theatres, Canada is in a unique position to take the initiative. It is prepared to do so."

Already, of course, Canada had proven an impressive capability to dispatch its contingent to Cyprus immediately. The manifold reasons for participating in the United Nations Force in Cyprus (UNFICYP) were succinctly identified by Paul Martin on 4 May 1964. There was the "urgent need for international cooperation to preserve peace in Cyprus"; the future of the UN was at stake; Canada's NATO membership "obligates us to do our utmost to prevent conflict between Greece and Turkey and exposure of the Eastern flank of the alliance"; "Cyprus and Britain are members of the Commonwealth"; and, finally, the "suffering of the people of Cyprus ... demanded the attention of all who believe in human decency and dignity."[33]

The UNFICYP was just one of Canada's peacekeeping operations. Apart from the International Commissions for Supervision and Control in Vietnam, Cambodia, and Laos, not under the aegis of the UN, Canadian "Blue Berets" were now active in various locations. As Paul Martin recounted in the summer of 1963: "We have provided a reconnaissance squadron, administrative troops and the RCAF personnel for the United Nations Emergency Force in Gaza, observers for Kashmir, Palestine and Indochina, specialized Air Force personnel for the Congo and the Yemen and signallers for the Congo.[34]

In addition, an important Canadian-sponsored conference was held in November 1964. Called the Ottawa Meeting on Peace Keeping Operations, the five-day conference attracted delegates from twenty-two other countries. They came primarily from Third World states and from the like-minded middle powers of Denmark, Finland, the Netherlands, New Zealand, Norway, and Sweden. The Canadian chairman, Commodore R.W. Murdoch, concluded that the Ottawa conference was a success "simply by its happening, by the wealth of talent and experience among the delegates, and by the fullness and frankness of the exchange of information." In addition, the Canadian standby battalion's demonstration apparently impressed the UN secretary general's military advisor. Indian Major-General Indar Rikhye suggested that the airlift for peacekeeping operations might be supplied by Canada.[35]

To be sure, the UN was finding it frustrating trying to translate peacekeeping into peacemaking and to decide who should pay and how. Nevertheless, Canadians and the Pearson government remained committed. Charlotte Girard concluded about 1963–5 that "Few Canadians had any quarrel with the Prime Minister's view that this was what Canada *should* be doing."[36] Indeed, while the Canadian people were appreciating the country's solid accumulation of diplomatic credit, their "idealist impulse" was one major source of this result. As Peter

Dobell has stressed, "Canadian attitudes to UN peacekeeping have always been highly idealistic." Simultaneously, of course, Canada's peacekeeping role "had contributed so much to Canada's international reputation."[37]

FOREIGN AID

Paul Martin made clear on various occasions Canada's entrenched commitment to help developing countries. He also premised it explicitly on a synthesis of idealism and pragmatism.

In his March 1964 statement to the United Nations Conference on Trade and Development (UNCTAD), he quoted Lester Pearson, for whom the developing world's economic and social life "is strengthened by the function which outside assistance performs and by the evidence which it brings of widespread interest, sympathy and support." That was why, Martin explained, "Canada actively encouraged the formation of United Nations programmes and we backed up our support with substantial contributions." Through programs targeting first South and Southeast Asia, and later Africa and the Caribbean, Canada had already provided "substantial development resources, by far the greater part of which has been on a grant basis requiring no repayment." Recognizing, however, that more must be done, the Pearson government "decided to increase Canada's economic aid by more than one-half ... We expect our aid expenditures during the next twelve months to reach $180 to $190 million."[38]

Speaking to a domestic audience in February 1965 in Quebec, Paul Martin reviewed the motives behind foreign aid in general; he then turned to the humanitarian impulse:

For my own part, I have no hesitation in saying that I regard humanitarian considerations to be foremost in the minds of those who have supported and sustained the principle of Canadian aid to the developing countries ... In essence I would say [the humanitarian approach] rests upon the recognition that, as flagrant disparities in human wealth and human welfare are no longer morally acceptable within a single community, whether it be local or national, the same principle is applicable to the larger world community.[39]

Then, in what sounds like an echo from St Laurent's Gray Lecture, he quoted Barbara Ward: "To me, one of the most vivid proofs that there is a moral governance in the universe is the fact that when men or governments work intelligently and far-sightedly for the good of others, they achieve their own prosperity too ... Our morals and our interests – seen in true perspective – do not pull apart."[40]

This was a sophisticated endorsement of the moral dimension of pragmatic idealism. But Martin also focused on Canada's enlightened self-interest when he presented four Canadian benefits from foreign aid: Canadian economic growth is stimulated "by contributing to the level of production, exports and employment"; "Canadian producers, engineers and educators" can "gain valuable experience" while "Canadian products and skills" can "become known in new areas"; "the horizons of Canadians are enlarged and Canada's image abroad is more clearly projected"; and finally, "the use of Canadian goods and services gives Canadians a stake in foreign aid which, I am sure, has helped to enlist and maintain public support in Canada for an expanding aid programme."[41]

The Pearson government really meant what it said: its development assistance rose by some 280 per cent between 1964 and 1967. While Colombo Plan recipients still got the lion's share of Canadian aid, French-speaking former colonies now benefited as well. In 1964–5, Canadian assistance to African countries of la Francophonie was increased by more than thirteen times. In a conference held in Montreal in early 1965, Martin acknowledged that Canadian-African relations were "still in their initial stage," but he noted that funds given through the External Aid Office had been increased from $300,000 to $3.5 million annually in the previous three years. More funds had been given through the United Nations for civilian projects in the Congo. Much of this aid was for education; but projects were also forthcoming for bridges and hydroelectric power.[42]

By 1966 the grant component of bilateral Canadian aid to French-speaking African states had risen to $6.1 million; when food aid and soft loans are added, the 1966–7 figure for francophone Africa becomes $11.1 million.[43]

Canadian multilateral assistance under UN auspices also rose by leaps and bounds. A new program was initiated in 1964, when Ottawa allocated $10 million for concessional loans to be administered in association with the Inter-American Development Bank. By 1966–7 these funds were raised to $30 million. Quite remarkable also was the nature of these loans, which were intended for economic, technical, and educational projects: "These funds are used for loans which may have maturities up to 50 years, including grace periods up to 10 years, and may be free of interest or bear such concessional rates of interest as are agreed to by the Bank [IADB] and Canada."[44]

The increase in Canada's multilateral aid can be further illustrated by three programs. First, Canadian allocations to the International Development Association (IDA) rose from $8,510,000 in 1960–1 to $15,030,000 for each of the fiscal years 1965–6 and 1966–7. Second,

Canadian disbursements to the UN Development Program rose from $3,880,000 in 1960–1 and $4,900,000 in 1962–3 to $9,500,000 for 1966–7. And third, Canada's cash contributions to the World Food Program quadrupled in two years: the $400,000 for 1962–3 rose to $600,000 in 1964–5 and then to $2,500,000 for 1966–7.[45]

Foreign Aid in the Commonwealth

Canadian development aid, channelled primarily through the Commonwealth's Colombo Plan, continued to rise. India remained the chief recipient; however, Malaysia received special attention, the allocation to Africa improved dramatically, and the same occurred for the Caribbean states.

As regards India, in addition to assistance in the traditional fields of food, commodities, transportation, and public utilities, Canadian aid also covered the military and the nuclear sectors. Military assistance was requested by India in view of China's challenges in 1963. Canada supplied New Delhi with surplus equipment and a loan towards the purchase of sixteen Cariboo aircraft. In the atomic energy field, Ottawa agreed to provide valuable knowhow on heavy water systems and a CANDU reactor. The latter agreement envisaged that Canada would contribute about $35 million, representing half of the project's costs. Moreover, it was agreed that Canada would provide "half of the initial charge of uranium fuel" and that India would use the Canadian technology for peaceful purposes only.

In September 1963 Malaysia was created out of Malaya and other former colonies. Canada promised an increase of aid from $1 million to $5.5 million. Besides disbursements through the Colombo Plan, Ottawa provided the Asian country with teacher training and vocational schools. When the Malaysian prime minister visited Canada in July 1964, the Kuala Lumpur press was elated by the reception he received, describing his visit as "fruitful beyond all expectations."[46]

Additional Colombo Plan countries which benefited from Canadian assistance included Pakistan and Ceylon. In 1963, for instance, Canadian-funded projects covered hydroelectric studies and plants in Pakistan and Ceylon, while similar projects continued in India and Malaya. But Canadian aid was also allocated for such purposes as medical improvements, airport expansion, electrification, and educational training up to the university level. Thus, by 1966–7, the total Canadian Colombo Plan allocations had reached $147.25 million. The top recipients were India ($109 million), Pakistan ($27 million), Ceylon ($4.5 million), Malaysia ($2.7 million), and South Vietnam ($2.0 million).[47]

The Pearson administration's aid disbursements for African Commonwealth and Caribbean countries were also expanding. They addressed primarily the field of education and the provision of Canadian technical advisors in such areas as health, forestry, geology, transportation, and television. Grant disbursements and development loan assistance for the Commonwealth Caribbean Aid Program reached $13.4 million in 1966–7. The three top recipients were Jamaica, Trinidad-Tobago, and Guyana. In Africa, the top recipients were Nigeria, Ghana, Tanzania, and, after 1965–6, Kenya and Uganda. Clearly, the general allocation of grants to Commonwealth Africa increased dramatically: from $3.5 million in 1961–2 to $11 million in 1964–5, and then $18.5 million in 1966–7.[48]

In sum, the Pearson government's internationalist promises on aid were fulfilled. Total Canadian allocations for grants and loans were $48.98 million in 1956–7 and $112.97 in 1961–2. By 1966–7, they had risen to $307.33 million.[49]

CANADIAN ANTI-RACISM

Canada's reputation under the Commonwealth aegis was strengthened in other areas. This multilateral forum, while satisfying the Canadian interest in a counterweight to Washington's power and influence, was also capable of celebrating Canada's values and fulfilling its functionalist needs. Paul Martin repeatedly praised the Commonwealth's role in Canadian foreign policy, and vice versa.[50] And Lester Pearson summarized his own conception of the organization's nature and value. "It is not," he wrote in his memoirs, "an empire, an alliance, a power bloc, or a mutual security group. It is neither a diplomatic unit nor a trading and currency system for its members."

It is, if I may use the word, a fellowship, the great value of which stems from the fact that it is an association of peoples of every race, freely joined together as equals in the hope that they have something to offer one another and can give the world an example of inter-racial as well as international friendship and co-operation.[51]

According to Dale Thomson and Roger Swanson, Pearson's personal prestige was Canada's most important contribution to the deliberations of the Commonwealth in the 1960s: "At a special meeting held in Lagos in 1966 he succeeded in drafting a statement concerning Rhodesia that was accepted by all members, and may have prevented the organization from breaking apart."[52] This is true, and constitutes the best among numerous Canadian contributions. Although incapable of blowing his own diplomatic horn, Pearson referred to the functionalist activism of the Canadian delegations on various occasions.

First, during the July 1964 Commonwealth meeting in London, the Canadian delegation "actively tried to use its influence to prevent disintegration." Letting the new members "know that we were entirely on their side in principle" when the burning issue was racial discrimination in Southern Africa, the Canadians performed in the Pearsonian manner. They took "an active part in the discussions and a leading part in drawing up the Declaration of Racial Equality, which became a virtual charter for the New Commonwealth."

Second, in 1965 in London, responding to the request by some new African members, Canada "took the major step of setting up a permanent Secretariat, and this has worked extremely well ... Now we were instrumental in founding the Secretariat, and the first Secretary General was a Canadian, Arnold Smith."[53]

Third, Pearson referred to the January 1966 Lagos conference, dominated by the Rhodesian situation. But, with customary modesty, he praised British Prime Minister Harold Wilson's "masterly skill" in defusing temporarily the crisis.[54] It is therefore important to note that Paul Martin later spoke of Pearson's contribution during the Lagos conference: "Britain welcomed the proposal of Prime Minister Pearson which led to the establishment of two continuing Commonwealth committees." The sanctions committee was chaired by the Canadian high commissioner in London; the second committee was formed to plan "a large-scale programme of training for Rhodesian Africans." Finally, and most tellingly, Harold Wilson said about Pearson's mediation that "only Mike could have done it."[55]

Fourth, regarding the next Commonwealth meeting (London, September 1966), Pearson elaborated on his speech against general mandatory sanctions and against the use of force in Rhodesia. He added that "only in Rhodesia ... is racial equality still denied as a basis of government and of society ... This is abhorrent and intolerable to the great majority of people and must be changed." Pearson then concluded: "The conference finally reached a compromise, with a good deal of effort on Canada's part, between the African desire to employ force against the illegal Smith regime and the British hope of negotiated settlement."[56]

It follows that Canada had demonstrated again its passionate commitment to the idealist values of its thoroughgoing internationalism. Once again it had saved the Commonwealth from a fatal cleavage along colour lines. It had sided with the African and Asian members in condemning racism while resisting the use of force. This, then, was another reason why "after 1965, Pearson was seen internationally as one of the best friends the Third World had in the industrialized West."[57]

OTTAWA, PARIS, AND QUEBEC

Traditionally, foreign policy analysts have treated the post-1965 malaise in Pearson–de Gaulle relations, and the concomitant federal-Quebec sensitivities, as grounds for the claim that they explain Pearson's limited energy in foreign policymaking. Then, David Dewitt and John Kirton, propelled by their idiosyncratic framework, conceived of Canada and France as "two emerging principal powers competing for influence and international presence."[58] That the traditional conclusion is unwarranted is by now demonstrated: far from being anemic, Canadian foreign policy under Lester Pearson and Paul Martin was as energetic and effective as Canadian internationalism needed to be. Dewitt and Kirton's conclusion amounts to a *non sequitur,* if only because Pearson and Martin repeatedly stated or implied that Canada is, and ought to remain, a pragmatic idealist middle power. Thus, what needs to be shown is how Pearson reacted to the convoluted conundrum and, if possible, why.

The brief sketch of the Ottawa-Paris-Quebec triangle can begin by recalling that Québécois self-assertion amounted by the early 1960s to restlessness accompanied by manifold pressures on Ottawa. Lester Pearson was sensitive to the underlying perceptions and realities. As leader of the opposition he had called for the re-evaluation of Canada's bilingual and bicultural character. Five months later, in the May 1963 speech from the throne, the Pearson government gave the Royal Commission on Bilingualism and Biculturalism pride of place in its program. In November 1963 Pearson designated his approach "cooperative federalism," and signalled his conviction that "there would no longer be a federation if French Canada was not satisfied." Therefore, many domestic decisions and programs, from the flag to pensions, from bilingualism to equalization, came from Pearson's recognition that national unity was the most important issue facing the country.[59]

Already, in October 1961, Quebec had opened a *délégation générale* in Paris. But when Quebec and Paris signed an educational agreement in February 1965, Pearson's concern was heightened, and Ottawa proceeded to sign a framework agreement with France in November 1965. The Liberal government embarked on further initiatives intended to pre-empt Quebec's nationalist assertiveness and to provide guidelines for federal-provincial foreign policy coordination in matters of provincial interest. As Pearson explained later, he did believe "that we should bring the provinces much more into these external matters because so many subjects discussed at international conferences fell, according to our constitution, under provincial jurisdiction." He also saw it as reasonable "for the Quebec government to have special contacts with Paris, to make special arrangements, to have a special understanding and special liaison with the French government." After all, other provinces had pursued such policies with London. Therefore, Pearson "was not impressed by the horror felt in certain quarters because Quebec was at last discovering France, or rather France was discovering Quebec."[60]

Pearson, however, was now also convinced that the Quebec provincial government wished to move into the area of foreign affairs. This, of course, contravened "the essential constitutional fact that only the federal government could speak for Canada abroad." It also implied "the intervention of France in our domestic affairs."[61] What embittered Pearson especially was the disconcerting contradiction between the developing Quebec-Paris flirtation and the "fine and noble words" uttered by General de Gaulle in January 1964. During Pearson's official visit to Paris, the French president had made "a very moving speech." He described as natural the "special regard for French people in Canada"; he admitted that they "interest us especially and deeply"; and then he added:

However, there need be nothing in this particular and natural connection which would interfere with the happy relations of the French Republic with your Federal state ... in which we see a faithful and courageous ally whose blood was shed on our soil in two world wars ... and whose independence we wish to see assured.[62]

Thankfully, we do not need to untangle the precise motives of this complex leader who was known to believe that "States do not have friends – they have interests."[63] We need only note that a number of irritants in the Ottawa-Paris liaison preceded the 24 July 1967 provocation, "Vive le Québec libre!" Paris was disappointed that the Caravelle jetliner was not bought by Air Canada, and found Ottawa's restrictions on uranium sales to France discriminatory. But Pearson could not have acted on the former; on the latter, he announced a compromise in June 1965. Canada would apply the same uranium sale conditions to the French as to the British. Paris, however, resented international supervision, and additional disagreements on the uranium contract caused the negotiations' collapse. Ottawa, for its part, was disappointed when de Gaulle's assertiveness vis-à-vis "les Anglo-Saxons" culminated in his country's March 1966 withdrawal from

NATO's integrated military structure. Moreover, the Canadian NATO troops were asked to leave French soil and move to Germany. This sufficed to rouse Pearson's indignation; when a high-ranking French official regretted that the Canadians were requested to leave, "I could not refrain from asking him whether he thought we should take our hundred thousand dead with us to German territory."[64]

Pearson's memoirs are inconclusive on de Gaulle's motives. But he knew how to respond after the "Québec libre" challenge: "The people of Canada are free. Every province of Canada is free. Canadians do not need to be liberated." He also knew that, as John English wrote, "he would not fight another day." But, with the rise of Pierre Trudeau, Pearson finally knew that he had those who would.[65]

CONCLUSION: LESTER PEARSON'S OPERATIONAL CODE

The main goal of this chapter has been to show the uninterrupted continuity of Canadian internationalism and the sophisticated coherence among the 1963–8 premises and deeds of Canada's foreign policy-makers. Despite the domestic and external odds, this period extended and entrenched Canada's post-1945 multilateralism, functionalism, mediation, moderation, caring, and sharing – in others words, its pragmatic idealism. This was manifest in its internationalist agenda, exemplified by arms control and disarmament, peacekeeping and peacemaking, support for human rights and anti-racism, foreign economic and technical assistance, de-ideologized trade, energetic support for international organizations, and constructive relations with the Third World.

This picture permits the drawing of a stark methodological lesson. When the analytic perspective of the foreign policy observer is incompatible with the declared or implied intentions of the foreign policy-makers themselves, fallacies become inescapable. That is why some conclude that these years yielded meagre results, while others find their favourite thesis falsified by a record that did not aspire to such status at all.

By supporting the thesis of pragmatic idealism and by identifying the fallacies of competing perspectives, the continuity thesis can again be seen as confirmed. It now remains to add some observations on Lester Pearson's operational code to explain more fully what inspired him and spurred him on. It is arguable that his worldview was premised on his own principles, on the valuable experience of his diplomatic practice, and on their dialectical relationship.

With respect to his diplomacy, Denis Stairs has summarized perceptively some of Pearson's main lessons.[66] Starting from the premise that
his central preoccupation was "with peaceful methods of resolving
conflict," Stairs argued that Pearson's liberal pluralism explains this
preoccupation. Pearson understood that "in a world of endless diver-
sities and perpetual disagreements, the only principle of political
action which in the end is consistent with the pursuit of self-interest is
the principle of give and take." After all, Pearson's own war experience
had shown him that the failure to bargain or negotiate "ultimately
leads all too often to the battlefield." What followed was the need for
a willingness to deal, which is itself related to a host of other properties, "among them tolerance, moderation, an affinity for compromise,
a preference for the 'middle way', above all, a disposition to avoid
extremes."

Stairs added that Pearson's internationalist purpose "entailed support most obviously for the United Nations." Further, when statesmen
exhibited intolerance of opponents, extremism, immoderation, or a
reluctance to compromise, then "the obligation, and indeed the self-
interest, of third parties demanded that they go pragmatically in
search of common ground, in pursuit of some small basis for agreement." Finally, a wise formula was "to isolate the bargaining process
from the play of unreasoning influences"; for, as John Holmes wrote,
"the diplomat's primary responsibility is to 'cool' it."

All this is true and telling. It can be supplemented by what Pearson
said in his January 1948 Vancouver speech, and other instances, reflected in *Mike*, II and *Words and Occasions*. But what is missing in most
attempts to analyse Pearsonian internationalism is the parallel stress on
caring, sharing, and compassion. That is why Paul Martin's endorsement of Barbara Ward's philosophy is so revealing. For she stated explicitly what Louis St Laurent and Lester Pearson had implied: "That
generosity is the best policy and that expansion of opportunity sought
for the sake of others ends by bringing well-being and expansion to
oneself."[68]

Lester Pearson's own values have also been linked to the British-
Canadian Protestant tradition and the associated notion of "the interdependence of all creatures, the foundation of Pearson's internationalism." John English notes that Pearson, in his public life, "never spoke
of God or called upon him to explain or justify his ways ... Nevertheless, Pearson's thought, language, and ethics bear heavily the weight of
the tradition [of British Protestantism]."[69]

Denis Stairs, in yet another perspicacious essay, endorses English's
thesis and broadens the circle of the Pearsonian internationalists as

if to also imply that their collaboration with the Department of External Affairs is more comprehensible when the ethical source of their values and worldview is considered. After all, "Lester Pearson, Arnold Heeney, and Escott Reid were all sons of ministers. Chester Ronning and E.H. Norman were both 'mishkids', and they were far from alone. Walter Riddell was himself a Methodist minister, and Hugh Keenleyside, among others, came from a staunchly Methodist background. The manse, it seems, was a formative force in External Affairs as powerful as academia."[70]

It seems to follow that, if the goal is to explain the sources of Canada's international prestige, one should resist the temptation to assume that idealist values and attitudes are absent in the world of international relations. That this unqualified assumption is facile and artificial, and hence fallacious, has been amply demonstrated by the life and times of Canadian foreign policy from 1945 to 1968.

Finally, as regards Lester Pearson the person, and his implementation of the aforementioned principles and values, additional evidence came from an unexpected American source. Edward K. Hamilton, while deputy mayor of New York City, wrote about Pearson and about their collaboration in the Commission on International Development. He noted that "the vital point with regard to Pearson is that he honestly and deeply believed that the case based on narrow national interest was unnecessary." Pearson was also "absolutely firm in his conviction that if governments and peoples could be confronted with the fact that a better lot for the poor is possible, simple compassion and the will to justice would be ample justification for whatever effort was required." "In the end," Edward Hamilton concluded,

it was his humanity and his faith in its presence in others which distinguished Mike Pearson from lesser men. He led us by drawing out the best in us. He showed us that it was possible to be serious without taking oneself too seriously. He was an object lesson in nobility of spirit. He was the loveliest human being I have ever known.[71]

6 The Logic and Ethics of Trudeauvian Internationalism, 1968–1984

If the validity of analyses of Canadian foreign policy hinges decisively on the reasonable choice of a framework or perspective, it also derives from passing some elementary methodological tests. Except for vulgar post-modernists and thoroughgoing sceptics, we tend to regard as axiomatic that our theories must be verified by rich and relevant evidence; that we can also expect them to be falsifiable; that it is not enough to support a thesis without demonstrating the invalidity of its contraries; and that fallacies must, by definition, be eschewed.

This elementary code of methodology has been violated persistently in the analysis of Canadian foreign policy. That is why judgments about it are so contradictory as to make one wonder if the same empirical record is being analysed and assessed. The Trudeau era has generated more dramatically than any other the phenomenon of foreign policy mythologies. One such mythology is predicated on the notion that the years 1968 to 1980 were the "Era of National Interest."[1] Another influential view is premised on the thesis that Trudeau's foreign policy was rather "amorphous."[2] But the most severe set of fallacies was committed in terms of Trudeau's "overweening vanity and arrogance"; his sporadic interest in foreign affairs; the "quixotic" nature of some of his major projects; and his essential "inconsistency."[3]

This picture is nothing short of astonishing, and later, I will comment on its probable causes. But first I will try to show that Trudeauvian internationalism deepened, extended, and refined the pragmatic and the idealist elements of post-1945 Canadian foreign policy, and was also characterized by conceptual coherence, normative consistency, overall effectiveness, and widespread recognition.

THE 1968–70 FOREIGN POLICY REVIEW

In his 29 May 1968 statement, the newly elected Liberal leader and prime minister announced the decision to reassess Canada's foreign policy. His statement stressed that, in many respects, Canada's post-1945 record in international affairs "was a brilliant record," for which "we owe much to the inspiring leadership of the Right Honourable Lester Pearson ... Reassessment has become necessary not because of the inadequacies of the past but because of the changing nature of Canada and of the world around us."[4]

Both the language and the substance of the statement endorsed the internationalist framework. It gave pride of place to Canada's "legitimate responsibilities in world affairs." It accepted that Canada's "progressive involvement in international development and relations during two decades or more have given this country a position of prominence and distinction." The new government's broad objectives included the maintenance of peace and security, the expansion and improvement of aid programs, and general economic stability. The idealist dimension was represented by the repeated references to the needs of the developing countries and the acceptance "as a heavy responsibility of higher priority Canada's participation in programmes for the economic and social development of nations in the developing areas."

Trudeau's idealism could also be detected in his traditional Canadian response to the security challenges of the late 1960s. While "nations suffer the nervous exhaustion of living in an atmosphere of armed threat" and global and regional tensions abounded, Trudeau defused the notion of a monolithic communist unity and stated that there has been "a perceptible *détente* in East-West relations." And, since "China continues to be both a colossus and a conundrum," Trudeau was prepared to recognize the government of the People's Republic of China and take a hard look at Canada's role in NATO and NORAD. Finally, Trudeau registered the idealist-internationalist dimension of his worldview by declaring "our support for international organizations – and especially the United Nations family." While insinuating a possible pragmatic shift of emphasis, he stated that "there will be no slackening of our broad policy of support" for multilateral organizations.[5]

The pragmatic dimension cohabited with idealism and was quite explicit. National needs and resources had to be assessed; national unity was a crucial consideration; our "paramount interest is to ensure the political survival of Canada as a federal and bilingual state"; the "mutual confidence and respect in our relations with the United

States" should be maintained, and Canada should act "so as to widen the area of mutual benefit without diminishing our Canadian identity and sovereign independence." Finally, the pragmatic dimension was demonstrated by Trudeau's persistent stress on modesty and effectiveness. His call for better methods was motivated by the need to "keep Canada effectively in the forefront of those international endeavours which realistically lie within our national resources"; it was associated with the facts of a changed and changing world; and it was premised on the notion that we "should not exaggerate the extent of our influence upon the course of world events." Adopting policies "which will permit Canada to play a credible and creditable part in this changing world" did not mean harbouring excessive ambitions. Nor did Canada need "to preach to others or castigate them."[6]

The Trudeau government began implementing these promises and decisions. The foreign policy review also began in earnest. Canada recognized China and supported its UN membership. The External Aid Office was renamed the Canadian International Development Agency (CIDA) and Maurice Strong, the ardent internationalist, was appointed its first president. Soon thereafter, the International Development Research Centre was created. As Trudeau had announced on 29 May, the IDRC would, among other things, "ensure that Canadian and other moneys are put to the most effective use possible."[6]

It was clear, therefore, that foreign aid and cooperative international development were indeed Trudeauvian priorities. This could have been anticipated after Trudeau's 13 May 1968 speech at the University of Alberta. The speech contained what later became hallmarks of Pierre Trudeau's pragmatic idealism: the mobilization of the Canadian humanitarian impulse; the recognition of the pragmatic need for efficiency and for linking development and peace; and the admission of Canada's enlightened self-interest. This triptych, which I have called Trudeau's synthesis, will emerge as the best analytic device for understanding the logic and ethics of Trudeauvian internationalism.

The product of the foreign policy review was the June 1970 white paper, *Foreign Policy for Canadians.* Trudeau was personally involved in its production from start to finish, so it is not surprising, as Harald von Riekhoff noted, that the documents "incorporate much of his thought and even imitate his language."[7] The introductory section, "Canadians as Internationalists," is noteworthy:

During the post-war decades, Canada and Canadians acquired a certain taste and talent for international activities of various kinds. Canadians took pride in the skill with which their political leaders, their military and civilian peacekeepers, their trade and other negotiators conducted the nation's business abroad. The international reputation Canada had then was earned at a time when Canada enjoyed a preferred position and a wide range of opportunities … The Canadian people had broken out of the isolationism of the thirties and came to the realization that there was an interesting and important world outside where Canada should have a distinctive contribution to make.[8]

Among other things, "Canadians developed and exercised a substantial interest in international organizations"; they moved to and worked in the Third World "as technicians, teachers and administrators"; back home, they welcomed "foreign scholars, students, and trainees"; they "travelled far and wide in search of business, service and pleasure"; and decolonization "offered new challenges to religious groups, private aid societies, universities, humanitarian groups generally."

This varied activity by Canadians has stimulated and substantiated a deep-seated desire in this country *to make a distinctive contribution to human betterment.* It manifests itself in the various pressures which have been exerted on successive governments to do more in such international fields as peacekeeping, development aid and cultural cross-fertilization. This *altruistic aspiration* seems to be shared generally across Canada.

Then, immediately following the idealist celebration, the last sentence reiterated the pragmatic caution and moderation of the two Trudeauvian statements of May 1968: "What Canada can hope to accomplish in the world must be viewed not only in the light of Canadian aspirations, needs and wants but in terms of what is, from time to time, attainable."[9]

The 1970 white paper employed throughout this spirit of idealist and pragmatist balance. The basic national aims were three: Canada's security "as an independent political entity"; enjoyment by all Canadians of "enlarging prosperity in the widest possible sense"; and letting Canadians "see in the life they have and the contribution they make to humanity something worthwhile preserving in identity and purpose." These ideas were then unfolded in terms of "the main preoccupations of Canada and Canadians today." In addition to such familiar ones as sovereignty, unity, personal freedom, parliamentary democracy, economic growth, and balanced regional development, these main preoccupations also involved national identity, social progress, environmental improvement, "human values and humanitarian aspirations." The congruity between Canadian interests and values and those of the international community was stated explicitly. This central theme in the thought of St Laurent and Lester Pearson now assumed the following formulation: "Canada's action to advance self-interest often coincides with the kind of worthwhile contribution to international affairs that most Canadians clearly favour."[10]

The Trudeau government presented six policy themes to illustrate the point that foreign policy is the extension abroad of national policy. These themes were:
- fostering economic growth;
- safeguarding sovereignty and independence;
- working for peace and security;
- promoting social justice;
- enhancing the quality of life; and
- ensuring a harmonious natural environment.

The publication by the Department of External Affairs of "Canada–US Relations: Options for the Future" was added in 1972.[11] The government's programmatic conceptual and normative framework was thus completed. We now turn to the implementation of this framework.

TRUDEAU'S CANADA BETWEEN THE SUPERPOWERS

Trudeau's decisions in April 1969 to halve Canada's contribution to NATO Europe achieved considerable notoriety. The May 1968 promise of thoroughgoing reassessment had covered NATO and NORAD, and the Liberal party's protracted debate on security encompassed support for non-alignment or neutrality and withdrawal from Canada's alliances. Therefore Trudeau's option for the *middle way* appears eminently defensible from the pragmatic-idealist point of view.

This decision was amply defended by Trudeau. First, there was the question of availability of Canadian resources; as the prime minister emphasized, Canada's defence budget was one-sixth of its total budget. "That's a lot of money – $1,800 million for defence."[12] Second, Europe had now reached remarkable strength, in contrast to its paralysis at the time of NATO's formation. As Trudeau reiterated on the day of the decision (3 April 1969): "Perhaps the major development affecting NATO in Europe since the Organization was founded is the magnificent recovery of the economic strength of Western Europe." Therefore, by implication, the European allies could now safely increase their contribution to their own defence. Third, a new hierarchy of Canadian security commitments was adopted: the surveillance of Canadian territory and coastlines; the defence of North America in cooperation with the United States; "the fulfilment of such NATO commitments as may be agreed upon"; and the performance of international peacekeeping. Fourth, "flexibility," "effectiveness," support for the civil authorities, and even "renewed enthusiasm and a feeling of direction to the members of the armed forces" were mentioned in Trudeau's statement, which also referred to the Canadian armed forces' future contribution "to the maintenance of world peace."[13] Finally, the Canadian compromise was clear in the government's explicit rejection of a non-aligned or neutral role by Canada in world affairs.

The above statement was supplemented a few days later when Trudeau noted: "What we want to do with this $1,800 million is to defend Canadian sovereignty and to contribute towards world peace. Why else would Canadians want to spend money on defence? We don't want to go to war with anybody." He then employed the term "national interests" and hastened to explain:

... when I say national interests I am not thinking in any egotistical sense of just what's happening to Canadians. It's in our national interest to reduce the tensions in the world, tensions which spring from the two-thirds of the world's population who go to bed hungry every night, the two-thirds of the world's population who are poor whereas the other third is rich, and the tensions which spring from the great ideological struggle between the East and the West.[14]

This conceptual-normative framework explains why, despite the more pragmatic attitude towards peacekeeping adopted by *Foreign Policy for Canadians*, "the Canadian government remained responsive to appeals for forces to participate in peacekeeping operations and for aid in other emergencies." As Peter Dobell suggested, there were understandable reasons for the government's more modest stance and for its preparedness to continue honouring the Canadian tradition, including "the memory of past peacekeeping successes." In any event, the 1974 defence white paper stated explicitly that the Trudeau government "continues to support the concept of peacekeeping and will seek to utilize Canada's experience, to develop guidelines, with the United Nations and elsewhere for effective peacekeeping operations. The government will consider constructively any request for Canadian peacekeeping ventures when ... an operation holds the promise of success and Canada can play a useful role in it."[15]

By 1971, over six hundred Canadian armed forces personnel were serving in various UN operations, as well as in the international commissions in Laos and Vietnam. As *Canada and the United Nations, 1945–1975* reminded us, after detailing all the observer groups and operations under UN auspices until 1977, "Canada is the only member of the United Nations that has participated in all these operations."[16]

Trudeau's earlier comments also revealed his 1969 perception of the militarized nature of NATO, which contradicted the Pearsonian conception that led to article 2 of its charter. Trudeau argued that, after twenty years, "NATO had developed too much into a military alliance and not enough into a political alliance, not enough into an alliance which is interested not only in keeping the balance of deterrence of tactical power in Europe but into an alliance which is interested in arms control and de-escalation."[17]

This, then, was another Trudeauvian principle which adopted and extended the Canadian internationalist tradition of arms control and disarmament. The new emphasis on detente coincided with Trudeau's worldview and was, as we shall see, implemented throughout his prime ministership. Therefore, the decision to halve Canada's NATO contribution was, on reflection, a wise compromise. It appeased the nationalist (and occasionally anti-American) sentiment in the country; it strengthened the credibility of Ottawa's commitment to detente; it enhanced the legitimation of Ottawa's time-honoured commitment to arms control and disarmament; and it entailed once again the pursuit of Canada's treasured distinctiveness.

The authenticity of Ottawa's commitment to detente was demonstrated soon after the bitter frustration caused by the 1968 Warsaw Pact invasion of Czechoslovakia. Canada, of course, condemned the invasion. It co-sponsored a UN Security Council resolution to this effect, accepted 13,000 Czechoslovakian refugees in 1968–9,[18] and cancelled or postponed visits and exchanges planned earlier with Moscow. And yet, the principle that communication and bridge-building must continue at all costs – especially in periods of crisis – explains why Ottawa's representatives at NATO headquarters were urging talks with Moscow only a few months later. Visits and exchanges with the East Europeans were re-established. For instance, beginning in June 1969, Canadian officials visited Prague, Bucharest, and non-aligned Belgrade. Canada received Soviet foreign minister Andrei Gromyko, the Polish foreign minister, a Romanian delegation, and President Tito of Yugoslavia. Then, during the May 1970 NATO meeting in Rome, Mitchell Sharp argued vigorously for the discussion of a broad range of issues with the Soviet bloc, urging in particular "an early approach to the Warsaw Pact countries with a view to negotiating the mutual reduction of armed forces."[19]

Trudeau's Visit to the Soviet Union

Of all official Canadian diplomatic visits during this early detente period, the most significant was Pierre Trudeau's trip to the Soviet Union in May 1971. During his eleven-day visit, Trudeau had discussions with President Leonid Brezhnev and Premier Alexei Kosygin.

Apart from Moscow, he visited Leningrad, Kiev, Tashkent, Samarkand, Norilsk, and Murmansk. Trudeau and the Soviet government signed a Protocol on Consultations, agreeing "to enlarge and deepen consultations on important international problems of mutual interest and on questions of bilateral relations by means of periodic meetings."[20] During his Moscow press conference and upon returning home, Trudeau emphasized the importance of regular contacts with the Soviets on issues of mutual interest, of expanding bilateral trade, and of cultural, scientific, and educational exchanges. As Trudeau stated in the House of Commons on 28 May 1971:

I harbour no naïve belief that as a result of [the] protocol our two countries will find themselves suddenly in a relation that will reflect nothing but sweetness and tender feelings … But, surely, the only way to resolve these differences and eliminate these concerns is by increased contact and effort at understanding.[21]

The trip was planned to yield tangible benefits, beyond demonstrating Canada's preparedness to strengthen communication and dialogue with the Soviets at a fragile stage of detente. It also reasserted Canada's commitment to de-ideologized trade. A new round of wheat sales, totalling 130 million bushels, was negotiated with the Soviets in June 1971. In July the minister of Indian affairs and northern development, Jean Chrétien, made his own seventeen-day visit to the Soviet Union. Three months later Premier Kosygin paid a return visit to Canada and signed the Canada–USSR General Exchanges Agreement designed to facilitate exchanges in the technical, scientific, cultural, academic, and sports fields. The next year was also remarkable for three events: the Canadian National Defence College visited the Soviet Union in May; a $100 million wheat sale was negotiated in July; and, most important for many, the first Canada-Russia hockey series took place in September.

Canadian-Soviet trade relations continued to be strengthened. They were marked by an enormous imbalance in favour of Canada. For instance, while Canada's overall trade surplus in 1979 was $1.7 billion, the surplus in bilateral trade with the Soviet Union was $702 million or 40 per cent of the total.[22] Similarly, bilateral cooperation in the scientific and technical fields was intensified as were relations in the academic, cultural, and sports fields.[23]

The Vicissitudes of Canadian-Soviet Detente

The momentum for bilateral cooperation created by Trudeau's 1971 visit to the Soviet Union was not seriously interrupted until the December 1979 Soviet invasion of Afghanistan. Canada's reactions to irritants flowing from Moscow's sins and errors – from Soviet overfishing, to obstacles to family reunification, to human rights abuses – tended to be predicated on the expectation of their rational resolution. Both parties exhibited a sustained political will to contain the irritants and crises. Their multidimensional cooperation was important to both, and Canada's image as a distinct and significant international actor had been raised in Soviet eyes since May 1971.[24]

The December 1979 invasion of Afghanistan occurred in the brief interregnum when Joe Clark's Conservatives held power in Ottawa. A crisis in Canadian-Soviet relations ensued when Canada applied sanctions against Moscow on the entire spectrum of the bilateral relationship. *Pravda*'s Ottawa correspondent explained to his readers (in the words of Black and Hillmer) that "Canada was being forced – against the will of its people and most parliamentarians – to follow America's example by that troika of villainy, the White House, Wall Street, and the Pentagon."[25]

Pierre Trudeau's Liberals returned to power in early 1980. Moscow could count on prospects of renewed, and "de-ideologized," relations with Ottawa in the trade field. While most Canadian sanctions remained for some time, the Trudeau government lifted the grain embargo. Increased bilateral trade ensued: whereas Canadian exports to the Soviet Union in 1980 were $1,535 million, with imports of $59 million, the figures for 1981 were $1,865 and $77 million.[26]

Detente with all its advantages remained Ottawa's overarching commitment in conformity with *Foreign Policy for Canadians*. When the Polish crisis erupted in December 1981, Ottawa regretted the imposition of martial law and imposed some sanctions to Poland and the Soviet Union. Trudeau's statements, however, implied that Polish martial law was preferable to a Soviet military intervention. Meanwhile, as Ronald Reagan's rhetoric against the "evil empire" was escalating, Canada signed a new trade agreement with Moscow in 1982. In the same year, External Affairs Minister Allan MacEachen met Andrei Gromyko in New York, and Canada's deputy minister of external affairs visited Moscow to review the bilateral relationship. President Reagan's decision to intensify the Cold War was manifest in his declaratory toughness, Washington's massive rearmament programs, and his new containment (and even "roll-back") policy. By 1983, Paris and Bonn had also assumed an anti-Moscow posture. Ottawa's mood, however, was distinct. As Adam Bromke wrote about that year, "Canada remained virtually the sole major NATO member still committed to preserving 1970s style East-West detente."[27]

And yet, despite the indubitability of Canada's commitment to detente, it should not be supposed that Trudeau's Canada refused to pull its collective defence weight.[28] The myth about low Canadian defence expenditures must be dispelled. In absolute terms Canada's defence budget during Trudeau's years placed it in sixth place among NATO's fifteen (later sixteen) nations. Trudeauvian internationalism, therefore, did not contradict Canada's commitment to the West's collective defence. After all, Canada had always exhibited a broader conception of security. It was a non-European member of NATO with forces still stationed in Europe, it was genuinely serving the alliance's own professed commitment to detente, and it was, of course, also engaged in the defence of North America through NORAD. It thus seems to follow that the mythology of Canadian "free-riderism" under Trudeau was either alarmist or disingenuous, and certainly unfair.[29]

In September 1983 the fatal shooting down of a Korean Airlines 747 was unanimously condemned in the House of Commons, and MacEachen demanded compensation for the families of the ten Canadian victims. Aeroflot flights were suspended for sixty days. But Trudeau's statements were cautious. After all, the KAL tragedy had occurred in the bleak landscape of an ominous East-West crisis where the issue of the "Euromissiles" was only one component. He preferred to embark on his "Peace Initiative." This was his last major act as Canadian prime minister and world statesman. As we shall see, it too cohered with his commitments to detente, communication, de-escalation of East-West tensions, bridge-building, arms control and disarmament, and the associated principles of his pragmatic idealist worldview.

The Canada–United States Conundrum

These policies vis-à-vis the East-West conflict served to illustrate Canada's distinctiveness and Pierre Trudeau's worldview. The fundamental premises of this pragmatic idealism were clearly revealed in Canada's distinct perception of a less ominous Soviet threat; in Ottawa's decision to de-nuclearize Canada and to reduce its contribution, but keep participating, in NATO in Europe; in the commitment to de-ideologized trade; in rhetorical caution during the crises of the Cold War; in far less bellicose responses to Moscow's sins than favoured by other allies; in repeated bridge-building actions; and in the preponderance of Canada's appeals to, and policies of, moderation, anti-militarism, detente, and arms control and disarmament.

The spirit of these premises was already contained in the "Peace and Security" section of *Foreign Policy for Canadians*, which stated "the government's determination to help prevent war between the superpowers." This meant that "the confidence of the United States and other allies" had to be sustained by, among other things, "sharing in the responsibility for maintaining stable nuclear deterrence and by participating in NATO policy-making in both political and military fields." This pragmatic caution was combined with Canadian idealism:

The government has no illusions about the limitations on its capacity to exert decisive or even weighty influence in consultations or negotiations involving the larger powers. But it is determined that Canada's ideas will be advanced, that Canada's voice will be heard, when questions vital to world peace and security are being discussed.[30]

Needless to say, Ottawa's stance and Trudeau's initiatives frequently irritated the United States. Given the two neighbours' distinct political cultures and the associated discrepancies in power, size, interests, and values, bilateral irritants were bound to occur. Beyond security, Canada and the United States also experienced occasional tensions over foreign direct investment, trade, environmental issues, and culture. Consistent with the Pearsonian principles, Trudeauvian pragmatism generally preferred quiet diplomacy. However, if Canada's interests and values appeared threatened, different diplomatic devices had to be used, especially when Ottawa perceived the American propensity to take Canada for granted. In this case, quiet diplomacy would be left behind. Trudeau would not hesitate to employ public statements in various forums, or mobilize domestic legal means coupled with functionalist and multilateralist initiatives.

Important illustrations include the government's response to the ss *Manhattan* episode. This American supertanker decided to cross the Northwest Passage in 1969 without asking Canadian permission. Ottawa's concerns were both environmental, because major maritime oil spills had already occurred in the west coast of the continent and could occur in the pristine Arctic, and sovereignty-related, because Canada has always considered the Northwest Passage its own sovereign territory. The Trudeau government responded by speedily passing a number of environmental laws, the most famous of which is the Arctic Waters Pollution Prevention Act of 1970. Canada also established unilaterally a one-hundred-mile pollution control zone in the Arctic and asserted its responsibility for controlling the standards of navigation in the area. The flurry of domestic legislation was accompanied by Canada's extension of its territorial waters to twelve nautical miles from the traditionally accepted three miles.

The American government protested the Canadian laws on the Arctic. Ottawa, however, did not yield. Instead, it combined nationalist sensitivity with internationalist and functionalist experience to mobilize its technical and legal skills and talents. Ample use of all of these was made during the 1972 United Nations Conference on the Human

Environment in Stockholm. By winning new friends and solidifying relations with like-minded states, Canada succeeded in influencing the conference principles in a manner that addressed both its internationalist goals and its bilateral concerns with the United States. The logic and ethic of the Canadian position consisted of elevating ecological issues to a higher plane of interstate and international concern and helping shape a corresponding international consensus.

Meanwhile, as a result of his 1971 visit to the Soviet Union, Trudeau had the opportunity to articulate Ottawa's conception of the Canada–us relationship. He spoke of Canada's close friendship and alliance with the United States. But he also described his visit to the Soviet Union as "pour nous ... un pas important vers l'établissement d'une politique étrangère la plus autonome possible. Chacun sait que les Canadiens se sentent passablement dominés par la présence américaine et c'est important pour nous d'avoir d'autres interlocuteurs."[31]

Arguably, Canada–Soviet cooperation was, among other things, a counterweight to American influence. Moreover, the forging of ties in the Arctic could serve manifold ends, cultivated in the 1971 visits to the Soviet Arctic by both Pierre Trudeau and Jean Chrétien. As Thomson and Swanson noted, closer trans-Arctic ties could increase Canada's "leverage in Washington."[32] This observation was also made by the *New York Times* at the time of Trudeau's trip: "If this agreement [i.e., the protocol] makes the United States less inclined to take Canada for granted and more sensitive to Canadian concerns for protecting the Arctic and avoiding American domination, it will be all to the good."[33]

Public statements of Canadian disagreement were made in late 1971 in association with Washington's decision to perform an underground nuclear test, with a five-megaton bomb, on Amchitka, Alaska. Given "a groundswell of protest by the Canadian public from coast to coast," the Trudeau government introduced a resolution in the House of Commons calling "on all nuclear powers to cease all testing of nuclear devices"; but the resolution particularly called "on the President of the United States to cancel the test at Amchitka scheduled for this month." On 28 October 1971, the Ontario minister of the environment urged Richard Nixon to cancel the decision, asking "What more scientific knowledge can you gain by this affront to humanity?" Simultaneously, Ottawa made its opposition known at the United Nations. Addressing the un First Committee, the parliamentary secretary to Mitchell Sharp stressed Canada's concerns for the nuclear test: not only was it "on our doorstep"; it was part of the "poisonous, dangerous, and in the ultimate, futile" superpower contest.[34]

Canadian policies under Trudeau also diverged from Washington's in the fields of human rights, arms control and disarmament, foreign aid, and North-South relations. Indicative, for instance, was Canada's sustained condemnation of human rights abuses in countries supported by the United States. This occurred repeatedly at the UN Human Rights Committee and the UN Commission on Human Rights, to the occasional frustration of Washington, especially at the height of the "new Cold War" of the early 1980s. Similarly, when Canada decided in the early 1970s to contribute to civilizing the activities of the multinational corporations, it frequently sided with Third World countries, since their economic and political weakness offered fertile ground for quasi-exploitative practices. In December 1971 Canada proposed in the Legal Committee of the United Nations a Code of Ethics for the Multinationals. Then, in 1973, during the UN vote on Resolution 3171 concerning the "permanent sovereignty" of states over their natural resources, Canada voted in favour, Britain voted against, while the other NATO allies, led by the United States, abstained.

Even when Canada's stance was bound to cause direct conflict with Washington in a multilateral forum, Ottawa's internationalism could win the day. For instance, at the 1973 meeting of the Inter-American Development Bank, Canada disagreed with the American desire to impose sanctions against Third World states opting for nationalization. The Canadian support for developing countries "visibly angered u.s. Secretary of Treasury George Schultz ... This signals a fundamental and basic disagreement between the u.s. and Canada over bank policy." Michael Tucker has noted "Canada's sensitivity to the rights of developing states to nationalize MNCs." He found it in the 1971 case of the Guyanese nationalization of a bauxite company which was a subsidiary of Alcan. Trudeau's officials made representations but refused to pressure the Guyanese government and "there was no hint of retaliation." Tucker saw Canada's conflict with George Schultz as "a Canadian aversion, as a matter of policy, to using developmental assistance as a weapon of statecraft" coupled with Canada's "concern over its own right to direct its economic future without fear of intimidation."[35]

This picture, however, does not warrant the conclusion that Canadian–United States relations during the Trudeau era were marked by unmitigated crisis. Overall, the bilateral relationship rested on defence association, manifold cooperation, many common values, economic interdependence, and mutual benefits. Canadian pragmatism recognized all these, even if Canadian idealism kept asserting itself either for reasons of Canadian identity and distinctiveness or in order to stress and implement Canada's cosmopolitan values.

Canadian pragmatism had recognized primarily the country's dependence on the American market which, as *Foreign Policy for Canadians* put it, was "a fact of life." There was also a recognition that Canadian energy resources were needed by the United States, that American capital was to continue flowing in, and that "the Canada-United States economic relationship will be affected by agreements between governments and arrangements by multinational corporations and trade unions." But because of the simultaneous "danger that sovereignty, independence and cultural identity may be impaired," the Trudeau government also recognized the need for an "active pursuit of trade diversification" and for "technological cooperation with European and other developed countries," among other things.[36]

Canadian nationalists remained unconvinced. They would point to the fact that, from 1945 to 1970, Canada's indebtedness had reached $40 billion, four-fifths of which were owed to the United States. Figures on foreign control of crucial sectors of the Canadian economy also showed the remarkable degree of American penetration. For instance, 1968 figures revealed American control of mineral fuels (67.1 per cent), rubber products (84 per cent), machinery (64.8 per cent), electrical products (58.1 per cent), and petroleum and coal products (76.4 per cent), with comparable percentages for other sectors of manufacturing and mining.[37] Ottawa was being accused of apathy towards the expansion of United States' multinationals in Canada. And economic nationalists joined cultural nationalists to predict the inevitability of economic penetration into the political and cultural spheres, resulting in the loss of Canada's integrity and autonomy.[38]

The Trudeau government responded with a series of papers, parliamentary reports, and legislative measures. In 1972 Mitchell Sharp's "Canada–US Relations: Options for the Future" (known as the "Third Option" paper) opted for lessening "the vulnerability of the Canadian economy to external factors, in particular, the impact of the United States." The goal of strengthening Canada's economic base would also assert Canada's separate identity and distinctive character. In this way, the Liberals were hoping to contain the nationalist critique and begin diversifying Canada's economic activities and trade relations.

It transpired that the Third Option was not, and perhaps could not be, fully implemented. But at least the "contractual link" with the European Community was concluded, after energetic personal diplomacy by Trudeau, in 1975 and 1976. Economic activities in the Pacific Rim were also intensified. Another contractual link was concluded with Japan in 1976. And a number of domestic initiatives were taken, of which the Foreign Investment Review Agency (FIRA) and the 1980 National Energy Policy (NEP) are best known for generating vehement American reactions.[39]

To protect Canada's cultural distinctness, threatened by the massive avalanche of cheaper and generally "low-brow" American products, the Trudeau government took initiatives and formed commissions and task forces whose recommendations led to legislative measures. They include the 1976 transformation of the Canadian Radio and Television Commission into the Canadian Radio-Television and Telecommunications Commission; the 1978 formation of the Social Sciences and Humanities Research Council, which assumed granting functions from the Canada Council; the creation of the Canadian Film Development Corporation; the direct support of cultural and artistic activities by subsidies from the three levels of government; and the introduction of tax incentives, such as the 1976 Bill C-58, an amendment to the Income Tax Act, which allowed the tax deduction of the cost of advertisements directed to Canadian audiences, if these expenses were incurred on Canadian media.[40] In sum, the American cultural challenge stimulated manifold domestic Canadian measures, which helped strengthen Canada's cultural autonomy and productive energy. Indirectly, they may have gone some way to protecting the very political culture which is one of the main sources of Canadian internationalism.

Finally, conflicts on the environmental front frequently marred the bilateral landscape, especially during the Trudeau-Reagan period. Canadians can be excused for feeling frustrated regarding American attitudes to conservation issues. President Reagan, apparently in the process of implementing his neo-conservative philosophy, also attracted the wrath of his compatriots. The National Audubon Society accused his administration of "deliberately undercutting the nation's environmental laws and programs," and the *Chicago Tribune*, friendly to the Republicans on other issues, concluded that "as far as the environment is concerned, Mr. Reagan is a menace."[41]

This state of affairs, however, did not always hold. Earlier American administrations (including that of Richard Nixon) were either more ecologically alert or prepared to seek bilateral compromises. Important bilateral Canadian–United States environmental issues have been handled cooperatively through the International Joint Commission (IJC). Established in 1909, the IJC's mandate had evolved to cover the monitoring and studying of water levels and ecological problems, water-related concerns at the Canadian-American boundary, air pollution, and more. The commission has generally exhibited remarkable political neutrality, since its decisions have given pride of place to technical standards and considerations. Of the approximately eighty cases treated by the IJC until 1970, only four had been decided along national lines.[42]

A celebrated instance of a politically neutral decision by the IJC involved the Garrison Diversion Project, which was intended to divert water from the Missouri River through the Lonetree Reservoir Dam into rivers flowing into Manitoba. By the late 1960s Canadian officials began expressing concerns that the project would be detrimental to Manitoba's ecology. Federal members of Parliament were mobilized in 1974, and other Canadian voices joined like-minded Americans – Congressmen, farmers, environmental groups, Washington bureaucrats, and some editorial writers – to oppose the project. Ottawa decided again to transcend quiet diplomacy and Mme Jeanne Sauvé, the minister of the environment and fisheries, took the opposition side against the project's continuation. With the consent of the head of the American Environmental Protection Agency (EPA), she submitted the dispute to the IJC in late 1975. In its September 1977 recommendations, the commission agreed that the Garrison Project was "a biological time bomb," capable of harming Canadian agriculture, fish stocks, and wildlife. The Carter administration had already called for a moratorium on the construction of the Lonetree Reservoir Dam, days before the scheduled summit between Pierre Trudeau and Jimmy Carter in February 1977.[43] After the publication of the IJC report, Washington opted for a seriously revised project of a reduced scope. Thus, President Carter's non-antagonistic stance towards Ottawa, the manifold pressures from popular and political bilateral forces, and the politically neutral IJC report all contributed to the cooperative handling of the dispute. In early 1984, however, the Reagan administration increased tenfold the federal funding for the project, causing a new round of Canadian concerns.

To conclude, it bears repeating that even in the fundamentally cooperative, mutually beneficial, and generally civil Canada–United States relationship, irritants and conflicts were inevitable. Canada's distinctive political culture and sense of pressure from the gigantic power of its southern neighbour led it to the frequent assertion of its differing perceptions, interests, and values. The most effective and satisfactory results came from combining domestic measures with the functionalism of Canadian multilateralism. When, however, the nature of the case did not allow Canada to "multilateralize" its bilateral frustrations, other measures had to be used, including public (as opposed to quiet) diplomacy. Such instances, of course, kept reminding Canadians of their need for counterweights. Thus, the presence of the elephant at the border served as an additional stimulus to Canadian internationalism. In other words, Trudeau's and Canada's pragmatic idealism was clearly manifested even towards the United States – at times primarily as self-protecting pragmatism, with Canada's kinder and gentler worldview as the solid backdrop. Moreover, Canada's desire to not only be, but simultaneously to be perceived as, distinct from the United States also explains its passionate projection abroad of its cosmopolitan values, including moderation, communication, compassion, compromise, and caring and sharing. We now turn to the further implementation of Trudeau's internationalist agenda.

ARMS CONTROL AND DISARMAMENT

The cosmopolitan normative foundation of Trudeau's worldview has been demonstrated already. It was evident *inter alia* in the ethical premises associated with detente, the de-escalation of East-West tensions, Canada's partial demilitarization, the stress on bridge-building, de-ideologized trade, and the broader conception of "security" manifested as early as the May 1968 speech in Edmonton. The underlying logic of Trudeau's ethic was unabashedly idealist both in language and in substance. If his repeated calls for a "global ethic" were primarily linked to foreign development assistance, in the field of arms control and disarmament they took the form of "the better ordering of the affairs of our planet."[44]

One of the most eloquent statements of this ethic was presented by Trudeau on 26 May 1978. In the context of the first United Nations Special Session on Disarmament, the Canadian prime minister advocated his "suffocation strategy." The heart of his proposal was to stop the arms race "in the laboratory" by cutting off the "oxygen supply" to its development. Four concrete measures were proposed: a comprehensive test ban to impede the further development of nuclear explosive devices; an agreement to stop the flight-testing of all new strategic delivery vehicles; agreement to prohibit all production of fissionable material for weapons purposes; and agreement to limit and progressively reduce military spending on new strategic nuclear weapons. This strategy would deliver three principal benefits: the freezing of fissionable materials, the prevention of testing technology developed in the laboratories, and the reduction of military expenditures. Trudeau articulated several other quintessentially idealist propositions. First, detente was in real danger, because inter-state trust was lacking, communication was becoming problematic, as was "cooperation based on common interests and concerns." Second, while the arms race continued and the world was spending annually about $500 billion on weapons, "basic human needs remain unsatisfied." Third, security is only a means, not an end in itself; "it is only the setting that permits us to pursue our real ends: economic well-being, cultural attainment, the fulfillment of the human personality."[45] Finally, middle powers such as

Canada had an obvious role to play in slowing down the insanity of the nuclear arms race.

Trudeau's speech defended additional measures in the spirit of pragmatic idealism, such as the reduction of conventional defence expenditures, strengthening peacekeeping, regional security arrangements, and the strengthening of the role of the United Nations. He concluded: "What we must try to achieve is a reasonable consensus on broad objectives and on a plan of action for the next few years. If we can do that, if we can hold out hope that the arms race can be reversed, we will have taken a significant step toward the better ordering of the affairs of our planet."[46]

Trudeau's personal involvement in arms control and disarmament fitted in perfectly with Canada's traditional commitment, despite the self-evident constraints placed on it by "alliance obligations." Just as Canada was the first country in the world which refused to produce nuclear weapons, it also became, with Trudeau, the first country which decided to "divest itself of the nuclear weaponry which it acquired under defensive alliances." Moreover, by the mid-1970s, Canada was one of the first countries to impose safeguards on nuclear transfers to foreign countries. In fact, especially after the bitterness caused by India's 1974 nuclear explosion, Canada's regulations on nuclear safeguards became the most stringent in the world.[47] Simultaneously with enacting the relevant domestic legislation, both through personal diplomacy, and in such forums as the Commonwealth and the London Suppliers Group (of nuclear exporters), Canada insisted on international measures to strengthen nuclear safeguards. To be sure, Trudeau's personal involvement frustrated some Ottawa mandarins and those eager to sell CANDU reactors. But this, of course, demonstrated tangibly the authenticity of Trudeau's cosmopolitan ethic.

Canada also devoted its energy to the goals of partial and comprehensive test bans. From 1969 to 1973 Canadian delegates introduced three draft resolutions in the General Assembly (joined by Australia and New Zealand in 1973) calling on states to assist the development of seismological verification techniques, encouraging the superpowers to negotiate a treaty halting underground tests, and urging the negotiation of a comprehensive test ban and a stop to all atmospheric testing. Canada's diplomatic credit and internationalist prestige were being further enhanced by the manifestation of its technical expertise, for instance, through research into the seismological detection and identification of underground nuclear testing.

But Canadian expertise was being accumulated in other areas, one of which was the control of chemical and bacteriological weapons. By the time of the Trudeau governments, "Canadian expertise in chemical weapons would also allow Canadians to play a major role in the technical definition of chemical and bacteriological weapons, and in the control of chemical weapons. From 1970 to 1988, Canada would present a score of texts and documents in Geneva on these major issues."[48]

Whereas cynics may designate as quixotic some of Canada's performances on arms control – as if Canada harboured any illusions about the immediate implementation of all of its proposals – it is far wiser to see the Canadian intentions as multidimensional. Among other things, the Trudeau government kept alive the country's post-1945 disarmament legacy; it gave voice to the Canadian people's anti-nuclear sentiments; its rhetoric implemented an obvious pedagogical goal; the country's example could well inspire imitators rendering Canada a "mentor state"[49]; and the functionalist mobilization of Canadian skills and talents was bearing fruits. Canadian diplomats and legal/technical experts kept contributing to the entire spectrum of arms control and disarmament sub-fields, primarily through consensus-building, mediation, active participation in multilateral negotiations, proposal-modification, expertise in verification, and so on. During the Trudeau years Canadians contributed with knowledge and energy to the diplomacy concerning such diverse issues as the Seabed Treaty, the Diplomatic Conference on the Reaffirmation and Development of International Humanitarian Law Applicable in Armed Conflicts, nuclear-weapon-free-zones, and the negotiations concerning the Mutual and Balanced Force Reductions (MBFR) in Central Europe.

Finally, Trudeau's 1983 peace initiative deserves special mention if only because it demonstrated his commitment to cosmopolitan principles even against apparent odds. Begun essentially with his 27 September 1983 speech at Guelph University, the campaign called on political decision-makers to take over from the "nuclear accountants." The downing of the Korean jetliner by the Soviets a few days earlier had cast an additional ominous shadow over the planet, after the breakdown of Moscow-Washington communication following the protracted crisis surrounding the Soviet ss-20s and the us nuclear missiles to be deployed in NATO countries in Europe. Trudeau stressed the urgent need to raise the nuclear threshold, to repair the lines of East-West communication, and to pursue a sane strategy of confidence-building. The Canadian prime minister embarked on a round of visits to European capitals (including London, Paris, Brussels, the Hague, Bonn, and Rome) as well as meeting with the leaders of the United States, the Soviet Union, and China in their capitals.

Sceptics and cynics, once again, doubted Trudeau's motives. The major criticisms were summarized by Geoffrey Pearson in an *International Perspectives* article. Some suspected political motivation as the explanation. Others objected to Canada's acting unilaterally without prior consultations with the allies, and thought the prescriptions were beyond Canada's interests and skills and unfitting the urgency of the situation. Still others criticized the alleged implication that both super-powers were equally to blame for the nightmarish impasse. Geoffrey Pearson's own considered judgment was as follows:

Who can say whether the improvement in East-West relations over the course of 1984 was due in part to his private conversations with many leaders, or on the impetus he gave to arms control negotiations, or to his musing aloud about sacred cows and sleeping dogs? Nothing can be conclusively proved. But in Canada there was new confidence that the government would and could act in the interests of the global community if the occasion appeared to demand it.[50]

On 9 February 1984, in the House of Commons, Trudeau himself said: "Let it be said of Canada and of Canadians that we saw the crisis; that we did act; that we took risks; that we were loyal to our friends and open with our adversaries; that we lived up to our ideals; and that we have done what we could to lift the shadow of war."[51]

ECOLOGICAL CONCERNS

The importance of the environment for Canada's self-definition is a familiar stereotype. It is, however, a stereotype with a difference, capable of inspiring even hard-nosed scholars. For instance, Harald von Riekhoff put it eloquently: "For Canadians, with more wilderness per capita than any other nation and a history of struggle in settling in an inhospitable environment, the concept of uncontaminated nature transcends the purely physical implications and acquires a deep symbolic meaning which promotes a sense of national identity and purpose."[52]

Similarly, Pierre Trudeau's pronouncements on the matter have included sophisticated and insightful statements, including the conviction that Canada's wilderness "encourages a reluctance to selfishness, a stimulus to self-confidence, and a reticence to find fault in others."[53] On 1 May 1971, in Vancouver, Trudeau indulged in a discourse combining the metaphysical and the ethical with the poetic, and with a clear eye on policy consequences:

Surely we are not so ignorant as to assume that, somehow, the earth will begin producing more resources at an inexhaustible rate. Surely we do not prefer to live beside garbage dumps, to breath smog, and to look out on polluted oceans. Are we totally indifferent to the world in which our children and grandchildren will be forced to live? Have we, in short, permitted our common sense and our value system both to be so distorted that we equate "good" with "consumption" and "quality" with "growth"?

A little later in his speech, Trudeau asked: "Is it possible for Canadians to contribute to the solution of these vexing problems; to help in the evolution of a metaphysic and an ethic to write a new discourse on method, for the technological age? I believe it is."[54]

Trudeau's style might have seemed recherché. But the substance of his views coheres perfectly with his ethic, the cosmopolitan worldview has emphasized ecological sanity, and *Foreign Policy for Canadians* had already enunciated deep normative commitments in this field. The goal of ensuring "a harmonious natural environment" was explicitly linked with enhancing the quality of life. It was said to include "policies to deal not only with the deterioration in the natural environment but with the risks of wasteful utilization of natural resources." Such policies had to include both domestic initiatives for the rational management of Canadian resources and international action. The latter envisaged the promotion of "international scientific cooperation and research on all the problems of environment and modern society"; assistance "in the development of international measures to combat pollution in particular"; and policies that would "ensure Canadian access to scientific and technological information in other countries."[55]

We have already noted the Trudeau government's two-track response to the voyage of the *Manhattan*. Domestically, a number of laws were enacted, during the period from 1968 to 71: the Canada Water Act; the Clean Air Act; amendments to the federal Fisheries Act and the Canada Shipping Act; the Northern Inland Waters Act; and, of course, the Arctic Waters Pollution Prevention Act of 1970. Moreover, a new Department of the Environment was created in 1971, to handle the management of renewable resources and the natural environment, including meteorology and atmospheric research, fish and marine water management, fisheries, forestry, wildlife, land use, and inventory and environmental protection. Simultaneously, Canada was preparing for the internationalization of its ecological concerns and sensitivities. One of the most celebrated of such instances involved Canada's role in promoting the 1972 United Nations Conference on the Human Environment at Stockholm.

The Conference on the Human Environment

The decision to hold a UN-sponsored conference on environmental issues was taken in 1968. The relevant Swedish resolution was co-sponsored by Canada. The Canadian preparations for the Stockholm conference were long, serious, and multi-layered. A Federal Interdepartmental Committee, a National Preparatory Committee, and a Federal-Provincial Preparatory Committee were created. Public hearings were held in eleven Canadian cities in April 1972: twelve hundred

Canadians attended and over four hundred participated through written and oral briefs. The establishment of interdepartmental mechanisms of collaboration and the clear sense of purpose to produce legal
and technical submissions help explain the success of Canada's participation at the conference, which Tucker has called "the epitome of
effective functionalism."[56]

Canadian Maurice Strong was the secretary-general of the Stockholm
conference. The idealism surrounding the meetings was conveyed by
the British economist Barbara Ward: "It is impossible to take part in this
conference without wondering whether we may not be present at one
of those turning points in man's affairs when the human race begins to
see itself and its concerns from a new angle of vision." Similarly, the
indefatigable internationalist, Maurice Strong, said: "We have taken
the first step on a new journey of hope for the future of mankind."[57]
This enthusiasm proved justified. The conference, attended by over two
thousand delegates and advisors from 113 countries, had an impact on
the entire cluster of environmental issues. It proclaimed a Declaration
on the Human Environment containing twenty-six principles. The delegates approved 109 recommendations constituting an action plan to
handle global environmental degradation, to protect humans and
their habitat, and therefore to enhance human well-being. In addition,
a resolution was passed recommending an environmental fund to
encourage and support international initiatives and outlining a new
machinery under United Nations auspices.

Two principles of the Stockholm Declaration were put forward
by Canada. Principle 21 recognized that "States have ... the sovereign
right to exploit their own resources pursuant to their own environmental policies, and the responsibility to ensure that activities within
their jurisdiction or control do not cause damage to the environment
of other states, or of areas beyond the limits of national jurisdiction."
Canada's special interests and sensitivities were evident in this principle. But numerous other states, especially those of the Third World,
were gratified by the Canadian initiative. For, in addition to a stress on
sovereign rights, the responsibility of other states was also emphasized
and "in accordance with the Charter of the United Nations and the
principles of international law."

Moreover, in the wake of the *Manhattan* crossing, Canada's particular concerns assumed a legal formulation in Principle 22, whereby
"States shall co-operate to develop further the international law regarding liability and compensation for the victims of pollution and other
environmental damage caused by activities within the jurisdiction or
control of such States to areas beyond their jurisdiction."

Canada's activism throughout the conference transcended the
principles adopted. Legal-technical preparatory work by the Canadian

delegation resulted in influence and coalition-building in all the areas of the conference's deliberations and agreements. Among numerous other things, Canada's contributions figured prominently in the establishment of an international referral service for the exchange of environmental information; the program of setting aside areas of environmental significance for international research; its offer to host a conference on Experimental Human Settlements; its promised increase of economic assistance to less developed countries to help them tackle environmental problems; the acceptance of the Canadian proposal to establish a World Registry of Clean Rivers; and the adoption of more than twenty Canadian-sponsored principles on marine pollution.

The Stockholm conference was followed by the creation of the United Nations Environment Programme (UNEP). The new agency was located in Nairobi, Kenya, and Maurice Strong was the natural choice to become its first executive director. Canada offered up to $7.5 million over five years and promised an immediate transfer of $100,000 to help the conference secretariat prepare for the presentation of the Stockholm conference recommendations to the UN General Assembly.

Habitat: Conference on Human Settlements

The seriousness of Canada's environmental commitments was widely recognized. As promised in 1972, Canada hosted "Habitat" in Vancouver in 1976. The new UN conference addressed the problems of the "man-built environment" in a world that expected to see its population double by the year 2000. Solutions were put forward to the constellation of problems already identified at Stockholm, such as urbanization, housing, land use, water supply, community development, and related issues. The recommendations included in the Declaration of Vancouver contained such specific proposals as public participation in decision-making, safe water for Third World countries, the status of women, and the improvement of international coordination in the field of human settlements by restructuring existing agencies of the United Nations.[58]

Canada's functionalist stamp continued to be placed on the international ecological momentum which Canada helped sustain, as we shall also see in the next chapter. When the secretary general of the UN invited Gro Harlem Brundtland to chair the World Commission on Environment and Development in December 1983, the work of the her commission began, culminating in the Brundtland Report, *Our Common Future* in 1987. Of the twenty-three members of the commission, two were Canadian: Maurice Strong and Jim MacNeill. But Canada's international activism also comprised less visible but equally recognized successes. For instance, as Professor von Riekhoff noted in 1978, Canada's assertive diplomacy on the environmental front, coupled by its own domestic practices, have borne fruits: "Rather than aborting the emergence of international rules, Canada's pollution control measures have had a catalytic effect in promoting international consensus within the context of LOS [Law of the Sea] negotiations. The right of coastal states to take steps to control marine pollution in accordance with accepted international norms is now widely recognized, as is the need for special provisions to govern Arctic waters." Hence von Riekhoff concluded sympathetically: "In retrospect, Trudeau's finesse appears to have succeeded."[59]

THE HUMAN RIGHTS RECORD

Foreign Policy for Canadians observed that, primarily because of the divided federal-provincial jurisdiction on relevant matters, Canada's approach to the issue of human rights under UN auspices "has tended to be cautious." It then promised: "Canada's future approach to human rights at the United Nations should be both positive and vigorous."[60] In the early 1970s, however, international human rights issues were highly sensitive and convoluted, given the widely different interpretations of their nature, lack of consensus on implementation, the subjection of the matter to Cold War antagonism and manipulating double standards, and the dilemmas confronting even committed advocates. For example, Canada, which promoted human rights abroad, could also be constrained by various obstacles, including "alliance obligations." Only by the mid-1970s did human rights become a critical test of a state's development and of the globe's level of civilization. This occurred primarily after the 1975 conclusion of the Conference on Security and Cooperation in Europe (CSCE) and the Helsinki Final Act. It was further inspired by President Jimmy Carter's decision to give these rights pride of place in Washington's foreign policy agenda, by the genocidal atrocities of the regimes of Pol Pot in Cambodia and Idi Amin in Uganda, and by the frustration and anger of the world at South African racism.

Countries generally pursue their human rights policy in several ways: in multilateral forums such as the UN, the CSCE/OSCE, and the Commonwealth; through bilateral measures (in terms of carrot-and-stick diplomatic, economic, cultural, and military policies); and by the activities of non-governmental organizations (NGOs). Canada has employed all these strategies. The evidence seems to suggest that, overall, Canada's record in the multilateral context has been quite successful – that is, energetic, principled, and effective. According to some critics, whereas the bilateral record has been less satisfactory, NGO activism has been remarkable.[61] The present discussion will address primarily Canada's multilateral policies, if only because the bilateral context is most convoluted. As late as the early 1980s, Amnesty International reported that torture or abuse of prisoners was occurring in at least one-third of the world's states; ninety-eight countries had documented abuses of human rights; sixty-six states were treated as serious offenders; and 115 countries were identified as abusing human rights in various degrees.[62] It follows that the human rights field is mind-boggling, and if sensitive countries were to condemn all abusers simultaneously, their foreign policies would be severely restricted.

A note on bilateral measures, then, must acknowledge that Canada's activism employed well most of the bilateral instruments. When compared impressionistically to that of most countries, Canada's record emerges as vastly superior. Canadian internationalism never hesitated to condemn a country whose human rights violations were morally repugnant. Canada, for instance, immediately cut off aid to the Ugandan regime of Idi Amin in 1973, and Trudeau "was instrumental in obtaining Commonwealth condemnation of the regime" in 1977.[63] Similarly, Canada cut its aid to Guatemala in 1981 and "Canadian officials have apparently raised concerns in bilateral talks more frequently and more energetically in Guatemala than elsewhere in the region." As Frances Arbour reported regarding "America's Backyard," Allan MacEachen's tenure as minister of external affairs included a Central America policy of emphasis on the local socio-economic sources of domestic crises, support for diplomatic-political solutions, concern for human rights violations, and concern for continuing militarization.[64] All these principles, of course, are pragmatic-idealist. What makes their implementation more praiseworthy is the fact of American opposition to Canadian meddling in Washington's "security interests."

As regards South Africa, the Trudeau government took some symbolic measures in the mid-1970s, operating in part on the pragmatic principle that engagement was preferable to ostracism. But it also acted humanely in 1977–8. A voluntary code of conduct was introduced by Ottawa regarding racial equality and trade union rights for Canadian firms operating in South Africa. Moreover, in 1978 Canada withdrew its official commercial counsellors from Johannesburg and Cape Town. The governmental Export Development Corporation was ordered to stop promoting exports to South Africa. In addition, the Trudeau government endorsed the mandatory 1977 United Nations ban on arms trade with Pretoria. If, however, Trudeau's Ottawa cannot be praised for exhibiting fully the humanitarian impulse towards the apartheid regime, Michael Tucker's relevant comment appears compelling. Given that Canada resents the extra-territorial application of other states' laws to itself, it seemed hard for the Canadian government to punish Canadian multinationals with investments in South Africa, such as Massey-Ferguson, Bata Shoes, Ford of Canada, and Falconbridge Nickel.[65] Thus, it was only later, when Canadian and world opinion had had enough of the institutionalized racism of Pretoria, that Mulroney's government acted as it did. It must also be stressed, however, that Trudeau's Canada channelled its South African concerns multilaterally, in the contexts of both the Commonwealth and the United Nations.

Before leaving the bilateral framework, it is important to recall a crucial dimension of Canada's humanitarian response. In addition to the honourable Canadian record on UN-sponsored relief of refugees and displaced persons, Canada's immigration policies have made clear efforts to facilitate the admission of victims of human rights abuses. The 1966 white paper on immigration policy by the Pearson government had endorsed Canada's "fair share of international responsibility for refugees." The Trudeau government followed suit. In 1970 it adopted new immigration guidelines. According to a 1977 Department of External Affairs document, these guidelines included "a provision authorizing the responsible minister to admit certain categories not specifically covered in the United Nations Convention and Protocol (such as people still within their own countries, like the Ugandan Asians and many Chileans)." From 1946 to the mid-1970s, approximately 10 per cent of the immigrants to Canada have been refugees or members of oppressed minorities. In addition, Canada welcomed refugees from victimized states. Just as 38,000 Hungarians entered Canada in 1956–7, in 1968–9 the country welcomed 13,000 Czechoslovakians, 228 Tibetans in 1970, and 5,600 Ugandan Asians in 1972–3. Also, up to the end of March 1976, 4,510 Chileans and 6,518 Indochinese were refugees authorized to enter Canada.[66]

Multilateral Forums

Canada's involvement with UN-related support for human rights dates back to the drafting of the Universal Declaration of Human Rights in 1947. John Humphrey, the Canadian who was instrumental in that drafting, became the first director of the Geneva-based Division of Human Rights. In fact, Humphrey served as director of the division for twenty years, from 1946 to 1966. In addition, Canada was elected member of the UN Commission on Human Rights in 1963, and then three more times from 1976 to 1984.

John W. Foster has shown that Canada's participation in the commission during the early 1980s was characterized by a large delegation, active and committed involvement, overall effectiveness, and success in handling the work of standard-setting activities, investigation of gross and systematic violations, and implementation. Supported by the Department of External Affairs, which increased the staff and resources devoted to human rights, the Canadian delegations embarked on the classic functionalist role of a pragmatic-idealist middle power: sponsoring and co-sponsoring resolutions, working on drafts, strengthening the resources of the commission, building consensus, and so forth. For instance, focusing on the thirty-seventh session of 1981, Foster reported Canada's activism regarding resolutions on the study of conscientious objection, on the right to development, the study of mass exoduses, and numerous resolutions on countries either suspected or perceived to be gross and persistent violators of human rights.

Canadian delegates were especially active in African and Latin American cases. In 1981 Canada sponsored a resolution on Uganda, co-sponsored another on the Central African Republic, and sponsored yet another on the restoration of human rights in Equatorial Guinea. Thus, of ten resolutions dealing with specific situations of violation, Canada introduced five. This work was coupled with active involvement in the more sensitive Latin American cases, including Argentina, Chile, El Salvador, Guatemala, and Uruguay. For instance, "Canada engaged in a project on Guatemala that no other Western power seemed willing to initiate." Admittedly the Canadian approach was overly cautious and moderate. It is equally arguable, however, that precisely because no other Western delegation dared to touch the case, the Canadians deserved praise.

In general, John Foster's conclusions on the 1981 session constitute a celebration of Canada's diplomatic skill, energy, moral commitment, and effectiveness. He writes that the Canadian government "was strongly committed to the forum," and that the Canadians worked hard and "undertook a number of positive actions." The delegation head, Yvon Beaulne, "took satisfaction from Canada's re-election to the commission with Third World rather than eastern or western European support and expressed shock at the aggressive misbehaviour of American delegation head Michael Novak."[67]

Similar conclusions have been drawn from Canada's performance at the Human Rights Committee.[68] According to Cathal Nolan, Canada's cooperation has been "full and enthusiastic," drawing flattering remarks from senior officials at the UN Centre for Human Rights in Geneva. One of Nolan's interviewees called Canada's efforts "first class, supportive and active"; another saw Canada playing "a leading role in setting an example of cooperation with the reporting procedure and even more so with the optional protocol." In fact, Canadian activism was also praised in off-the-record conversations "in which the performances of other countries were discussed frankly."[69] Ironically, it was precisely this concerned activism that blocked the re-election to the committee of Canada's nominee in the mid-1980s.

Cathal Nolan's assessment praised Canada's role in the UN Human Rights Committee and explained some of its underlying motives. First, this role represents Canada's "humanitarian concern to see rights respected in other countries." Second, Canada defends thereby the values associated with the upholding of civil and political rights. Third, it satisfies the middle power's need to see the strengthening of "respect for international law and institutions." Fourth, it increases Canada's diplomatic prestige through membership in multilateral bodies. Finally, "support for the UN system as a potential guarantor of security has been a central priority in Canadian policy since 1945."[70]

In sum, Trudeau's synthesis remains the best tool for explaining Canada's pragmatic-idealist concerns, and the benefits accruing from the country's prestige are manifest both broadly and with respect to human rights in particular. As another participant observer has attested concerning the Human Rights Commission (where Canada was an elected member from 1976 to 1984), "Canada was viewed by many as one of the leading and most active of the delegations." In fact, "Canada gained the respect of other countries and was well viewed by NGOs who could rely on the Canadian delegation to raise their issues at the Sessions and to lobby on their behalf."[71]

Just as Canada's internationalist prestige had many concurrent sources beyond human rights, its human rights activism was also channelled into other UN and non-UN forums. For instance, the Trudeau government certainly placed it in the broader anti-racist context of its policies towards Southern Africa. Trudeau's visit to the UN General Assembly in November 1969 can be seen as the catalyst for a series of actions oriented towards condemning all colonial practices in the area:

Thus began Canada's staunch support, independently of the positions of the United States and other Western allies, for Third World resolutions condemning the Portuguese role in Africa. On five such resolutions passed in the General Assembly from 1964 through 1973 ... Canada voted in favour of all, while the United States abstained on one, in 1969, and voted negatively thereafter.[72]

Throughout these years the voting pattern of Trudeau's Canada diverged from that of Washington and other Western states on issues "dealing with racism, colonialism and the deprivation of human rights in colonial ... territories in southern Africa." As John Humphrey himself concluded, by 1971 Canada was the "leading protagonist among the developed Western countries in opposition to racist policies." And as Michael Tucker (echoing Robert Matthews) observed, "It was in the United Nations that this growing sensitivity in Canadian foreign policy to Third World perceptions of socioeconomic injustices took root and grew."[73]

It was evident that the Trudeau government was addressing the South African dilemmas by walking on a pragmatic-idealist tightrope. When a Carleton University student had asked him in February 1970 "how Canada's policy of trading with South Africa could be reconciled with Canadian condemnations of apartheid," Trudeau replied *inter alia*: "We are not very proud of this approach. It's not consistent. We should either stop trading or stop condemning."[74] What the stress on pragmatism yielded was to buttress the idealist condemnation with the bilateral measures we saw earlier and with the broadening of the declaratory attacks against Portuguese colonialism and Pretoria's racism. The idealist component was cultivated simultaneously, as we have just seen.

In 1973, Canada supplemented its UN votes condemning Lisbon by offering humanitarian assistance to the liberation movement fighting Portuguese colonialism in Angola and Mozambique. Mitchell Sharp, in September 1973, declared Canada's moral judgment on the matter in the Political and Security Committee of the General Assembly, stating that Canada recognized "the legitimacy of the struggle to win full human rights and self-determination in southern Africa." In early 1974 Sharp explained the relevant moral reasoning: "To refuse humanitarian aid to people who happen to be politically militant would be discriminatory; peaceful humanitarian aid is one tangible method of demonstrating where we stand on the issue of racist and colonialist injustices."[75]

Other more subtle, if less visible, ways were also designed to relieve the plight of victims of human rights violations. Development assistance was itself an important tool, on the principle that such victims should not be doubly victimized through the cancellation of aid. For instance, when the UN General Assembly asked the world community in late 1979 to help the victims of Idi Amin's overthrown regime in Uganda, Canada responded. It sent bilateral aid for rehabilitation and reconstruction, as well as $2 million in emergency food aid. When it transpired later that the Ugandan army was committing atrocities, Ottawa did not suspend its bilateral aid because it had been "designed largely to reach those most in need."[76] Similarly, in addition to mainstream aid reaching the developing countries of the Commonwealth, Canada responded with special assistance projects. For example, the Special Commonwealth Program for Assisting the Education of Rhodesian Africans, living as refugees outside Rhodesia, was established in 1966. In May 1972 the Trudeau government agreed to provide additional funds which raised Canada's annual contribution to over $25,000.[77]

Finally, mention should be made of Trudeau's own contribution to the legacy of Canadian prime ministers saving the Commonwealth from a break-up. It occurred when London decided to resume arms sale to South Africa. First, Canada protested strongly, but privately. When the London press revealed the story after a mysterious leak, some tension in Canada–United Kingdom relations ensued. And while the Conservative government of Edward Heath was determined to pursue its arms sale, various African members of the Commonwealth threatened to boycott the forthcoming Singapore summit. Trudeau reacted again, by sending Ivan Head, his foreign affairs advisor, to Presidents Kaunda of Zambia and Nyerere of Tanzania to persuade them to attend. The 1971 meeting in Singapore took place. Moreover, Trudeau's mediatory role included another Canadian compromise formula.[78] This saved the Commonwealth from another serious crisis over an issue of race and human rights.

FOREIGN DEVELOPMENT ASSISTANCE

The dearth of studies recognizing Canada's multifarious foreign policy successes explains in part Canadians' limited appreciation of the country's distinguished place in the world. Fair-minded observers, however, have noted both that Canada's internationalist credentials derive in great measure from its record in Official Development Assistance (ODA) and that the Trudeau years gave such aid a quantitative and qualitative boost.[79] This discussion will try to expand on this conclusion and sketch the logic and ethics of Pierre Trudeau's relevant worldview. It will also demonstrate, first, that Canada's motives exhibited the pragmatic idealism of Trudeau's synthesis – that is, humanitarian considerations, the conception of development as enhancing peace, and tangible benefits accruing to Canada itself; and second, that Canada's record, when compared to most countries, is highly distinguished and reached, in absolute ODA terms, one of the top rankings in the world.

The Moral Logic of Trudeau's Conception

We noted earlier the genuine passion in support of the world's poor exhibited in Trudeau's 13 May 1968 speech in Edmonton. The parallel logic of this passion is what I have called Trudeau's synthesis. The same principles were reiterated two years later in the white paper, *Foreign Policy for Canadians*. Despite the moderate tone of this document, one cannot miss either the moral authenticity of the Trudeauvian commitment or the concomitant logic of his pragmatic-idealist worldview.

The 1970 white paper articulated additional reasons for ODA. First, Canada's interests and responsibilities in the international community are related to its being "one of the most international of nations"; therefore, not only the values of Canada but also "the future prosperity and security of Canadians" are linked inextricably to the future of the world community. Second, Canada needs to contribute to the strengthening and improvement of the international system because the problems of humankind require multilateral handling. Additional global problems include population growth, environmental problems, technological change, and an increasingly interdependent international economy. Development assistance, therefore, would contribute significantly to the rationalization and progress of the international system. Third, tangible benefits to Canada will be the strengthening of the country's general economic interests abroad, not only by the short-term enhancement of the export of Canadian goods and services but also because, in the long run, the economic development of the developing countries will provide a growing market for Canadian goods and services. Finally, the logic of Trudeau's synthesis implied crucial political and politico-cultural consequences for Canada's domestic interests: "By providing an outward-looking expression of the bilingual character of Canada, our development assistance role also helps contribute to our sense of internal unity and purpose."[80]

In short, humanitarian, economic, and political interests would be served by a strengthened ODA program; these interests have parallel domestic and international dimensions; and while the values dear to Canadians – and central to their worldview – would thus be promoted, so would Canadian internationalism as pragmatic idealism. What follows *inter alia* from this succinct moral logic is a policy that would attain for Canada the status of a "mentor state."

It is noteworthy that this set of explicit values and their associated premises predated the formulation of cosmopolitanism in the relevant academic literature.[81] Equally important, this philosophy would not only guide Canada towards a highly civilized international performance; it would demonstrate simultaneously and palpably an enlightened alternative to *realpolitik* and show how countries can in fact make a moral difference in global politics.

The reasoning of pragmatic idealism which was entrenched in Trudeau's conception of development assistance was demonstrated repeatedly over his sixteen years in power. For instance, in his 16 June 1974 speech to the Canadian Jewish Congress, Trudeau stated that a narrow foreign policy would not serve Canada's real interests. Moreover, "Canada's foreign policy would be meaningless if it were not caring, for it would not reflect the character of Canadians."[82] Then, in his Mansion House speech in England, on 13 March 1975, Trudeau articulated explicitly "a global ethic" involving caring and sharing on a world scale. This global ethic was predicated, among other things, on the notion that "the human community is a complex organism linked again and again within itself and as well with the biosphere upon which it is totally dependent for life." From this general proposition of interdependence, Trudeau deduced two concrete functions: first, "the maintenance of an equilibrium among all our activities"; and second, "an equitable distribution, world-wide, of resources and opportunities." The speech's rhetoric amounted to an unabashed celebration of idealism: "We are one on this earth"; "we are all brothers"; and "in this global village we are all accountable." Pragmatism, however, was cohabiting harmoniously with Trudeauvian cosmopolitanism. He referred to the need for more imaginative and bolder initiatives to improve the present international monetary system and trading mechanisms, in a cooperative manner, in view of the facts of global interdependence. After all, "Co-operation is no longer simply advantageous; in order to survive it is an absolute necessity." In the final analysis, the essential prerequisite is the endorsement of a global ethic, which "extends to all men, to all space, and through all time"; it is predicated "on confidence in one's fellow men," and it is a presupposition for attaining real freedom, human dignity, and justice.[83]

From Words to Deeds

Pierre Trudeau's cosmopolitan ethic began to be implemented even before the publication of *Foreign Policy for Canadians*. As announced in his 29 May 1968 statement, the External Aid Office was renamed Canadian International Development Agency (CIDA) and Maurice Strong was appointed its first president. In 1970, the International Development Research Centre was established with the mandate to let Third World countries articulate their own conception of their developmental needs, in such areas as health, education, energy, and agriculture. As Peter Dobell commented, this was "a unique governmental institution, funded generously by the Canadian government ($30 million for its first five years of operation) with a board of directors of whom ten out of twenty-one are foreign nationals."[84]

When the Trudeau government took over in 1968, Canada's foreign aid disbursements represented 0.29 per cent of GNP. At this level, Canada ranked eighth among the Development Assistance Committee (DAC) members of the OECD.[39] Within two years, Ottawa's commitment had jumped to 0.41 per cent of GNP, placing Canada fifth among OECD members and, therefore, fifth in the world. While France, Australia, the Netherlands, and Belgium exceeded the 1970 Canadian percentage, countries that ranked below Canada included the United States, the United Kingdom, Norway, Sweden, Denmark, Italy, and Japan. Needless to say, whereas Canada is not burdened by any legacy of colonialism, France and Belgium are former colonial powers with evident historical interests and associated moral obligations.

If Canada's disbursements are considered in terms of volume of aid, the Canadian record from 1968 to 1984 is even more impressive. In three of those years (1968, 1970, and 1975), Canada was sixth among the OECD countries. In 1984 Canada ranked in fifth place. Moreover, the only countries whose volume of aid exceeded Canada's in 1984 were the United States, Japan, France, and Germany. Yet all these countries had enormous differences in GNP, size of population, foreign policy interests, and the "strategic" and "image-related" considerations of their role in the world. Similarly, it is notable that the Nordic countries, the Netherlands, Italy, and the United Kingdom were all surpassed by Canada, even though the latter two members of the Group of Seven (G-7) also have a much higher GNP than Canada.[85]

If the above figures show that the Trudeau governments had indeed taken ODA seriously, how about the qualitative aspects of their record? As Peyton Lyon wrote in 1976, the ratio of grants to loans became exceptionally high. Furthermore, a large portion of the loans would "bear no interest and are repayable over fifty years with an initial ten years of grace." These terms, Peyton Lyon concluded, "are softer than those of almost any other donor and mean that the grant element in the Canadian loans is about 90 percent."[86]

A sensitive ODA dimension concerned the amount of aid the recipient had to take in the purchase of Canadian goods. This degree of tied aid was 80 per cent when Trudeau assumed office, but it was soon reduced to 66 per cent. The commitment of *Foreign Policy for Canada* ("International Development") was to reduce the proportion of tied bilateral aid to 53 per cent. In fact, by 1982–3 the percentage of Canadian tied aid had gone down to 51.7 per cent. To be sure, this percentage was among the highest for Development Assistance Committee countries. But, then, it must also be stressed that Canada's *multilateral* component was among the highest in OECD, at 37.7 per cent.[87] And given that, by definition, multilateral aid is untied and disbursed without donor specificity, Canadian generosity rises again above suspicion.

Finally, additional attributes of Trudeauvian ODA can be seen in the early years of CIDA, as the agency expanded the caring range of Canadian aid. This is demonstrated by the decision to increase assistance to needy African countries, the consideration of the social impact of aid projects during their planning stage, and the stress on rural development, and especially on food production and the satisfaction of basic needs. To the same end, in what Peyton Lyon described as "another instance of Canadian pioneering," CIDA began a close and highly successful collaboration with Canadian non-governmental Organizations (NGOs). The government's humanitarian concern was here manifest because the NGOs chosen placed their attention primarily on education and social development.

In sum, the Trudeauvian foreign aid record far exceeded the modest tone of its promises in the foreign policy review. Trudeau fulfilled thereby the commitments of the 13 May 1968 speech and misled those who fastened on the white paper's cautious style but failed to perceive the moral logic of his pragmatic-idealist worldview.[88]

TRUDEAU AND HIS CRITICS

Just as no discussion of Canadian ODA is ever complete without a serious dose of self-flagellation, the general foreign policy record of Pierre Trudeau has been subjected to variegated attacks and challenges and to intriguing misinterpretations. Therefore, in keeping with a main promise of this book – to contradict Canadian self-deprecation and to promote the good news – a critical comment on such critics is called for.

Two foreign policy crises, exploited ad nauseam by Trudeau's academic and political opponents, have concerned the Nigerian civil war and cruise missile testing. We must, therefore, address them since, among other things, they can serve to clarify the nature of Canadian pragmatism in Trudeau's pragmatic idealism.

As regards Biafra, it is true that public and party political criticism of the new government's "inaction" had reached a disconcerting degree by mid-1968. It may also be true that the cautiousness of External Affairs (which determined Ottawa's initial stance) erred on the side of excessive legalism. In retrospect, however, it seems fair to conclude both that Ottawa finally mobilized Canadian humanitarianism and that the reasoning behind the initial hesitancy to interfere represented principled pragmatism over knee-jerk idealism. First, this reasoning was solidly premised on the twin international legal principles of sovereignty and territorial integrity. Moreover, consideration was given to the special sensitivity attached to the African fears of balkanization. Second, Trudeau's advisors at External Affairs "took the view that the interest groups' demands were impractical and that Canada should not become involved in an external issue in which it could have little effect." Third, Canadian diplomats had actually approached their United Nations colleagues with a view to raising the issue at the world organization. The Canadian diplomatic contacts included those with three members of the Security Council – France, the United States, and the Soviet Union. In part because of the clearly expressed opposition to outside intervention by the Organization of African Unity, the heads of missions of these three powers "were all unwilling to have the subject discussed."[89] And fourth, the connection between Biafran secession and Quebec separatism could not be underestimated.

Thus, when the crisis was over in January 1970, "the standing of the Canadian government with other African states was preserved and enhanced by the general Canadian policy of non-involvement in African affairs,"[90] while the humanitarian impulse was satisfied by the November 1968 Canadian decision to provide additional relief (to the tune of $1.6 million) to Nigeria and Biafra.

Arguably, the public discontent generated by Ottawa's decision to test the American air-launched cruise missile (ALCM) was partly attributable to the anxieties caused by the sorry state of East-West relations in the early 1980s and the perceived contradiction to the established anti-nuclear credentials of Pierre Trudeau. Many Canadians, therefore, could have expected that Canada's relevant contribution should have reinforced his "strategy of suffocation" instead of partaking in a new round of the pernicious arms race of the superpowers. These Canadians (38.5 per cent in the fall of 1983) could not be blamed for utterly misplaced expectations; by the same token, the 41 per cent who supported the testing might have been swayed by the Trudeauvian rationale as presented in his 9 May 1983 "Open Letter to All Canadians."[91] The essence of the explanation amounted to arguing that, while the decision was taken with moral anguish, it was primarily determined by the pragmatic consideration that Canada had to prove its broad support for the Western alliance at a time of profound crisis. After all, Canada had endorsed NATO's December 1979 "Twin Track" decision concerning the Euromissiles to which the cruise was linked. Moreover, as Trudeau emphasized, Canada was committed to insisting "that progress be made simultaneously on both tracks," thereby combining "steadfastness of purpose and willingness to negotiate." Finally, whereas Andropov's Moscow had rejected the Canadian strategy of suffocation, Trudeau still concluded that it represented the best strategy.[92]

Pierre Trudeau's reasoning on cruise testing was later amplified during an interview with the *Toronto Star*. He recalled both his anti-nuclear record and the fact that Canadians neglected to protest against both the Soviets and the European allies "who have asked for Cruises and for Pershing IIs and who have said they want them deployed on their soil."[93] (These Europeans, of course, included such socialist leaders as Helmut Schmidt and François Mitterand.) Prime Minister Trudeau, however, did not mention two additional explanatory grounds (one which he need not, and one which he could not have mentioned). First, since the early months of Ronald Reagan's reign, Canadian-American relations were undergoing an obvious, deep, and multilayered crisis. And second, all indications point to the fact that Washington was exercising unbearable pressure on Canada, including the threat of economic santions, to compel it to accept the tests. It is therefore arguable that such a withdrawal from anti-nuclear idealism, at low domestic political cost, was the pragmatic thing to do. It complied with Canada's *sui generis* commitment to NATO; it conformed with major European socialists' stance on the Euromissiles; it implied strengthening Canada's economic self-defence; and it permitted breathing space for idealist battles at other times.

Therefore, as regards both Biafra and the cruise missiles, it may be concluded that both crises lent themselves to political exploitation, especially by those on the Canadian left whose high ethical principles frequently tended towards moral perfectionism. Furthermore, both crises constituted classic cases on which honest and reasonable persons can rationally disagree: for it is as arguable that both decisions bordered on political realism (in terms of predominantly self-regarding or national interest considerations) as it is to assert that they were fully pragmatic (that is, adaptable to difficult and idiosyncratic contexts). Finally, one thing is, I think, certain: to perceive the two episodes as anomalies to Canadian internationalism – as the left seems to have implied – is to reveal once again the romantic presumption that Canadian foreign policy is permanently supposed to endorse even self-sacrificial projects.

Returning to the critics of Trudeauvian foreign aid, one can distinguish the following primary grounds for discontent: Canada's suspect motives; too much tied aid; and absence of a broader developmental strategy. The more vehement critics who launch such complaints seem to be separable into the cynics and the pure idealists – although the two sets are not always mutually exclusive. Therefore, the identification of the critics' premises, if done fairly, should suffice to show why their disapproval may be totally misplaced. By definition, the cynical critics could never be convinced that Trudeauvian ODA could contain humanitarian elements and enlightened Canadian self-interest; for if they could, they would not be cynical. In this logically economical manner we may therefore treat Bob Bothwell and Jack Granatstein's *Pirouette*, which contains this sentence: "Trudeau's foreign policy began to place a Pearson-like emphasis on international do-goodism ... to offer foreign aid (though with only a little more money)."[94]

Although Cranford Pratt's work's general tone is authentically concerned (implicitly endorsing the radical version of humane internationalism), he seems also to have embraced a variety of cynicism. Thus, he recently wrote about Canadian ODA of the mid-1960s that it was an extension of Washington's Cold War commitment to contain the influence of the Soviet Union; that the growth in disbursements in the second half of that decade (when Trudeau was also in power) "had its origins in a foreign policy concern to maintain Canada's standing within the US-led anti-communist alliance" and that, in the late 1960s, foreign aid would serve "three central objectives of Canadian foreign policy – containment of Communism, expansion of overseas markets potentially open to Canadian exports, and promotion of international security in ways suitable for a liberal, internationally responsible middle power."[95]

Such a decision, Pratt proposes, was reached "after decisionmakers had concluded that such a policy would be shrewdly anti-Communist and appropriate for Canada both as a member of the Western alliance and as a middle power anxious to conduct an independent foreign policy."[96] This kind of conspiracy theorizing will not do. First, there is the internal contradiction of treating Canada simultaneously as a satellite and an independent middle power. Second, we do know both Trudeau's NATO-related attitudes and the role played by the United States, the Soviet Union, and their conflicts in Trudeau's worldview. Finally, behind it all lurks Cranford Pratt's morally respectable, but quite fallacious, conception of foreign aid, as just owed to the poorest of the poor and as having no valid place in Canadian foreign policy.[97] This error, which I have called the "fallacy of supererogation,"[98] amounts to the demand always to go beyond the call of duty to help those beyond our borders. While such sentiments are certainly most honourable, they fall outside even the realm of the ethical. Therefore, especially at junctures of serious economic, fiscal, and social anxieties and problems, they are not only politically impracticable – they can well be counter-productive.

To be sure, idealist critics are always important since their voice is a refreshing corrective to the cacophony of hard-hearted, cynical realism. But Trudeauvian ODA could not be suspected of narrow or sinister motives, given the evidence surveyed above. What this evidence clearly established is that the Trudeau government exceeded its own promises and never misrepresented the threefold goals of Trudeau's synthesis. To think otherwise borders on accusing the Trudeau administrations of orchestrating a massive and protracted deception. As regards tied aid, it is wiser to acknowledge the progressive reduction of its proportion throughout the Trudeau years and to compare Canadian ODA multilateralism to that of other major donors. Moreover, romantic calls for the total untying of Canadian aid – while the other donors "tie" it to an extent – may amount to the notion that recipients of Canada's aid can be free to use Canadian funds to purchase goods and services from Canada's commercial competitors. Such a notion, of course, is akin to a kind of political and economic masochism rarely performed in the real world. Finally, although there may indeed have been more room for a broader developmental strategy – as indeed envisaged in *Foreign Policy for Canadians* – it should always be remembered that foreign policy decision-making is subjected to manifold domestic pressures, as Cranford Pratt has clearly shown about the Trudeau years.[99]

More broadly, Trudeau's foreign policy record has attracted various types of bizarre complaints. Whereas sophisticated analyses by Peter Dobell, Michael Tucker, and Tom Axworthy (among others) have captured the essential decency, consistency, and overall effectiveness of Trudeau's internationalism, there are also unwarranted judgments which attempt a holistic undermining of the "good news."

Perhaps the milder of such critiques was contained in an influential 1978 essay in the *International Journal.* Harald von Riekhoff concluded that, as opposed to Mackenzie King's isolationism and Lester Pearson's internationalism, "No single label can encapsulate Trudeau's more amorphous foreign policy." The use of the word amorphous is intriguing because von Riekhoff emphasized Trudeau's personal commitment in at least three areas: "safeguards against nuclear proliferation, protection of the environment, and aid to developing countries." Furthermore, von Riekhoff recognized explicitly the crucial Trudeauvian linkages between domestic unity-stability and Canada's international role, a role ultimately conceived by Trudeau in terms of Canada's status "as a mentor for other states." The essay also praised Trudeau's leadership role which, among other things, "has made for greater speed and consistency of response than would otherwise have been the case." Von Riekhoff's final sentence noted approvingly that Trudeau's policies prepared Canadians for the new global environment. Whereas the older emphases were placed "on issues of military security and deterrence," the new environment exhibited "relatively more concern for problems of international economic disparities, resource scarcity, human rights, and environmental deterioration."[100]

Harald von Riekhoff, therefore, identified correctly a constellation of Trudeauvian attributes tantamount to rare perspicacity and moral vision. However, the range of Trudeau's sustained foreign policy concerns transcended the three areas discussed by the 1978 essay. This is because Trudeau's activist worldview entailed the parallel handling of North-South and security issues premised on the redefinition and radical broadening of the very concept of security. This broadening, as we have seen, embraced the manifold commitment to East-West detente; the energetic involvement in arms control and disarmament; uninterrupted peacekeeping; Canada's relative demilitarization; de-ideologized trade; support for human rights and anti-racism; the dramatic increase in Canadian foreign aid; the 1983 peace initiative; the passionate defence of ecological sanity; and the enthusiastic support of multilateralism in the forums of the United Nations, the Commonwealth, and la Francophonie.

It therefore follows that the epithet "more amorphous" was a *non sequitur.* But then it also follows *a fortiori* that Bothwell and Granatstein's reading is fallacious. For while von Riekhoff was convinced that Trudeau's thought "fits comfortably into the classical tradition of nineteenth-century liberalism exemplified by John Stuart Mill," the two historians concluded that "Trudeau's foreign policy ... was made up of a mishmash of ideas and attitudes."[101] In fact, as we have seen, Trudeau's foreign policy was predicated squarely on pragmatic idealism. This synthesis clearly contained a cosmopolitan philosophy, before the academic literature rediscovered this term and began exploring its content. This philosophy, which is anathema to cynical realism, is a species of idealism and is far wider than the liberalism of J.S. Mill. Its central concepts (all Trudeauvian favourites) include the primacy of distributive justice, freedom, self-realization, compassion, communication, cooperation, moderation, ecological sanity, anti-militarism, caring, and sharing. Trudeau's idealism, however, was tempered by the domestic Canadian exigencies which frequently required the substitution of political necessity for pure virtue. This pragmatism, therefore, was arguably the price that the philosopher had to pay to the statesman. By the same token, Trudeau might justly claim that the Canadian implementation of the cosmopolitan vision demonstrates the realism and overall effectiveness of pragmatic idealism as a model for the international community.

Michael Tucker first identified many telling elements of Trudeauvian internationalism in his important 1980 book. Then Tom Axworthy presented a compelling picture of Trudeau's worldview, including its idealist components, under the aegis of liberal internationalism.[102] Because, however, the latter term has been variously and misleadingly employed (so that even Richard Nixon and Ronald Reagan have been classified under its rubric),[103] I submit that pragmatic idealism may serve clarity best. After all, it has the additional advantage of emphasizing the idealist dimension that Trudeau's global ethic unabashedly endorsed. In addition, our use also signals that pragmatic idealism is, by definition, flexible enough to allow revisions and refinements according to changing circumstances, being also solidly premised on the constellation of the values we have identified and illustrated above.

For all these reasons it is sad to see Bothwell and Granatstein's fixation on the terms "sporadic" (Trudeau's interest in foreign policy); "quixotic" (to expect the rich nations of the North to do much to help the starving countries of the South); and "inconsistent," essentially because of his "mishmash of ideas and attitudes" and his "overweening vanity and arrogance."[104] Most of these judgments commit the fallacies of begging the question, distorted sample, and insufficient evidence. They flow from the authors' disregard of the powerful evidence about the internationalist agenda.

Finally, a word on the two distinguished foreign policy analysts who attempted to revolutionize the study and the making of Canada's foreign relations by their powerful book, *Canada as a Principal Power* (1983). David Dewitt and John Kirton resisted the continuity thesis regarding Canadian internationalism and insisted on detecting the "neo-realist" dimension throughout the 1945–83 period of Canadian foreign policy. Their insistence entailed the conflation of explanation and prescription and presupposed the arbitrary selection of "salient" decisions and of bizarre case studies.[105] This implied, among other things, that issues of the internationalist agenda were generally suppressed and frequently missing. In the case of Trudeau, the *petitio principii* is first committed by labelling 1968–80 the "Era of National Interest," and 1980–3 the "Era of Bilateralism." The same fallacy is then perpetrated by the choice for discussion of only eleven salient decisions in fifteen years of foreign policy-making, including the Namibia Contact group, the Argentine reactor, the Jerusalem embassy, the Indian nuclear explosion, cooperation with the United States, and defence spending increases.[106] Thus, it was hardly surprising that their considered assessment of the 1968–80 Trudeau years was as follows: "Although, as in the previous eras, the three perspectives coexist, foreign policy in this era was increasingly weighted towards interest-based involvement through bilateral relationships the world over."[107] Such a conclusion can only follow by employing a biased sample. Once the internationalist agenda is addressed, in conjunction with Trudeau's operational code or worldview, then the two authors' conclusion becomes a *non sequitur.*

CONCLUSION

This chapter must have suggested why the designation "internationalist" was fixed on Trudeau by such experts as Tom Axworthy, Peter Dobell, Peyton Lyon, and Michael Tucker. If we substitute the term "pragmatic idealism," the continuity thesis will be established for the entire 1945–84 period of Canadian foreign policy. The propriety of opting for this term for the Trudeau era follows from the realization that Pierre Trudeau as foreign policymaker operated with a well-crafted normative framework which extended the range and refined the style of classic Canadian internationalism while retaining its defining principles, interests, and values. Therefore, if his operational code is neglected or distorted, it follows inevitably that the analysis of his logic and ethics is either absent or fallacious. Most critics of Trudeau's foreign policy embarked on their negative assessments by assuming that Pierre Trudeau could not possibly be a pragmatic idealist. As realists or crypto-realists, therefore, they were bound to reach unwarranted conclusions, perpetuating thereby yet another mythology about Canadian foreign policy.

7 Mulroney's Constructive Internationalism, 1984–1993

Our lengthy elaboration on Pierre Trudeau's pragmatic idealism was justified by his reign's duration, its relative controversiality, and the richness of its internationalist results. Moreover, our present perspective permitted informed judgments about both Trudeau's sophisticated worldview and the foreign policy associated with it. It may be too early to evaluate the Mulroney period. Yet in presenting the primary motives, principal patterns, and major results of Canadian foreign policy during 1984–93, it will transpire that the internationalist legacy was respected, reaffirmed, and at times celebrated by Mulroney's "constructive internationalism."

. This conclusion may be unexpected by some, in view of the Progressive Conservatives' neo-conservative economic philosophy and the hawkish early phase of their defence policy. But a survey of their foreign policy record will establish the proposition that their constructive internationalism was an authentic case of pragmatic idealism. This conclusion should not be surprising for at least the following reasons. First, the accumulated internationalist legacy of the years from 1945 to 1984 was too strong and deeply rooted to be altered. Second, Canada's political-cultural parameters (which inform its foreign policy patterns) remained all but constant during the Mulroney years, in spite of the fiscal and economic malaise of the period. Third, Mulroney's Ottawa conducted copious opinion polls which established beyond doubt that the idealist impulse of Canadians remained entrenched. It therefore follows that the Mulroney governments would have been highly unwise (if not masochistic) to change Canada's forty-year-long prestigious, effective, highly popular and widely respected internationalism.

Thus, the central preoccupation of this chapter is to exhibit the 1984–93 record of Canada's internationalist agenda, to explicate the nature of constructive internationalism as pragmatic idealism, and to demonstrate thereby the continued validity of the continuity thesis.

THE MULRONEY REVIEW OF DEFENCE AND FOREIGN POLICY

After his 1984 electoral victory, Brian Mulroney initiated a thorough-going review of Canada's defence and foreign policy. Beginning with the 1985 green paper, *Competitiveness and Security*, the new government introduced a number of foreign policy goals to which it invited responses. The discussion paper led to the formation of a Special Joint Committee of the Senate and House of Commons, which presented its reactions in the June 1986 report, *Independence and Internationalism*. The Department of External Affairs, in turn, produced the government's reply, *Canada's International Relations* (1986), which endorsed most of the recommendations of the Joint Committee. Finally, Canada's new defence white paper of June 1987 completed the cycle of the new government's defence and foreign policy review.

A remarkable continuity in Canada's overall foreign policy goals, interests, and values was reflected in *Independence and Internationalism*. The continuity had been demonstrated already in *Competitiveness and Security*, which had endorsed six "objectives that derive from our values and aspirations." Five of these objectives were all but identical with the six policy themes of the Trudeau government's foreign policy review. The only real difference was that the Mulroney Conservatives substituted "unity" for Trudeau's "quality of life," thereby returning to a theme found in both Paul Martin and Louis St Laurent. On the other hand, two shifts could also be detected: the review placed more emphasis on deterrence and defence; and in enunciating preparedness to negotiate a free trade agreement with Washington, the Conservatives were signalling the decision to align Canada's economic interests with those of the United States.

The heart of post-1945 Canadian internationalism was endorsed by the response of the Department of External Affairs: "As the Committee report makes clear, Canada has '… the capacity as well as the inclination to work actively for international peace and well being.' It has economic influence. It has renewed credibility as an ally. It has moral influence as a workable and humane society. Most important, it has an informed and concerned public whose role in foreign policy is growing." To this end, the review endorsed the central importance of multilateralism for enhancing Canada's international influence. It called for an "amplification" of this influence in the United Nations and its specialized agencies. And it adopted the notion of Canada's contribution to the strengthening of the United Nations mandate:

Canada promotes by its actions, statements, and policies the peaceful settlement of disputes. Canada supports various techniques depending on the circumstances including bilateral and multilateral negotiation, good office, fact finding, arbitration, and judicial proceedings. Canada is active in moderating regional conflicts and participating in peacekeeping operations around the world, which it believes ideally should be brought under the aegis of the United Nations whenever possible.[1]

Both the committee's report and the response by Joe Clark's Department of External Affairs embraced unambiguously Canada's commitment to international development. Special attention was given to the issue of Third World debt and the need for coordinated Western efforts to handle this mounting problem. Equally important, two central tenets of Canadian internationalism were strongly reaffirmed: Official Development Assistance should represent at least 0.5 per cent of GNP; and the duty to promote human rights was designated "a fundamental and integral part of Canadian foreign policy."[2]

On arms control and disarmament, the Mulroney review endorsed the traditional Canadian stance. Thus it supported serious cuts in the nuclear arsenals, endorsement of the Anti-Ballistic Missile Treaty, strengthening of the non-proliferation regime, negotiations for a global ban on chemical weapons, and confidence-building measures to encourage reduction of conventional forces in Europe. The Arctic region was elevated further as a significant area of Canada's defence and foreign policy. Given that the Arctic was attracting increasing international attention, it was concluded that "Canada's huge stake in the region requires the development of a coherent arctic policy, an essential element of which must be a northern dimension for Canadian foreign policy."[3]

The review emphasized the special importance of Canadian–United States relations. It recommended the internal coordination of Canadian policies so as to manage more effectively the bilateral relationship; it advocated that Canada should seek advance bilateral consultation on matters affecting its interests; and it proposed that Canada communicate its views to all levels of the American political system.

Regarding Canada's international economic relations, both the report and External Affairs endorsed trade diversification and improvement of Canada's international competitiveness, while insinuating the further strengthening of bilateral trade with the United States. The latter design, however, was seen as harmonizing with Canada's general commitment to the trade liberalization strategies of the General Agreement on Tariffs and Trade (GATT).

Finally, the Special Joint Committee's report endorsed the concept of constructive internationalism which was introduced by the 1985 speech from the throne. Demonstrating its respect for the established pattern of Canadian foreign policy, the report concluded: "Canada has a great deal more to gain from a posture of confident idealism than from one that is mean-spirited and ungenerous to the world at large."[4]

The Department of External Affairs' official response to this fundamental premise began with these words: "The government warmly endorses the committee's recommendations on constructive internationalism."[5]

IMPLEMENTING THE PRAGMATIC DIMENSION OF THE MULRONEY DOCTRINE

It is clear from these reports that the Progressive Conservatives would introduce a synthesis whereby orthodox Canadian internationalism would cohabit with continental pragmatism. From the outset, it was evident that the new government did not wish to deviate from the entrenched idealistic traditions of post-1945 Canadian foreign policy. Simultaneously, however, the Mulroney government intimated its pragmatism by reorienting Canada's economic and security emphases towards a harmonization with American and allied choices.

The Economic Sphere

Concerns for rapid and destabilizing developments in the global and North American political economy formed the first backdrop to Mulroney's continentalism. Attention was drawn to increasing globalization, the formation of regional economic blocs, and perennial calls for protectionist measures from quarters that included American labour and the United States Congress. Moreover, the Canadian experience of the early 1980s was marked by frequent instances of economic conflict, and Canada's occasional attempts to strengthen the protection of the domestic economic base caused repeated and at times vehement American retaliations. Thus, in this climate of international economic interdependencies and Canada–US economic idiosyncrasies, the government decided to negotiate a free trade agreement (FTA) with Washington.

As far as the Conservatives were concerned, the debate about the FTA was to be conducted in exclusively economic terms. In particular, the economic arguments in favour of the agreement concentrated on asserting the numerous benefits to Canada. These included unfettered access to the enormous American market, increase in Canada's competitiveness, decrease in prices for Canadian consumers, an influx of new investment, and a buffer against American protectionism. For their part, critics of the FTA stressed the likely costs to Canada's socio-economic well-being, including rise in unemployment, dislocation of the labour force, unwanted arrival of powerful American corporations, departure of Canadian corporations for south of the border, problems for Canadian regional development, loss of Canadian control over its energy and other resources, and a host of implications for Canada's social support system.

In addition, the critics raised concerns over Canada's political sovereignty. There were doubts about the autonomy of its foreign and defence policy, fears about loss of cultural independence, and problems for Canada's identity or distinctiveness, deriving from the harmonization with American economic policies. In reply, the Mulroney government's assurances stressed that no aspect of the FTA would possibly affect Canada's socio-political sovereignty and its power to decide autonomously. In fact, more income in Canadian hands would entail more funds for social programs. As regards the cultural alarmism and foreign policy fears of the nationalists, the government emphasized that, just as more freedom of exchange would be involved on the cultural front, Canada's independence need not, and would not, be jeopardized in the spheres of defence and foreign policy.

Since the two positions operated with inherently conflicting starting premises, they were bound to reach contradictory conclusions.[6] And since the entire debate was futurological, empirical evidence alone could not be decisive.[7] Therefore, the FTA was more akin to a sociopolitical-economic-philosophical leap of faith. Brian Mulroney's economic philosophy exhibited a certain affinity with Ronald Reagan's, which lent credence to the view that Ottawa's continentalist promises were being deduced from neo-conservative premises.

When the agreement began to be implemented on 1 January 1989 the opposition's concerns were centred around the issues of energy, investment, the service sector, the dispute settlement mechanism, banking, and the resource sector. Moderate critics also lamented that, contrary to the "benign interdependence" assumption in the FTA negotiations, Washington out-negotiated Ottawa.[8] Finally, the fear was expressed that Canada's community values would be eroded because of the possible indirect effects of economic harmonization on Canadian public policy. For instance, domestic and American economic interests could press for concessions in such areas as taxes and regulatory controls – the Canadian producers protesting at the higher costs of production in their country relative to the United States, and Americans objecting to Canadian policies that result in reducing Canadian producers' costs, such as subsidies and social security programs. In this manner, and in the longer term, the "kinder and gentler" Canadian political culture might be transformed.[9]

By early 1997, the effect of the North American free trade agreements is sufficiently mixed to discourage assertive judgments. It is telling, however, that by the time the federal Liberals regained power in October 1993, their animus against the FTA had disappeared. Making a liberal virtue out of apparent continentalist necessity, they did not push for substantial changes, implying thereby that North American economic integration had become a trilateral inevitability.

It seems to follow that the pragmatism of Mulroney's economic continentalism may no longer be couched in alarmist terms of betraying essential Canadian values. Controversial and uncomfortable though it may be, the trilateral – Canada, Mexico, United States – economic harmonization need not become a public policy straitjacket. Rather, it could remain a twofold challenge for productivity growth and simultaneous diversification of Canadian trade.

The Security Sphere

In tandem with the envisaged Canada–United States economic honeymoon, Mulroney's government was establishing a close security rapport with Washington. To be sure, its security policy was to be conducted in the broad framework of constructive internationalism. As we discuss below, the government would soon assert Canada's internationalist credentials on the entire spectrum of what I have called the internationalist agenda. Moreover, Ottawa clearly differentiated its position from American policies on such major security issues as the future of South Africa and instability in Central America. And yet, for at least three years, the Conservatives followed a harmonization of broad security thinking with Washington just as – and probably because – they had opted for the pragmatism of economic continentalism.

Soon after taking office, the Mulroney government increased Canada's personnel in NATO Europe by twelve hundred. In March 1985 the agreement to upgrade and modernize the NORAD system was signed by Mulroney and Reagan. The old Distant Early Warning (DEW) line was to be replaced by a North Warning System (NWS). The total cost of the project was $7 billion of which the Canadian portion was 12 per cent, and Canada agreed to underwrite 40 per cent of the NWS. In their March 1986 summit, Mulroney and Reagan renewed the NORAD agreement for another five years. Opposition to the perceptible shift towards the primacy of deterrence over detente focused on the government's projected increase in defence expenditures. Fears were also expressed that Canada's bilateral security arrangements under NORAD would entail dragging Canada into Reagan's Strategic Defence Initiative (SDI). In September 1985, however, Ottawa decided to allow only Canadian private firms to bid for SDI contracts; it refused to participate on a government-to-government basis in the Star Wars project.[10]

In June 1987 the government tabled its defence white paper, *Challenge and Commitment*. The paper reaffirmed the Conservatives' commitments to NATO, NORAD, peacekeeping, arms control, the protection of Canada's sovereignty, and the closure of the "commitments-capabilities gap." While the pragmatic idealist dimension was represented by the continued endorsement of arms control and disarmament as well as peacekeeping, the white paper was also marked by an oddly Cold War tone. For instance, noting that "Canadian security policy must respond to an international environment dominated by the rivalry between East and West," it added: "It is a fact, not a matter of interpretation, that the West is faced with an ideological, political and economic adversary whose explicit long-term aim is to mould the world in its own image." There followed a justification for Canada's increased European commitment, the "growing importance of the Asia-Pacific region," and the reassertion of the strategic significance of the Arctic Ocean.[11]

Ironically, six months later Mikhail Gorbachev and Ronald Reagan signed the historic Intermediate-Range Nuclear Forces Treaty. Thus, the hyperbolic pragmatism of Canada's defence white paper bordered on alarmism. Apparently, the document was long in the making and its relative obsolescence had soon to be acknowledged. To its credit, less than a year after *Challenge and Commitment* the government published a *Defence Update*. The new document of March 1988 recognized in positive, if still cautious, terms Gorbachev's revolution in defence and foreign policy:

The past 12 months have confirmed that major and dramatic shifts in [Soviet] domestic policy and in the conduct of foreign relations are occurring ... *Glasnost* has engendered greater candour in the presentation of East-West and other issues to the Soviet people and, indeed, to the world. For his part, Mr. Gorbachev has placed less emphasis on the alleged implacable hostility of the Western democracies. Instead, he has stressed the common interests of East and West in enhancing global stability...

> While the Soviets remain convinced of the intrinsic superiority of their own
> system, they are demonstrating unprecedented interest and flexibility in im-
> proving East-West relations ... Canada will continue to work to reduce tensions
> and to improve East-West relations. We will remain alert, however, to the differ-
> ence between rhetoric and substance.[12]

In addition to the publication of the *Defence Update*, the acquisition
of expensive new equipment began to be shelved. Under the pressure
of public opinion, for instance, the government cancelled the purchase of ten to twelve nuclear-powered attack submarines. And when
the Berlin Wall fell in November 1989, the Department of National
Defence began a thorough re-examination of Canada's security commitments and justified capabilities. In fact, before the end of 1989
"the government of Canada embarked on one of the most comprehensive reviews of Canadian defence policy in the post-war period," even
if its completion "was repeatedly diverted by commanding events both
at home and abroad."[13] Such events included the crises at Oka and
Chateauguay, Canada's participation in the 1991 Gulf War, and the
beginning of the end of the Warsaw Pact.

Still, the early post-Cold War months were marked by thoroughgoing uncertainty, mainly as a result of the proliferation of potential
regional crises, fears of disintegration in Yugoslavia, and the collapse
of the Soviet Union. Pragmatic caution, therefore, was the rational
tone in Marcel Masse's April 1992 Statement. Canada's current security identity was still based on time-honoured fundamentals: collective
defence through NATO, continued commitment to NORAD, and an
emphasis on peacekeeping and on arms control and disarmament. A
new stress, however, was now placed on support of the civil authorities
by the Canadian armed forces. Canadian internationalists could also
detect some "greening" of Canadian security thinking, since the statement promised that "the Department will place increased emphasis on
the ability to assist civil authorities in areas such as fisheries protection,
drug interdiction, environmental monitoring, deterrence of illegal
immigration, search and rescue, and protection of economic zone
resources."[14]

REAFFIRMING TRADITIONAL CANADIAN INTERNATIONALISM

The probable greening of official Canadian security thinking coincided
with an unprecedented demand for Canadian peacekeepers. In addition, if the Department of National Defence had somewhat prolonged

the pragmatic stress on strategic caution in volatile times, the internationalist agenda was reasserting itself among concerned Canadians. Together with calls for a "peace dividend," a new discourse was being cultivated concerning post-Cold War conceptions of security. A new normative framework was attracting ever-increasing adherents, including ecologists, the erstwhile peace groups, church groups, intellectuals and academics, labour unions, retired diplomats and military officers, and mainstream political figures.[15] Identified as "common security," "cooperative security," or "mutual security," it had received special impetus since its adoption by Mikhail Gorbachev. The idea was anchored on the principle that "peace and security can no longer be attained at the expense of one's adversaries but only in concert with them."[16] Moreover, security was now forced to transcend the frontiers of the state, since the sources of the new threats did not themselves recognize fixed borders. This, of course, had long been one of the intellectual contributions of Canadian internationalism and a central personal commitment of Pierre Trudeau.

Canadian think-tanks, such as the Canadian Institute for International Peace and Security (CIIPS), followed by the Canadian Arms Control and Disarmament Agency, actively promoted relevant analysis until their demise in the wake of the 1992 federal budget. In this spirit, Bernard Wood, the second and last director of CIIPS, called in mid-1990 for concerted internationalist action through multilateral institutions:

Surely it is the time for a group of like-minded governments, from all regions of the world, to advance the cause of these institutions for handling challenges like regional conflict, the arms trade, drug trafficking and terrorism, and environmental protection, as well as the continuing desperate need for economic improvement in the Third World.[17]

Soon after, the Mulroney government communicated its apparent decision to cultivate simultaneously the caution of pragmatism with traditional Canadian idealism. In his 26 September 1990 speech at the UN General Assembly, Minister of External Affairs Joe Clark stated:

Security has ceased to be something to be achieved unilaterally. Security has ceased to be something to be attained through military means alone. Security has become cooperative.

In a world where poverty and underdevelopment plague most of the planet, the developed world cannot pretend to be secure simply because it alone is prosperous. In an era of nuclear and chemical weapons, of ballistic missiles, of terrorism, of interdependent markets and economies, of diseases, the development of prosperity throughout the world is not a question of charity but of security.[18]

If pragmatic idealism was thus officially reasserted by a leading Canadian policymaker, it had also remained anchored in Canadian public opinion. For instance, in a major study commissioned by CIIPS and conducted between June and September 1987, Canadians were asked about their perceptions of East-West relations and the concomitant threats. Only 5 per cent of respondents "said Soviet actions on the international scene were the greatest threat. About the same number (8 per cent) thought it to be American actions." More important, Canadians expressed deep concerns over the arms race and Soviet-American relations. But of those who detected improvements in these relations, "many more regarded the USSR as responsible for this improvement than thought the US responsible (40 per cent to 10 per cent)." And of those who perceived a deterioration in East-West relations, "more blamed the United States than the USSR (28 per cent versus 7 per cent)."[19]

Such data supported the Canadian people's entrenched attitudes to international developments and Canada's internationalist role in the world. The Department of External Affairs commissioned "comprehensive public opinion polls on foreign policy issues" in 1984 and 1985 "for the first time in its history." The results were published in early 1986. P.H. Chapin, then director of the Political and Strategic Analysis Division of the department's policy development bureau, drew the following conclusions: "While Canadians may claim only modest knowledge of international affairs, the data makes clear they possess an impressive grasp of the world and its complexities and have sophisticated views on a broad range of international issues."

Among the issues addressed by these polls (conducted by Goldfarb Consultants and Decima Research) were international peace and security, cruise missile testing and Star Wars, Third World needs, and Canada–United States relations. As Chapin observed:

The picture that emerged was one of a society in which the vast majority express an interest in international events, believe that Canada can and should exert its influence internationally, and expect their government to be actively engaged in finding solutions to international problems. The two issues Canadians care most about are international peace and security, and relieving the hunger and poverty of the Third World.[20]

Canadian public opinion, then, may well explain why, as I suggested at the outset, the hard-nosed phase of the Mulroney government's security thinking was short-lived. In addition to the 1988 *Defence Update* and Joe Clark's September 1990 statement at the United Nations, the evidence clearly suggests the government's self-conscious reaffirmation of the logic of pragmatic idealism. Among other signals, this confirmation of Canadian internationalism was entailed by the two-track approach of Ottawa to Moscow.

Ottawa and Moscow under Mulroney

Illustrative of the underlying continuity in Ottawa's thinking on relations with the Soviet Union were decisions and actions that both preceded and followed the publication of the June 1987 defence white paper. Thus, in early 1987 bilateral ties over the Arctic were strengthened. The first meeting of the Coordinating Group of the Canada-USSR Arctic Science Exchange Program was held in Ottawa. Besides providing a forum for the exchange of scientific information, the program was a substantive component of the continued betterment of bilateral relations. As an External Affairs communiqué put it in February 1987, the program "also served to improve and broaden Canadian-Soviet relations, and to open the door to fruitful commercial cooperation in certain areas of Arctic development where Canadian capabilities, equipment and machinery could match Soviet needs."[21]

Then, a joint Canadian-Soviet trans-polar ski journey took place in 1988 with the approval of the Canadian government. The "Polar Bridge" involved thirteen skiers who travelled eighteen hundred kilometres from the Severnaya Zemlya Islands in the Soviet Arctic to Cape Columbia on Ellesmere Island. The expedition, which collected scientific data, was also the occasion for a daily quiz on Canada in a major Soviet youth magazine.[22]

In December of the same year, Mikhail Gorbachev made his historic announcement at the United Nations, to the effect that Soviet forces would be reduced by 500,000 and would assume a purely defensive posture in Eastern Europe. Ottawa responded with evident satisfaction. The Canadian prime minister welcomed the Gorbachev speech and described it as "a positive contribution to arms control and improvement in East-West relations."[23] Meanwhile, Canadian-Soviet trade had presented a notable change between 1985 and 1987, with Canadian exports to the Soviet Union falling to $800 million from $1.6 billion and Soviet exports to Canada rising from $27.6 million to $35 million. But by late 1989, exploiting the 1987 changes in the

Soviet law, Canadians had signed agreements for twenty-three joint ventures, while about fifty more were being negotiated. These ventures ranged "from pizza outlets to oil-drilling equipment to the breeding of Holstein cattle."[24]

In November 1989 Brian Mulroney paid the first official visit to Moscow by a Canadian leader since Pierre Trudeau's in 1971. The prime minister was accompanied by Joe Clark and, as the trip intended to expand bilateral economic relations, they were accompanied by some 250 business people. The visit resulted in the signing of a number of trade agreements, including some in such new sectors of cooperation as protection of foreign investment, outer space, film co-productions, and the fight against drug-trafficking. During his meeting with Mikhail Gorbachev, the Canadian prime minister signed "a several-page joint declaration on various bilateral and international issues," and the two countries endorsed thereby "a common vision of the world as a 'community of interdependent nations'."[25]

The shift in Brian Mulroney's attitudes towards Moscow had thus occurred. It was soon crystallized during the Open Skies conference in Ottawa. On 12 February 1990 Mulroney was among the first world leaders to be so explicit:

Confidence was impossible while basic values were in conflict. But the confrontation of ideologies has at last subsided. We are no longer hostage to the frozen political meteorology of suspicion and animosity. The Cold War is over. And today, in Ottawa, former adversaries work together to ensure that such a long and bitter winter never comes again.[26]

Ironically, when Canadian pragmatic prudence was finally transcended, the Soviet economy began to deteriorate. Canada, having invested more than political hope in Mikhail Gorbachev, supported the 1990 G-7 initiatives for economic assistance to Moscow as the best means towards its experiment's success. But in January 1991 came the military crackdown in Latvia and Lithuania, causing numerous deaths. Ottawa warned the Soviets that any escalation of violence would have serious consequences for bilateral relations; and Joe Clark announced "a review of offers of technical assistance and lines of credit for the Soviet Union."[27] However, during the July 1991 G-7 economic summit in London, after meeting Mikhail Gorbachev, Mulroney announced that Canada "was lifting the freeze on $150 million worth of food credits" imposed in January, and agreed also to help the Soviets in the areas of agriculture and energy.[28]

The dramatic, indeed world-shattering, Moscow events of the next few months began with the August military coup. The disintegration of central power in Moscow was unfolding. A few days later, the Baltic states were the first to leave the Soviet Union. Canada, before Washington, announced the re-establishment of diplomatic ties with the newly independent states of Lithuania, Latvia, and Estonia. The minister of international trade, Michael Wilson, immediately visited the three capitals to explore the possibilities of economic and technical cooperation. And when Ukrainian independence was legitimized by a popular referendum on 1 December 1991, Canada was the first Western state to recognize it formally.

Canada was consistently supportive of the Commonwealth of Independent States, created on 21 December 1991 by the former Soviet republics (except Georgia and the Baltics). Ottawa also implemented its decision to assist the new states in economic and technical terms, beginning in March 1990 with the establishment of the Task Force on Central and Eastern Europe by External Affairs and International Trade Canada. By the middle of 1992, the task force's Economic Development Fund could claim support for "numerous projects, from reforming financial institutions and training business managers to privatizing industries and educating dairy farm workers." Food assistance was also provided, so that Canada could argue that, proportionally, its "food assistance to the former USSR has outpaced that of any other Western country."[29]

By late 1993 Canadian internationalism had solidified its credentials vis-à-vis the countries of the former Soviet Union and its Central and Eastern European former Warsaw Pact allies. Thus was completed a full circle, initiated in the early Cold War. Canada's distinct interests and values informed its special foreign policy style and substance which resisted facile bellicosity and opted, for the most part, for the implementation of a constructive internationalism.

IMPLEMENTING PRAGMATIC IDEALISM

Commenting on the response of External Affairs to *Independence and Internationalism* in 1986, Dan Middlemiss and Joel Sokolsky found that its "tone was decidedly Pearsonian." The department called for "increased Canadian involvement in all aspects of international politics, from trade to development to arms control."[30] Constructive internationalism was also explicitly associated by the Mulroney government with "a posture of confident idealism." The authenticity of this early declaration can be amply demonstrated through a review of their decisions and actions in the entire spectrum of the internationalist agenda.

Arms Control and Disarmament

The Canadian functionalist momentum in the arms control and disarmament forums continued unabated. Ambassador for Disarmament Douglas Roche joined his distinguished predecessors (from General Burns to George Ignatieff) in asserting Canada's genuine endorsement of arms control and gradual disarmament. Even if the early Mulroney government's position fastened more on pragmatic caution rather than internationalist boldness, the fundamental principles remained unaltered. As John Barrett has noted, Brian Mulroney restated in May 1987 six arms control objectives first articulated by Pierre Trudeau's friend and advisor, Michael Pitfield, in November 1983. These objectives involved negotiated reductions in nuclear forces, promotion of the effective nuclear non-proliferation regime, help to prepare a convention to prohibit chemical weapons, support for a multilateral comprehensive test ban treaty, prevention of an arms race in outer space, and finally, active participation in negotiations to limit and reduce conventional military forces in Europe and elsewhere.[31] It is remarkable that the objectives, first presented at the height of the "new Cold War," implied that Canada could give assent to policies and initiatives that might not be necessarily shared by other NATO partners.

Canada's activism was again demonstrated by its expertise in the scientific and technical areas of arms control and disarmament. One of these areas concerned the Biological (and Toxin) Weapons Convention (BWC) which banned the development, production, and stockpiling of biological/toxin weapons or agents for non-peaceful purposes. The weakness of this convention, however, derived from inadequate verification provisions. Thus, two review conferences were held, in 1980 and 1986, to strengthen its effectiveness. Canada, which adhered to the BWC in 1972, participated actively in the review conferences. Ottawa pressed for confidence-enhancing measures, especially regarding the exchange of data on research facilities. Canada also participated fully in the exchange of information and data, since an ad hoc group of experts met in Geneva in 1987. As of 1 January 1990, the BWC had been signed by 137 states of which 112 had ratified it.

In January 1989 the Paris Conference on Chemical Weapons was convened primarily in response to the confirmed use of chemical weapons by Iraq, both during the Iran-Iraq war and again, in March 1988, against its own Kurdish population. At the Washington summit of June 1990, the two superpowers agreed to set in motion the destruction of their chemical weapons, down to a common level of 5,000 agent tonnes over a period of ten years which began in 1992. Canada welcomed this agreement as well as the September 1989 treaty between the United States and the Soviet Union concerning the exchange of information on the location, size, and composition of the two superpowers' chemical weapons stockpiles. More generally, Canada continued working for the success of the multilateral negotiations at the Geneva-based Conference on Disarmament.

In the new climate of East-West relations stubbornly cultivated primarily by Mikhail Gorbachev, an agreement was signed in January 1989 mandating new talks between NATO and the Warsaw Pact on mutual and balanced force reductions.[32] Their formal name became Negotiations on Conventional Arms Forces in Europe, or CFE. Canadians participated energetically in these talks, which aimed at lowering tensions by reducing forces.

Canada's role in arms control forums consisted in active support for the various negotiations, and in working for the conclusion of treaties. Throughout the 1980s Canadians tabled a number of working papers on legal, conceptual, and technical issues. For instance, in 1985 Canada tabled a "Survey of International Law Relevant to Arms Control and Outer Space at the CD"; and in 1988 it produced a review of various technical, military, and political developments associated with outer space. In 1987 Canada presented the results of its "PAXSAT" research project concerning the verification of arms control agreements. The project studied the feasibility of developing a system of satellites capable of verifying arms control agreements in outer space.[33]

In the spirit of the continued utilization of Canada's relevant technical sophistication and expertise, in 1990 Bill C-16 established the Canadian Space Agency. According to the act, "The objects of the Agency are to promote the peaceful use and development of space, to advance the knowledge of space through science and to ensure that space, science and technology provide social and economic benefits for Canadians."[34]

Canada also continued its active support for a number of other multilateral ACD measures in the post-Cold War landscape. For instance, after attaching high priority to the Conference on Disarmament negotiations on a convention barring chemical weapons, Canada signed the finalized Convention in Paris, on 13 January 1993.[35] Under United Nations auspices, Canada continued the allocation of Canadian expertise and resources in support of conventional and nuclear verification regimes. It is this area primarily – including the seismic detection of underground nuclear tests – that Albert Legault referred to when he wrote that "Canada makes a far from negligible contribution of expertise ... There is no question that Canada leads the pack in this area."[36] And again under the UN aegis, Canada called for an arms register in the fall of 1990, when External Affairs Minister Joe Clark proposed to the General Assembly the reporting to the UN of military expenditures, procurement and arms transfers. In a major diplomatic success, his Canadian arms control initiative was adopted by the General Assembly with 150 votes in favour, none opposed and two abstentions (Cuba and Iraq).[37]

Finally, Canada was an active participant in the discussions of confidence-building measures (CBMs) in Europe under the auspices of the Conference on Security and Cooperation in Europe. After the signing of the Helsinki Final Act in August 1975, a follow-up meeting established in Stockholm the Conference on Confidence- and Security-Building Measures and Disarmament in Europe. The conference was concluded in 1986, producing the Stockholm Document, signed by the thirty-five participants of the Conference on Security and Cooperation in Europe. Canada was actively involved in the CSBM process by contributing to the development of the Stockholm Document, by meeting its reporting obligations, by having Canadian troops observed and inspected, by sending observers to all military activities to which the country was invited, and by inspecting military exercises of other countries, as in the June 1989 Canadian visit to Czechoslovakia. In addition, Canada made available its experience and expertise in the fields of verification and telecommunications, to assist in the exchange of data regarding both CSBM and CFE matters.

Once again, therefore, Canada cultivated its functionalist talents and skills and accumulated corresponding prestige which enhanced its internationalist image. As two leading Canadian experts concluded, "Canada's influence on arms control and disarmament went much further than might have been expected from a country both as small and as large as Canada." After surveying Canada's contributions to all subfields of arms control and disarmament, Legault and Fortmann expressed appropriate praise. Proving, however, that French-speaking Canadians can also exhibit a penchant for self-effacing understatement, they wrote: "Concerning the peaceful uses of outer space, Canadian competence, whether legal or technical, took a back seat to no one." But they also admitted:

Several European countries even seek "information sessions" with Canada on these important issues of the day ... Doubtless the problems [on CFE negotiations] will be addressed in the future as they were in the past, with much tact and patience, recognizing that Canada is only one player amongst others but one which is frequently expected to set the tone of leadership. Canada can be proud of her accomplishments.[38]

Peacekeeping

The meteoric rise in the demand for United Nations peacekeeping missions coincided with the second Mulroney government, elected in fall 1988. As the UN secretary general, Boutros Boutros-Ghali, wrote in 1992, "Thirteen peace-keeping operations were established between the years 1945 and 1987; 13 others since then. An estimated 528,000 military, police and civilian personnel had served under the flag of the United Nations until January 1992."[39] Canadians formed an impressive percentage of this personnel. Their success has constituted a principal source of Canada's international prestige and internationalist credentials. The Mulroney government's persistent commitment to the functions and goals of peacekeeping contributed decisively to this Canadian success.

Apart from playing a central role in the conception and refinement of classical peacekeeping, Canada has been recognized universally as a peacekeeping leader. The Canadian peacekeepers have distinguished themselves for their training and technical expertise, military and interpersonal skills, and overall professionalism. Furthermore, Canada has responded unfailingly since the mid-1940s to calls for peacekeeping assistance around the globe, having participated in more operations and missions than any other nation. Finally, Canada has been prepared to pay directly, rather than through the United Nations, for its commitments.

Canada's achievement was no historical accident. It was the result of a rational design, as shown by considering the functions and goals of the Canadian vocation in peacekeeping:

– to employ the credibility of middlepower status in order to reduce, contain, terminate, or manage armed conflict;
– to pre-empt conflict escalation, thereby preventing its spreading and causing any consequent involvement by the superpowers;
– to substantiate Canada's ambition of being an energetic international actor constructing a better world order while serving its own enlightened self-interest;
– to strengthen multilateralism, thereby also increasing its own diplomatic credit and prestige;
– to strengthen its counterweights by a global presence through further UN-sponsored activism; and thus, ultimately,
– to solidify its distinct identity.

Some of these goals are associated with the nature of classical peacekeeping; others follow for the general interests and values of Canadian internationalism. The Mulroney government adopted the associated reasoning, as can be inferred from its rhetoric[40] and from its unqualified commitment to peacekeeping – even when the going got tough, as we shall see.

From 1984 to 1987 the Conservatives inherited the peacekeeping engagements of the Trudeau era. These comprised Canada's participation in the UN Truce Supervisory Organization Palestine (UNTSO), which had began in 1954; the UN Peacekeeping Force in Cyprus (UNFICYP), in existence since 1964; and the UN Disengagement Observer Force (UNDOF), created in June 1974 to supervise the ceasefire between Israel and Syria.

Following the December 1987 signing of the INF Treaty between Washington and Moscow, the new detente began taking shape. Manifested, among other things, in its retrenchment from Central and Eastern Europe, the abandonment of global activism or interventionism, and its support for the goals and methods of the United Nations, the Gorbachev regime decided to resolve or contain Third World (regional) conflicts in cooperation with the United States under United Nations auspices. In this spirit of early post-Cold War collaboration, five new peacekeeping operations were implemented. They involved either areas from which Moscow was withdrawing or areas in which the Soviet Union had long had special interests. Indeed, none of them could have been possible unless Gorbachev's Moscow, after years of UN obstructionism, had given its assent in the Security Council.[41]

Canada agreed to participate in all post-1988 UN-sponsored observer missions or full-fledged peacekeeping operations. By the end of 1992 Canada's armed forces were providing their personnel, equipment, resources, and their highly acclaimed experience and skills to fourteen multinational peacekeeping commitments. The most important of these engagements, with their dates and mandates, were as follows:

1 Iran/Iraq Military Observer Group (UNIIMOG), to supervise the ceasefire and withdrawal of forces, from 1988 to 1991.
2 Transition Assistance Group Namibia (UNTAG), to help Namibia's transition to nationhood, 1989–90.
3 Observer Group in Central America (ONUCA), to verify compliance with the Esquipulas Agreement, involving Costa Rica, Guatemala, Nicaragua, Honduras, and El Salvador, from 1989 to 1992.
4 Iraq/Kuwait Observer Mission (UNIKOM), to monitor the demilitarized zone after the Gulf War, which began in 1991.
5 Advance Mission in Cambodia (UNAMIC), to monitor the ceasefire, 1991–2.
6 Transitional Authority in Cambodia (UNTAC), to help the transition to Cambodian order, which began in 1992.
7 Protection Force (UNPROFOR I and II), to provide "observation patrols, mine clearance, construction and maintenance of shelters, and to help ensure the delivery of humanitarian aid in the former Yugoslavia," which began in 1992.

8 Operation in Somalia (UNOSOM), created in 1992 to stop the famine, help control the civil war, and distribute aid.[42]

With 2,400 Canadians engaged with UNPROFOR in the former Yugoslavia, the number of Canadian men and women participating in UN peacekeeping by early 1993 had exceeded 4,400. However, the pressures, responsibilities, and risks involved in peacekeeping for the new world order generated intense debates and necessitated revisiting the conceptual and political map. In other words, because of the geopolitical uncertainties of a world in post-Cold War transition and the astronomical costs involved, the inevitable debate between realists and idealists resurfaced.

The international debate was stimulated by the publication of Boutros-Ghali's *An Agenda for Peace*. While classical peacekeeping retained its essential validity in the secretary general's reflections, the concept was expanded to cover "both the prevention of conflict and the making of peace." *Preventive diplomacy* was understood as action "to prevent disputes from escalating into conflicts and to limit the spread of the latter when they occur." *Peacemaking* was meant to mobilize chapter VI of the UN Charter and bring hostile parties to agreement. And *peacebuilding* was proposed as action "to identify and support structures which will tend to strengthen and solidify peace in order to avoid a relapse into conflict."[43]

Boutros-Ghali's concerns naturally extended to the necessities of increased logistical and financial support to cope with the host of ambitious activities that precede, accompany, and follow peacekeeping. He called for member states' contributions to be financed from defence budgets rather than from those of foreign ministries. Canada's energetic responses to these developments included a seminar organized by Barbara McDougall on 8 and 9 February 1993. Summarizing participants' views on the definitions of peacekeeping, Alex Morrison reported:

It was acknowledged that, until recently, the single term "peacekeeping" has served to cover a multiplicity of United Nations activities. However, the recent dramatic increase in the types and numbers of peacekeeping operations has given rise to the more frequent use of such terms as peacemaking, peacebuilding, peace-enforcement, peace-restoration and peace-establishment.

There are those who hold that each of these terms ought to be defined precisely and related to a spectrum of action. Others, trying to avoid a definitional morass, believe that peacekeeping has such a positive reputation that it ought to be the only term used. The latter group uses the illustration of a "peacekeeping umbrella," under which stand missions ranging from an observer type, through the classic interpositional model of Cyprus, all the way to operations such as those in the former Yugoslavia and Somalia. The umbrella also covers an expanding range of tasks, including those of an environmental, anti-crime or maritime nature.

Some participants expressed the need for a philosophical, intellectual and conceptual framework to be used in determining and refining future approaches. The "aggression-anarchy" spectrum could be a starting point.44

Canada's debate on the future of peacekeeping and peace-building began addressing such questions as the conditions under which Canadian peacekeepers should join the increasing number of multilateral interventions, the sources of funding, the rules of engagement, and the probability of translating peacekeeping into peacemaking. Yet Ottawa's commitment to this Canadian vocation never wavered, because of the entrenched notion that peacekeeping serves ideally both Canada's humanitarian impulse and its enlightened self-interest. The official rhetoric of the day was quintessentially Canadian internationalist. As Barbara McDougall put it, "In the postwar period, we quickly earned an envied reputation as a nation of peacekeepers. In so doing we were extending the values on which we had built our own country into the international arena."45 A few months later, Ms McDougall expressed pride that "with under 1 per cent of the world's population, we provide about 10 per cent of the world's peacekeepers." She then noted:

Peacekeeping is an invention that we have been most willing to share with the world, one that has already saved untold numbers of lives and prevented untold amounts of damage to property and to the world's environment. It does not come cheap.

Peacekeeping this year will cost the United Nations US$3.7 billion, a staggering amount, but not excessive in a global economy of US$22 trillion. Nor is it excessive when one considers the costs of the alternatives: instability at best, anarchy, probably, and in many cases, war. These do not come cheap, either, as the economic costs alone can be measured in large multiples of the costs of peacekeeping. And the economic costs fade into insignificance when compared with the human devastation that results.46

As we have stressed, Ottawa continued to field its contingents in all post-1987 UN peacekeeping, peacemaking, and peacebuilding operations. Among other commitments, Canada announced in March 1989 that its contribution to the United Nations Transition Assistance Group (UNTAG) in Namibia would involve a 235-member logistics unit, military police and staff officers. In April 1989 the Vietnamese and Cambodian governments appealed to Canada, Poland, and India "to form a monitoring commission that would verify the withdrawal of Vietnamese troops from Cambodia." By December 1992, Canada's participation in the United Nations Advance Mission in Cambodia (UNAMIC) involved a contingent of nearly one hundred, while Canadians serving the United Nations Transitional Authority in Cambodia (UNTAC) numbered 213. Meanwhile, Canada's contribution to the United Nations Mission for the Referendum in Western Sahara (MINURSOS) involved 740 military personnel, which was at the time "the largest contingent Canada had fielded since 1974."[47]

As the Yugoslav crisis was intensifying in 1991, Mulroney urged the secretary general to call an emergency Security Council session and expressed Canada's willingness to be part of any international peacekeeping force. A month after the February 1992 creation of the United Nations Protection Force (UNPROFOR), Canadian General Lewis MacKenzie was appointed the force's chief of staff. Under his leadership, UNPROFOR performed a variety of new peacekeeping and peacebuilding (especially humanitarian) tasks. Canadian officers and troops, among other things, took actions to secure the Sarajevo airport in order to let humanitarian aid land; used a Canadian Forces C-130 Hercules transport plane to deliver relief supplies to Sarajevo; and participated in investigations into human rights abuses, allegations of "ethnic cleansing," existence of detention camps, and other atrocities.[48]

Referring to the Canadian participation in the Iraq-Kuwait Observer Mission (UNIKOM), and the operations in Cambodia and Western Sahara, Gregory Wirick observed:

It was a quintessentially Canadian performance: instinctively committed to the UN and a multilateral approach; anxious to be involved and helpful; fearful that non-involvement might lead to penalties of some kind or, what would be almost as hurtful to the Canadian psyche, might cause the country to be ignored; and finally, stretching diplomatic and military resources to the utmost.[49]

HUMAN RIGHTS

"Constructive internationalism" was pursued by the Mulroney Conservatives on the entire spectrum of Canadian foreign policy. But in some areas it was more internationalist than in others. For instance, building on the Trudeauvian legacy, they represented Canada's values in the same multilateral forums where human rights are being protected. In fact, they had the opportunity to outperform their predecessors in the

case of anti-apartheid diplomacy. The following discussion will demonstrate anew the validity of the continuity thesis, and will also provide
some insights into the idealist side of the Mulroney–Clark operational
code or worldview.

We begin with the commonly neglected aspect of human rights policy: Canada's protection of refugees as victims of human rights abuse.
In his succinct and informative 1988 study, Gerald E. Dirks recorded
Canada's recognized responses to the flight of those escaping war
zones, threat of violence, and other conditions of persecution, including the oppression practised by inhumane regimes:

Informed observers readily acknowledge that Canada has ... made a significant
contribution to the alleviation of worldwide refugee problems. More than half-
a-million people were allowed to enter and settle in Canada for humanitarian
and compassionate reasons during [the post-1945] period. In the 1980s, more
than 20,000 refugees have been sponsored annually through government
schemes and the private sector.

Dirks added that, since the late 1940s, Canada had donated over one
billion dollars in kind or in cash for the care of millions "who have
fled their homelands in search of a haven from prosecution, imprison-
ment, even death." The recognition was therefore inevitable: "In
1986, Canada was awarded the Nansen medal by the Office of the
United Nations High Commissioner for Refugees in recognition of
the humane and generous policy pursued by the public and private
sectors."[50]

Canada's genuine commitment to assist in further civilizing international life in the human rights field has been widely recognized. As
we have seen, senior officials at the UN Centre for Human Rights in
Geneva praised Canada's role. In fact, as regards the Human Rights
Committee, Cathal Nolan reported the belief in 1986 that "Canada's
nominee was blocked from re-election partly as a result of the
country's activism."[51] This belief was shared both in Geneva and by
External Affairs officials in Ottawa. Moreover, Canada's commitment
to human rights protection at the United Nations was passionately
exhibited by ambassador Stephen Lewis at various junctures. For
instance, only a month after Soviet Foreign Minister Eduard Shevardnadze's visit to Ottawa in November 1986, Lewis denounced the
Soviet occupation of Afghanistan at the General Assembly. After stating that the Soviet war against the Moslem rebels exhibited a "sickness
equivalent to depravity," Lewis asked: "What revolutionary fruitfulness
transforms an entire country into a killing-field?" Twenty days later, he
delivered a blistering attack against Soviet human rights abuses. He

also articulated the classic co-existence of interests and values in Canada's pragmatic idealism by stating that there was no inconsistency in attacking the Soviets regarding human rights while at the same time trying to form better ties with them.[52]

Brian Mulroney's and Joe Clark's sustained engagement with the role and opportunities provided by the United Nations simply extended Canada's love affair with the international organization. In fact, Canada's commitment was dramatically revealed by Joe Clark in September 1986, when he told the General Assembly: "We believe this institution is essential to the safety of the world, and we defend it even when its actions are foolish or infuriating or wrong."[53] This commitment was, of course, persistently supported by the Canadian people, who also perceived Canada's effectiveness in the area of international cooperation in the UN and other multilateral organizations.

As indicated earlier, the Department of External Affairs was constantly measuring Canadian public opinion on foreign policy matters since the mid-1980s. One telling survey was published in August 1987, and contains important insights into the Canadian public's attitudes towards the broad human rights field. For example, those polled favoured overwhelmingly Canada's benign involvement in Central America: 86 per cent wanted Canada to support Central American countries "to find a peaceful solution themselves"; and 60 per cent favoured increasing economic assistance to the area. Furthermore, 66 per cent saw "poverty and injustice as causing tensions in the region."[54]

The implication, of course, was that Canadians seriously disagreed with the Reagan administration's rhetoric and actions in Central America, and Ottawa had signalled its independent stance in the area. First with Mark MacGuigan and Allan MacEachen, and then with Joe Clark, Canada had endorsed the notion that the causes of the Central American crisis were socioeconomic and indigenous and therefore they required diplomatic negotiations and political solutions. Thus, since mid-1983, Ottawa supported the Contadora Plan for the peaceful resolution of the crisis. Economic aid to the region was strengthened. As Joe Clark reported in late 1987, from 1983 onwards "we have tripled our bilateral aid to over $105 million and, on a per capita basis, our aid to Central America is second only to what we do in the Caribbean." If support for Canadian non-governmental organizations was added, total direct Canadian aid to Central America was about $170 million.[55] Moreover, Canada responded generously to the plight of Central American refugees and displaced persons. Multilaterally, Canada contributed to the UN High Commission for Refugees and the International Committee of the Red Cross. Furthermore, from 1984 to 1988, Canada admitted almost 21,000 Central American refugees in the country.[56]

It is clear, therefore, that there was harmony between Ottawa's official policy and Canadian public opinion. There was also consistency between Ottawa's deeds and its words. As early as March 1982, Trudeau's minister of external affairs, Mark MacGuigan, had identified the principles of the pragmatic idealist policy towards Central America. The first such principle was "recognition that the problems of the region are rooted in social and economic conditions." The second principle was "the urgent need to foster economic growth and social reform, the benefits of which must be distributed more widely amongst the population. That is the heart of the problem."[57] Later Joe Clark would also distinguish Canada's stance clearly from that of Washington. As opposed to Ronald Reagan's infatuation with the Contras, Clark repeatedly adopted the rationality of the Contadora Plan. In addition, in August 1987 he sent a message to the foreign ministers of five Central American countries expressing support for the peace plan of President Arias of Costa Rica, and later visited all five countries – Nicaragua, Honduras, Guatemala, El Salvador, and Costa Rica.

When he reported to the House of Commons on 2 December 1987, Clark noted that some Canadians insisted on a public criticism of America's militaristic policy. This, he suggested, would reduce Canada's influence in Washington and might impede our capacity to actively help the region. He then added: "The five governments of Central America are in no doubt about the difference between Canadian and US policy, and our conduct should be guided by what makes us most effective in Central America itself."[58]

Finally, the same genuine commitment to a balanced policy of pragmatism and idealism was demonstrated in Joe Clark's September 1988 response to the report of the House of Commons Special Committee on Central America. The report essentially recommended Canadian support for the peace process, support for human rights and democratic development, economic and humanitarian aid, and diplomatic representation in the region. The external affairs minister endorsed "the main thrust of the report including most of its recommendations." He announced the opening of aid offices in Honduras, Nicaragua, and El Salvador. And he agreed to increase further Canada's economic assistance for reconstruction and development.[59]

Anti-Apartheid Policy as a Test Case

In previous chapters we surveyed Canada's dilemmas and actions against South Africa's racist regime. From John Diefenbaker to Pierre Trudeau, Canadian policymakers pursued a variety of policies, from embargoes of arms to ending trade promotion to cancelling sports participation to terminating preferential tariff arrangements for South African products in Canada. Yet none of these measures rose to the level of an almost passionate pursuit of anti-racism by the Mulroney–Clark administration. Despite opposition from important Western capitals, the government applied sanctions against Pretoria in June and August of 1986. It then assumed a powerful position against apartheid at the 1987 Commonwealth summit in Vancouver. Following these decisions, Canada remained the leading international actor, capable of guiding and maintaining the Commonwealth's anti-apartheid struggle. As a result, Canada attracted the respect and affection of the organization's Third World leaders. In the end, Canadian leadership was instrumental in the anti-racist victory. As a commentator reported, "by 1989 the sanctions imposed by Canada and other countries were indeed beginning to have an impact, as no less an authority than the governor of the South African Reserve Bank candidly admitted."[60]

Scholars have debated the reasons or causes of Ottawa's post-1986 moral leadership against apartheid. Realist scholars, such as Kim Nossal, have argued that Canadian policymakers after mid-1986 made a cost-benefit analysis in terms of economic and strategic interests in "coalition membership" and concluded that the threat to the Commonwealth had to be averted. In view of Margaret Thatcher's adamant refusal to apply economic sanctions against Pretoria, and given the bitter frustration of Asian and African member states, Nossal concluded that Canadian actions "were probably motivated by a desire to prod London into sufficient action to avert the threat to the Commonwealth."[61]

This interpretation is deduced from Nossal's "refined realist" premises. But interest-based interpretations remain incomplete if not supplemented by the missing values when it comes to a foreign policy like Canada's. Thus, Matthews and Pratt adopted the argument relating to Commonwealth interests and commercial considerations and then produced a more complex hypothesis by adding one more element: "the conviction of both the prime minister and the secretary of state for external affairs, against the advice of External Affairs, that Canada should assert a strong policy against racism in South Africa."[62]

If this last explanation insinuates a pragmatic-idealist improvement, there is yet another proposal proffered by Bernard Wood. The last director of the Canadian Institute for International Peace and Security drew on his direct experience in Commonwealth diplomacy and Southern African affairs to emphasize an almost idealist interpretation. He argued that Canada's anti-apartheid policy after the mid-1980s could not be properly explained by economic or "direct security" interests. Instead, "one has to accept a much wider definition of interests to understand the Canadian activism." Thus, Canada's "broad stake in the cohesion of the international community on the North-South axis" was its most important interest. It was related, more specifically, to the cohesion of both the Commonwealth and the United Nations. Ottawa "had a perceived political interest in exerting moral leadership and gleaning prestige and popularity on this question, and it would be naive to assert that these elements are ever entirely absent from the motivations of political leaders."

Bernard Wood, in fact, went far beyond a moderate pragmatic-idealist reading. He also added: "It is in the projection of Canadian values rather than the protection of narrow foreign policy interest that one can find the key motivator for the change of Canadian position. The Mulroney government, in its first Speech from the Throne, articulated a quintessentially Pearsonian approach of 'constructive internationalism.'"[63]

Wood also referred to the education and experience of Brian Mulroney and his fellow decision-makers regarding civil rights, human rights, and "the more brutal face of apartheid." He then reiterated his general proposition of the Conservatives' endorsement of Canadian idealist premises: "In terms of their general foreign policy instincts, it was clear from the outset that the key members of the new government adopted a Pearsonian approach of problem-solving idealism," for they had "grown up under the influence of the golden age of Canadian foreign policy under Pearson and his colleagues."[64]

As noted earlier, an additional factor prompting the Mulroney–Clark anti-apartheid policy was the well-established fact of the Canadian people's abhorrence. Don Munton and Timothy Shaw studied 1985–6 public and elite perceptions of Ottawa's anti-racist policies. They argued that such perceptions should be considered in addition to the Commonwealth-preservation thesis and the Mulroney government's concern for "constructive internationalism": "To a considerable extent, current Ottawa efforts also reflect a highly significant shift in Canadian public and elite opinion about the situation in South Africa, Pretoria's policies, and appropriate Canadian positions." This shift was captured by opinion research in June 1986 which showed that only 12 per cent of Canadians wanted Ottawa to put less pressure on Pretoria, 30 per cent "wanted the existing pressures to be maintained," and 45 per cent believed more pressure should be applied.[65]

Almost a year later, the April 1987 opinion research commissioned by External Affairs showed the following results: 58 per cent preferred "limited sanctions like those already imposed by Canada," and 26 per cent favoured "total sanctions." While 45 per cent said that Canada is doing enough to oppose the racist system and 15 per cent believed that Canada should "do nothing," 37 per cent said Canada should "do more."[66]

Summarizing the Mulroney government's policies, Kathleen E. Mahoney wrote recently:

After 1985 Canada adopted more than 150 measures designed to end apartheid and encourage dialogue. These ranged from financial and trade sanctions to assistance programmes for the education of blacks; from a ban on sporting contacts to support to the front line states; from an embargo on the export of arms to South Africa to support for workshops and conferences.[67]

As for the government's motivation, Mahoney endorsed the pragmatic-idealist view. She concluded that Ottawa's "position was that the immorality of human rights abuses, the illegitimacy of South Africa's tyrannical leaders, and the internal and external instability caused by apartheid justified Canada's hardening position."[68]

In sum, just as a single explanation for convoluted policies can never suffice, Ottawa's policies on South Africa's racism are best explained by the synthesis of internationalist reasons. The humanitarian impulse of the Canadian people and their elites deserves pride of place. And, once again, it is appreciated more fully when contrasted to the policies of Washington and London under Ronald Reagan and Margaret Thatcher.

Ottawa's antagonism to South African racism and its leadership role in the Commonwealth were greeted gratefully by African Commonwealth leaders. Joe Clark was elected chairman of the Commonwealth Committee of Foreign Ministers on Southern Africa in February 1989. Nelson Mandela was especially appreciative of Canada's leadership role, expressing it to the world's media during his visit to Lusaka in February 1990. At the same time, President Kenneth Kaunda of Zambia called Canada one of the "Front-Line states." This designation was most telling: for it was supposed to be applied only to the black African states neighbouring South Africa which, until recently, were being victimized by its policies.

ENVIRONMENTAL COMMITMENTS

Canada's environmentalism was established during the Trudeau era. The story of Canada's commitments was picked up by the Mulroney Conservatives for at least the following reasons: special domestic sensitivities, accumulated international prestige, and the need to play an ecological leadership role so as to be a model to the world.

In the previous chapter we noted the formation of the Brundtland Commission in December 1983. This World Commission on Environment and Development (WCED) had twenty-three members. Two of them, Maurice Strong and Jim MacNeill, were Canadians. The report, *Our Common Future* (1987), demonstrated the degree of Canadian concern and participation in deliberative meetings held by the commission. Whereas visits and hearings in Indonesia, Norway, Brazil, Zimbabwe, Kenya, the Soviet Union, and Japan typically lasted for three to four days and were held in the capital city (plus one in Brazil), the commission stayed in Canada from 21 to 31 May 1986, and visited Vancouver, Edmonton, Toronto, Ottawa, Halifax, and Quebec City.[68] The number of Canadians acknowledged in the report for "advice and support" is palpably higher than that from any other country. Moreover, the Canadian government was among the eight sponsoring governments which provided the initial funding for the commission's activities.

The Brundtland Report adopted what the Canadian secretary general of the WCED, Jim MacNeill, has called "the alternative agenda of environmental protection." This sustainable development agenda "embraces all of the issues that we have so long thought of as environmental, natural resources, and urban issues. The power of the concept is that it integrates them with the issues of growth, development, employment, energy, trade, peace, and security."

In MacNeill's succinct formulation, the commission "defined sustainable development in ethical, social, and economic terms," which include "living off Earth's interest, without encroaching on its capital." In a manner that echoes some fundamental premises of Canadian internationalism, MacNeill's own essay, "The Greening of International Relations," contains urgent prescriptions. As reformulated to reflect the thinking of the Brundtland Commission, these prescriptions derive from the fact that the ecological plight of the planet is conditioned by overpopulation, depletion of global resources, and massive environmental degradation. Therefore, immediate action is required to address the ecological catastrophe, in conjunction with socioeconomic reforms. It follows that, because the policies needed must confront resource depletion in tandem with population and poverty problems, none of these issues can be rationally (effectively) handled as "domestic affairs" or "low politics." As MacNeill put it, "These policies and the interests they serve are no longer national – they reach into the backyards of other states and the global commons." Fortunately, public opinion "is far ahead of governments" and promises always to keep prodding them. Therefore, "The politics of greening will continue to drive the greening of politics well into the twenty-first century."[69]

This was a sound assessment. As the world was being alerted to the global ecological malaise, and as the thaw in East-West relations began freeing the energies and imagination of governments, the international community was mobilizing. It thus began to intensify action regarding global warming, toxic pollution, ozone depletion, deforestation, acid rain, water and soil contamination, water shortages, and more. International conferences and high-level scientific, diplomatic, and political contacts and meetings were occurring in unprecedented numbers around the world. The mass media began reflecting the public anxieties and official concerns. In this atmosphere, and capitalizing on the post-1968 legacy, the Canadian government emerged as a committed participant, active host, and even leader in the environmental field. Some schematic illustrations from the 1987–90 period will suffice for our purposes.

Ozone Depletion. Global concern over the depletion of the ozone layer (which can cause skin cancer, eye diseases, and reduction of crop yields) led to the 1987 Montreal international conference. The Montreal Protocol was agreed to by sixty-two countries. It committed nations to reduce the use of chlorofluorocarbons (CFCs) by 50 per cent by 1999, since these substances contribute to both ozone depletion and the "greenhouse effect."[70] The protocol also contained provisions for trade sanctions against countries contributing to environmental degradation. In February 1989 the Canadian government announced its intention to reduce CFCs by 85 per cent by 1999, "exceeding by 100 per cent the objectives provided for by the 1987 Montreal Protocol."[71]

The first time the G-7 nations discussed environmental issues was at their 1988 summit in Toronto, when they endorsed the idea of sustainable development. At the G-7 summit in Paris the following year, the environment was again on the agenda, together with global warming and ozone depletion. The final communiqué acknowledged the need to "help developing countries deal with past damage and to encourage them to environmentally desirable action," urging common efforts to confront climate change which endangers the environment and the economy. Canada proposed the development of "environmental indicators" (analogous to the economic ones) to measure environmental change. The G-7 endorsed the idea and asked the OECD to pursue the matter in a detailed study.[72]

Canada continued its efforts to "sensitize" hesitant countries, and lackadaisical leaders, in various international conferences. For instance, in the March 1989 London conference, "Saving the Ozone Layer," Canada urged the one hundred participating countries to make substitutes

for CFCs available to less developed countries. By the end of this conference, twenty more states had ratified the Montreal Protocol. Canada
also participated in the May 1989 Helsinki Conference which reported
on progress regarding the Montreal Protocol, and recommended the
termination of CFC production and the elimination of other substances
harmful to the ozone layer no later than the year 2000.

Acid Rain. Although Canada's attention and deep concerns centred
around the bilateral acid rain problem with the United States,[73] Canada also signed the 1988 Sofia Protocol. This conference in the capital
of Bulgaria agreed to freeze at 1987 levels the emissions of nitrogen
oxides – that is, elements of acid rain which can react with hydrocar-
bons to produce lower-atmosphere ozone.

Hazardous Wastes. An international conference on trade in hazardous
wastes took place in Basel, Switzerland, in March 1989. It was attended
by 116 countries, including Canada. The conference approved unanimously the Basel Convention which will come into force three months
after its ratification by twenty countries. Canada's environmental diplomacy, conducted in association with some other participants, made a
proposal concerning the right of passage. Canada wished to be advised
when such waste was being transported through its territorial waters
and to have the right to refuse such transport. The proposal was
approved by Third World delegations. It was, however, opposed by
hazardous-waste producing states.[74]

Climate Change. In June 1988 an international atmospheric conference
was held in Toronto. Addressing the conference on the Changing
Atmosphere, Prime Minister Mulroney stated: "We, in Canada, believe
that there are no limits to economic growth, but we do recognize that
there are real limits to natural systems and resources. This is not just
about the atmosphere, it is not just about the environment, it is about
the future of the planet itself."[75]

A follow-up conference was held in Ottawa in February 1989 which
adopted the Ottawa Declaration, recognizing the atmosphere as a
"common resource of vital interest to mankind" which should, therefore, be protected by all states. The signatories from twenty-five countries called for an international treaty to reduce gas emissions and the
establishment of a World Atmospheric Trust Fund. At the conclusion
of the Ottawa conference an External Affairs spokesperson stated Canada's intention to promote these decisions at three upcoming multilateral meetings: of the Commonwealth, la Francophonie, and the G-7
summit.[76]

In March 1989 an environmental conference was convened at The Hague. It aimed at creating a monitoring agency empowered to impose sanctions on polluting states. The Hague Declaration was signed by the Canadian prime minister and over twenty heads of state and government. It provided for the establishment of a new institutional authority, under United Nations auspices, "to monitor and set international standards for pollution control." Decisions made by this new authority would be subject to review in the International Court of Justice. The Hague Declaration also called for the compensation by rich nations of Third World states for their efforts in pollution control. The spirit of this last measure was anticipated by Mulroney's statement at the June 1988 atmospheric conference in Toronto. There he had argued: "If the debtor nations of the tropics stopped stripping their rainforests to generate export earnings to service their debts, the industrialized countries would benefit." Therefore, to help Africa's poorest nations, Canada had forgiven $670 million in debt related to development assistance. Canada's motives were as clear as its goals: "It is *not just altruism*. It is in our self-interest."[77] In other words, it was squarely in the spirit of pragmatic idealism.

The UN Conference on Environment and Development

The Conference on Environment and Development (UNCED) involved far more than the actual meetings at Rio de Janeiro on 3–14 June 1992. It presupposed the two-year work by the preparatory committee which developed Agenda 21, the Earth Charter, and three additional important documents. Agenda 21 constitutes "a hefty package of environmental and economic proposals organized in 39 chapters and running to some 500 pages." The Earth Charter was finally refined as the Rio Declaration, and the three additional documents comprised the convention on forests, the convention on climate change, and the treaty on biological diversity.

Canada's contribution to the conference was considerable. Among other things, it co-sponsored the resolution calling for the UNCED. It contributed moneys to the United Nations, both for staging the conference and for assisting the participation of developing nations. Maurice Strong repeated his 1972 role at Stockholm, becoming the secretary general at Rio. And Canada's delegates played "a prominent part" in the preparation of Agenda 21 and in the negotiations for the three additional agreements.[78]

The conference was attended by 178 national delegations under the leadership of 117 heads of state or government. Canada was represented by a large delegation headed by the prime minister, and accompanied by the environment minister, Jean Charest. Mulroney used the opportunity to announce a number of Canadian monetary commitments. They included $50 million for humanitarian aid to the Southern African states victimized by drought; $25 million for the New Global Environmental Facility; $16.6 million for a rainforest project; $8 million to the Institute of Forest Management of the Association of Southeast Asian Nations; and Canada's preparedness to convert the ODA allocation to eight recipients into funds for use in environmental projects.[79]

As Andrew Fenton Cooper and J.-Stefan Fritz have argued, Ottawa's motives seemed to range from an attempt "to show its continued commitment to the international green agenda" to the effort "to be seen as prepared to take stronger action at home in implementing this agenda" to the demonstration of Canadian distinctiveness, both as a responsible ecological actor and as distinct from the United States. Noting that the Mulroney government entertained some self-regarding considerations, the two authors observed that, since 1984, Canada's relevant policy "has certainly shifted away from the bold style often adopted by the predecessor government of Pierre Elliott Trudeau." Yet it did not follow that Cooper and Fritz wished to question the essential respectability of the Mulroney government's international environmental record. Indeed, they explained that "to suggest that Canada's environmental diplomacy under Mulroney has lacked some of Trudeau's boldness is not to say that there has been a fundamental or dramatic break in its overall style." They also endorse the functionalist interpretation, in terms of Canada's "seeking consensus rather than acting unilaterally" and its "emphasis on detailed and persistent statecraft." Thus, "the standard operating procedure for much of Canadian activity on environmental issues under both the Trudeau and Mulroney governments has been the quiet functionalism traditionally displayed in Canadian statecraft."[80]

Finally, it is most notable that the Mulroney government extended another Trudeauvian first, namely, the rich participation of Canadian citizens and non-governmental organizations in the decision-making environment and even the decision-making process itself.[81] Thus, Canadian NGOs participated actively and effectively in the preparatory phase of the conference, under the auspices of the Canadian Participatory Committee for UNCED (CPCU). At the Rio conference itself, the official Canadian delegation included five representatives from the NGOs. While cynics and sceptics would tend to read this as an attempt by Ottawa to defuse domestic criticism, it is certain that much more was here at play. The empowerment of Canadian environmental NGOs and others can increase their influence on official decision-making.

It also enhances their pressure for Canada's domestic/international consistency on ecological concerns. And it encourages the interest of the NGOs' constituencies in the sustained greening of international politics.

FOREIGN DEVELOPMENT ASSISTANCE

The persistent evidence regarding the humanitarian impulse of the Canadian people remained unaltered during the Mulroney years. In fact, support for international development assistance remained at impressive levels even when the country was hit by the deep recession of the early 1990s. Thus, for instance, the External Affairs poll of April 1987 revealed that 52 per cent of respondents found Canada's aid budget "about right," with the remainder split equally between "too much" and "too little." Moreover, "Eighty per cent say the primary reason for aid is to relieve suffering."[82] Three years later, 84 per cent of interviewees agreed that "one of the best things about Canada and Canadians is that we are generous and prepared to help people in need." Only 7 per cent of respondents disagreed. On the proposition, "I'm proud of Canada's role in helping poor countries," 83 per cent agreed and, again, only 7 per cent dissented. Asked to respond to the proposition, "The main reason why Canada should assist poor countries is that their people are suffering and we have a responsibility to help," 10 per cent disagreed and 84 per cent agreed.[83]

Similarly, the 1990 CIDA report found that, when asked about Canada's foreign aid spending, "the majority of Canadians (70 per cent) believe that Canada is among the more generous of nations, and a significant proportion (39 per cent) believe that current funding of the aid programme is adequate. At the same time, one-third of Canadians would prefer that Canada play more of a leadership role in assisting developing countries, and are willing to increase government spending on aid."[84]

While the 1975–7 and 1984 aid level of 0.50 per cent of GNP was not duplicated by the Mulroney Conservatives, their percentage in the early years hovered between 0.48 and 0.49 per cent. With a 0.48 per cent average for 1983–7, Canada's place was seventh among the OECD states, a position it also occupied during 1991, even though Ottawa policymakers had by then reduced the percentage of GNP allocated to foreign aid to 0.45.

In terms of foreign aid volume, Canada was also ranked seventh in 1991. The other, and far richer, G-7 partners exceeded the Canadian disbursement in terms reflecting their GNP and population superiority over Canada – the only anomaly being that French overseas aid surpassed Germany's. While, then, Canada's 1991 allocation amounted to US$2,604 million, other like-minded middle powers such as Australia, Denmark, Finland, and New Zealand were far below Canada.[85]

We have already noted the various complaints of professional critics of Canada's performance.[86] In response to their perennial lament about tied aid, we argued that Canada's stance, far from being economically irrational, is also honourable when compared, as it should be, to other donors' policies. In any event, by 1988, 45 per cent of Canada's bilateral aid was untied. Moreover, in 1989–91, Canada's contributions to multilateral institutions such as the World Bank and UNDP were 32 per cent of total aid. This percentage was the fourth highest among OECD countries, when we exclude EEC contributions. The only donors with a higher multilateral percentage were Finland, Norway, and Denmark. It is, of course, informative to compare Canada's multilateral allocations of 32 per cent to those of the other G-7 members: France, 11 per cent; Germany, 18 per cent; Italy, 23 per cent; Japan, 23 per cent; United Kingdom, 22 per cent; and United States, 19 per cent.[87] By the same token, it should always be remembered that Canada's other-regarding multilateralist commitments are far broader, and richer, than any other G-7 member and even the like-minded middle powers themselves.

To be sure, when the recent protracted recession hit Canada (in conjunction with the fiscal malaise of astronomical deficits and debts), the cutbacks of aid allocations were felt in the federal budgets. The ODA share of these cuts in 1989–90 and 1990–1 were 23.3 and 17.3 per cent respectively.[88] Yet Canada's international aid performance did not come crushing down. If anything, numerous arguments can be adduced to demonstrate both Canada's persistent ODA dignity and the validity of the thesis of foreign policy continuity. First, Canada's manifold peacekeeping and peacebuilding activities must also be counted among the country's contributions to international aid, given the obvious linkages between peace, security, and socioeconomic development. Second, Canada's forgiveness of Third World debt amounted to $1.15 billion of ODA debt from 1980 to 1992. Third, Canada's commitment to sustainable development has been endorsed by CIDA's decision-making and planning for some time. Fourth, CIDA has also been committed to "environmental assessment procedures" regarding projects which may involve ecological risks.[89] Fifth, Canada has actively supported the linkage between foreign aid and human rights as implying that human development cannot be sustained in conditions of dehumanizing lack of freedom.

CIDA's *Sharing Our Future* guidelines received Mulroney's approval in late 1991, when he stated Canada's official policy of linking aid disbursements to human rights performance at the Commonwealth summit in Zimbabwe. He reiterated this policy in November 1991 at the Paris summit of la Francophonie.[90] Mulroney's declarations were soon implemented vis-à-vis Haiti, Indonesia, and Zaire, as Ottawa suspended its bilateral aid programs to these countries on grounds of human rights violations.

Finally, Canada exhibited genuine support for the broader economic interests of the less developed countries during the protracted last round of GATT negotiations. Among other things, Canada "acted as a bridgebuilder on issues such as investment measures and intellectual property rights, where it shares some common concerns with developing countries." Similarly, and despite the evident conflict with its own traditionally protected domestic industries, Canada has "also made offers on tariffs and on textiles and clothing and worked for the strengthening of GATT's institutional base. CIDA now recognized that it has the task of persuading our trade negotiators to keep the door open to Third World products."[91]

CONCLUSIONS

The above survey of characteristic actions and outcomes of constructive internationalism from 1984 to 1993 supports the following propositions. First, on the economic front, the Conservative government pursued a continentalist strategy, convinced that harmonization with the United States economy was rational because of both the emerging political economy of globalization and the need to protect Canada from American protectionism. Second, a similar emphasis on hard-nosed pragmatism was placed on the security sphere during the earliest years of the Mulroney rule. While the 1987 defence white paper echoed alarmist readings of global uncertainties, soon after the government nearly performed an about-face. At times, in fact, it led – rhetorically and tangibly – the allied movement towards burying the Cold War.[92] Third, constructive internationalism thus became synonymous with earlier Canadian internationalism which we have designated as pragmatic idealism. This was manifest in all issue-areas of the internationalist agenda, from arms control and disarmament to foreign aid through peacekeeping, human rights, and international ecological concerns. In each case the Mulroney Conservatives cultivated the same interests and values that have distinguished Canadian foreign policy since 1945. Fourth, behind this demonstrable continuity one detects the enormous influence of Canada's mainstream political culture. Canadian public opinion supported, and frequently guided, governmental policy choices, even when the times were tough. Finally, none of these propositions should be surprising, when we consider the evidence about the entrenched influence of the values of the pragmatic-idealist legacy. The spirit of this legacy was perhaps best captured by Joe Clark in October 1990: "When times are tough, an effective foreign policy is more necessary, not less. And if we do not choose to advance our values abroad, other values will take over and Canadians will be forced to live with an order we do not like."[93]

8 The 1993 Liberal Comeback: A Preliminary Sketch

After nine years on the opposition benches, the Liberals returned to power in October 1993. The country was preoccupied with manifold concerns, but the Liberal party's campaign had struck some optimistic notes. Domestically, Canada was experiencing chronic fiscal problems, serious unemployment, and lingering fears of disunity. Externally, the landscape was enveloped in the post-euphoria uncertainties of an alleged new world order. This period was characterized by the proliferation of regional crises (principally in the former Yugoslavia, the former Soviet Union, and Somalia), the concomitant demands for preventive diplomacy and peacebuilding, the increase in the United Nations' financial and administrative difficulties, and by a perceptible decrease in the developed countries' generosity towards the Third World.

In this disconcerting environment, the Liberal party's electoral platform, *Creating Opportunities* (the "Red Book"), gave pride of place to the domestic priorities of job creation and economic growth. Even so, the document confidently assumed the continuity of domestic and foreign policy and clearly asserted the party's commitment to "a more active, independent, internationalist role in this world of change." Thus, the collapse of the distinction between "low" and "high" politics was implied by the Red Book's treatment of the environment, sustainable development, and immigration. Similarly, chapter 8 ("An Independent Foreign Policy") was premised on the linkages between foreign and domestic policies, if only because Canadian interests and values were to be reflected in Canada's foreign affairs:

Canadians are asking for a commitment from government to listen to their views, and to respect their needs by ensuring that no false distinction is made between domestic and foreign policy. Finding jobs, protecting the environment, enhancing national unity, providing political security, and enriching the cultural identity of Canadians are all goals inextricably linked to how Canada acts in the global arena.[1]

Classical liberal optimism was manifested in the promise to "work to make change an opportunity – a chance for Canada to help develop greater international and intercultural collaboration in the interests of peace, justice, and the preservation of humankind." Multilateralism was espoused in explicit terms of "international law and the forum of the United Nations." All other traditional commitments of Canadian internationalism were adopted, including "a broader definition of national and international security, encompassing such goals as sustainable development, global economic prosperity, a capable defence, and the eradication of poverty and social inequality." Next, the Red Book's general principles covered support for democracy and respect for human rights worldwide as well as "a more open foreign policy-making process at home."[2] Finally, some elaboration was provided on four specific issue-areas: new directions in Canada-US relations; peace-keeping and foreign aid; multilateral forums; and an open process for foreign policy-making.

This chapter will attempt a preliminary assessment of the Chrétien government's implementation of its self-imposed agenda. Like all previous chapters, it will begin with official or programmatic foreign policy declarations. For, as we have argued, such "verbal actions" form part of the corpus of Canadian foreign policy and provide the best internal criterion to evaluate the coherence both among Ottawa's statements and between its words and its deeds.

THE FOREIGN POLICY REVIEW

The fourth component of the Red Book's promise for an "open process" emphasized the establishment of a National Forum on Canada's International Relations and the future role of Parliament. Both promises have already been fulfilled. In fact, the establishment in March 1994 of the Joint Committee of the House of Commons and the Senate to review Canadian foreign policy constituted a test of the authenticity of the government's promise – a test which it passed. The committee "held over 70 meetings, received over 550 briefs, heard from over 500 witnesses, and commissioned several studies from experts." It tabled its report in November 1994.[3]

Canada's Foreign Policy contained sophisticated perceptions of Canada's capabilities, interests, and needs. It responded to the emerging parameters of the dramatically altered post-Cold War landscape by stressing both the challenges and the opportunities. The committee was "impressed by the increasingly close link between foreign and domestic policies," a distinction further blurred by the phenomenon of globalization. A central theme of *Canada's Foreign Policy* was that "the most important global requirements for the 90s and beyond are for shared security, shared prosperity and shared custody of the environment." Shared security was seen to imply a close working relationship between the United Nations and such regional organizations as NATO and the Conference on Security and Cooperation in Europe. Shared prosperity "implies the widest possible liberalization of trade, combined with concerted international action to alleviate poverty." And shared custody of the environment "implies global action to promote sustainable development."[4]

Multilateralism thus emerged as a major premise of the committee's conclusions. But, as we saw in chapter 1, the members of the committee were also impressed by the idealism of the Canadians who testified.[5] Thus, the prescriptive foundations of Canadian foreign policy could not ignore these values, which the committee identified as: "The practice of dialogue, tolerance and compromise; the commitment to an open, democratic society, to human rights and to social and economic justice; responsibility for solving global environmental problems; working for international peace; and helping to ease poverty and hunger in the developing world."

These values have remained remarkably constant; and they are values "that Canadians have carried over to their approach to foreign affairs." Thus, in a clear endorsement of the heart of all post-1945 Canadian foreign policy, the committee embraced the very concept of pragmatic idealism: "These values can serve as criteria for consistent policies, policies that should be principled but pragmatic, idealistic in concept but realistic in application."[6]

Additional statements of the report's introductory chapter, "Rethinking the Foreign Policy Agenda," confirmed the conviction that Canadian functionalism must be encouraged to flourish in the areas of mediation, moderation, fighting pollution, promotion of conservation, helping the less fortunate, and peacekeeping. Pragmatism, however, must be pursued simultaneously. For even if these values and talents help define Canadian foreign policy, "the financial resources available to government are decidedly more tightly constrained than they have been for a long time, and this is unlikely to change soon."[7]

The conceptual framework of pragmatic idealism thus explicitly established, the report elaborated on rational prescriptions for future Canadian foreign policy. Rationality was predicated on the need for continuity, the requirement to satisfy Canada's special interests and values, and the necessity to respect existing financial constraints. Few surprises, therefore, were contained in the report's specific chapters which amplified the themes of shared security, shared prosperity, and shared environmentalism. Five items, however, deserve special mention. First, a new tone or penumbra surrounded prescriptions on Canada's relationship with the United States. Confidently affirming Canada's friendship with but distinction from our southern neighbour, the report emphasized the advisability of making Canada's concerns "known in a forthright way," the need for insisting "on respect for the rules of the game and the practice of true reciprocity," and the wisdom of "multilateralizing" Canada–US relations, by building coalitions with like-minded states and "bolstering multilateral institutions, in the hope of reinforcing the constraints on unilateral actions."[8]

Second, the strategy and tactics of regionalism were advocated. Canada was urged to pursue "strategic bilateral partnerships, based on a combination of a country's regional importance, its political or cultural ties with Canada, and its potential contribution to the achievement of Canada's objectives."[9]

Third, the concept of directed multilateralism was enunciated. The committee clarified the Canadian connotation of multilateralism by acknowledging the goal of fostering global cooperation. The recommended type of such policy should target "the multilateral institutions best suited to Canadian requirements": the Commonwealth, la Francophonie, the United Nations and its associated agencies, the World Trade Organization (WTO), the International Financial Institutions (IFIs), and the G-7.[10]

Fourth, an imaginative new policy was directed towards culture. The committee elevated Canada's cultural sovereignty, distinctiveness, and distinction to a foreign policy concern. This multi-dimensional recommendation could satisfy numerous Canadian needs, from further strengthening the domestic production of cultural goods and services to internationalizing education and academic/scientific/R&D exchanges.[11]

Finally, although it constituted an echo of the Red Book, the emphasis on "democratizing" Canadian foreign policy deserves special acknowledgment. Evidently, this sensitive and anti-elitist commitment would raise the government's obligations for wide consultation, thereby increasing potential controversies and political headaches.

By the same token, however, Ottawa has little to fear: for not only has Canada's mainstream political culture sustained Canadian foreign policy since 1945, but the experience of the joint committee demonstrated the impressive consistency of the corresponding profile. This, after all, was one reason why the penultimate sentence of the report reiterated that "Canadians want to make the world a better place."[12]

For all intents and purposes, the government's response endorsed the overwhelming majority of the report's recommendations.[13] By implication, therefore, it accepted the antecedent reasoning. From which it follows that both Canada's interests and values and the prescribed policy instruments and means were analogously conceived by the two bodies. Thus, the government's statement, *Canada in the World*, concurred on the identified values. It accepted the notion that Canada is "in a privileged position to influence change [in the world]," and promised to "exercise that influence responsibly to protect and promote Canada's values and interests in the world." The entire armoury of strategies and tactics, from bilateralism to regionalism to multilateralism, was happily adopted. Emphases were placed on the three key objectives of Canadian foreign policy: the promotion of prosperity and employment; the protection of our security within a stable global framework; and the projection of Canadian values and culture.[14] Numerous recommendations on the internationalist agenda were endorsed, albeit with a heightened sensitivity to limitations and constraints. Finally, it is arguable that both the government response (with its more austere tone) and the government statement manifested a clear preference for the pragmatic dimension of Canadian internationalism, but without ever questioning in the slightest the country's idealist legacy.

In sum, the picture emerging from the Chrétien government's foreign policy review justifies the designation of pragmatic idealism. Considering the domestic constraints and external conditions, this is quite remarkable. After all, few would have failed to understand and even tolerate a less generous and more self-regarding response at the present juncture. But this, apparently, would have been un-Canadian. Thus, classic Canadian pragmatic idealism was confirmed by the government's measured response to the more effervescent report of the parliamentary committee. Arguably, the response's tone may well be attributed to both the objective fiscal straits and the quasi-Trudeauvian refusal to raise expectations immodestly. In short, the style of Canadian pragmatism could once again be said to have shaped the idealist substance of the government's foreign policy designs.

FROM DECLARATIONS TO ACTIONS

Even before the publication of the Special Joint Committee's Report, the Chrétien government had begun to implement the major commitments of the Red Book and to substantiate the implied internationalist framework. The EH-101 helicopter program was immediately cancelled. The promise to revisit the FTA and the NAFTA was acted upon. A series of statements, decisions, travels, and official visits by leading cabinet ministers with foreign policy portfolios began confirming that the new government's activism was predicated on a coherent set of principles and goals. This conclusion can be verified by the following discussion whose structure reflects the major themes and promises of the Red Book, the foreign policy review, and the government's response.

Canada and the United States

The direct reference to this bilateral relationship in chapter 8 of the Red Book was laconic. This might have appeared as an evasion were it not for the confident assertion that Canada would reject "a camp-follower approach" and pursue a cooperative partnership with Washington, based on mutual respect and dialogue in the areas where American ideas "are particularly suited to our goals." These areas included "UN reform, strengthening international human rights and democracy, defence conversion, problem-solving through multilateralism, and protecting the global environment." In addition, the electoral platform endorsed the GATT (later the WTO) as the cornerstone of Canada's trade policy. This entailed that a Chrétien government would resist the fetishism of trade continentalism. In fact, the problematic nature of aspects of the FTA and the NAFTA was recognized explicitly. The Liberals promised to renegotiate these agreements to obtain a subsidies code, an anti-dumping code, some energy protection similar to Mexico's, and a better dispute settlement mechanism. Equally important, the Red Book stated clearly that Canada should actively promote a Western hemisphere trade bloc (as a counterweight to the United States) and expand trade and investment with the Pacific Rim, the former Soviet Union, and Western and Eastern Europe. In short – although the term was never used – the Liberals were gesturing towards the Third Option.[15]

International Trade Minister Roy MacLaren visited Washington in November 1993. The former foreign service official succeeded in extracting from the Clinton administration an agreement to maintain a working group on subsidies and anti-dumping. He also kept "on the negotiating table with the United States the damage that recourse to national trade remedy law has for both countries."[16] Pragmatism had revealed that these arrangements were necessary and (for the time being) sufficient. They also helped to set a positive tone in the bilateral relationship, at least by minimizing counter-productive friction. As the foreign affairs minister, André Ouellet, stated soon after, Canada's new approach in its relations with the United States was "one based on close cooperation where our interests coincide, and mutual respect where our opinions differ."[17]

Opportunities for such cooperation abounded, especially with a Democrat in the White House, with whom Jean Chrétien has obvious ideological affinity. Their first meeting, at the APEC forum in Seattle in mid-November 1993, was rather successful.[18] In December of that year the two neighbours agreed to a five-month shutdown of the Georges Bank fishery off Nova Scotia. Cruise missile testing was allowed to proceed in early 1994, but Washington was now advised that Canada's defence policy review was to reconsider the issue. In May 1994 Canada decided to apply unilaterally some conservation measures concerning salmon fishing in the Pacific, after the failure of negotiations with the Americans. American fishermen complied with the Canadian decision.[19] In September Canada claimed victory in the softwood lumber issue: a bi-national panel decided that American producers had not suffered injury and that Washington should reimburse about $800 million in illegally collected tariffs. Also in September 1994, the two countries signed a tax agreement to reduce tax rates on the cross-border payment of interest and royalties. Two months later, the United States government, after studying the evidence, recognized Canada's right "to manage and ensure the conservation of Icelandic scallops on its continental shelf." And soon after, long-held negotiations on liberalizing air travel between the two neighbours produced the expectation that an agreement was forthcoming.[20] Indeed, the agreement was signed in February 1995, during Bill Clinton's visit to Ottawa. The visit's atmosphere was positive; trade issues were raised but put on the back burner; the traditional friendship between the two countries was asserted; and President Clinton, addressing the House of Commons, spoke of the "remarkable" relationship of the two neighbours and friends.

Overall, recent Canada–United States bilateral relations have been conducted on a civil and businesslike plane, according to André Ouellet's predictions. Canadian officials, of course, do not harbour delusions of unmitigated trans-border bliss. Trade and economic issues periodically succeed in frustrating both sides. Occasionally,

Canadian policymakers tell American audiences what they think Washington does, or omits to do, with respect to the bilateral framework of cooperation. For instance, in his 24 May 1994 speech to the Canada–US Business Council, Roy MacLaren gently accused the United States of a relative lack of conviction in pursuing free trade and urged them to resist lobbying groups that were pressing for "devastating, short-sighted" protectionism.[21] After all, the bilateral economic landscape is dotted with relevant irritants which include, but are not confined to, softwood lumber, steel, durum wheat, live swine, Icelandic scallops, books, and beer. By the same token, this disconcerting list helps explain the very dynamism exhibited by Canadian ministers and officials in pursuit of the alternative trade strategies, to which we now turn.

Canada as a Global Trade Actor

The reality of globalization and its implications for Canada had been clearly perceived by the Liberal party at least two years before the Red Book. During the November 1991 conference at Aylmer, Quebec, where Lester C. Thurow gave the keynote address ("The Need for Strategic Approaches"), it became evident that the FTA need not be abrogated. Liberal pragmatism was making an ideological virtue of emerging economic necessity. And, as Jean Chrétien declared, "Protectionism is not left-wing or right-wing. It is simply passé. Globalization is not right-wing or left-wing. It is simply a fact of life."[22]

The conceptual-prescriptive foundations of the new impetus for Canada's globalized trade were solid. Roy MacLaren had worked on them for some time, having served as Liberal trade critic. In his June 1991 paper, "Beyond Continentalism: In Search of an Independent, Global Trade Policy for Canada," he enunciated the new doctrine. For MacLaren, after pursuing free trade with the United States, Canada "should take the next logical step and pursue free trade with the world – as the title of the paper suggests, move 'beyond continentalism' and become aggressively global."[23]

Once appointed international trade minister, MacLaren continued to articulate a coherent conception of Canada's aggressively global trade role. What is more, he and his colleagues began acting upon it. Within months of his ascent to the crucial portfolio, MacLaren emerged as a protagonist for hemispheric free trade, for a transatlantic (NAFTA-EU) link, and for an unprecedented network of bilateral agreements. Moving simultaneously were André Ouellet, as well as the secretaries of state for Latin America and Africa, Christine Stewart, and for Asia-Pacific, Raymond Chan.

As for Prime Minister Chrétien, within the first fifteen months of assuming power, he had travelled around the globe, promoting trade and deepening manifold Canadian roots. The first major visit, as noted, was to Seattle in November 1993. Chrétien participated in the Asia Pacific Economic Cooperation summit, aimed at enhancing trade liberalization in that gigantic marketplace. In late March 1994 he visited Mexico City to discuss bilateral trade promotion. In November of the same year, he visited China, Hong Kong, Indonesia, and Vietnam. And in January 1995, Chrétien and MacLaren visited Argentina, Brazil, and Chile, with brief stopovers in Costa Rica, Trinidad and Tobago, and Uruguay.

The Asian trade tour implemented the "Team Canada" concept. The delegation was the largest ever to visit China. Chrétien was accompanied by MacLaren, another cabinet minister, nine provincial premiers, the territorial government leaders, mayors, and about three hundred business executives. Cooperation with China was predicated on four principles: economic partnership, sustainable development, peace and security, and respect for human rights. The focus on China's human rights record appears filtered through an essentially pragmatic approach. Already in March 1994 André Ouellet had noted that this issue would be raised in quiet diplomacy. In May that year, he stated that Canada could influence China to move towards democratization through "methodical and diversified contacts based on economic partnership, sustainable development, peace and security and human rights." Canada would thus adopt dialogue instead of confrontation, but would denounce "all flagrant violations of human rights."[24]

In this pragmatic context, Canadian and Chinese companies signed about fifty commercial agreements in Beijing in November 1994. These contracts were valued at $5.3 billion, and a further fifteen contracts signed in Shanghai were worth about $330 million. Moreover, a deal was concluded between Atomic Energy of Canada and China's Bureau of Nuclear Power to sell two CANDU reactors for $3.5 billion. The Canadian prime minister told Chinese leaders: "We are not linking trade with human rights but we want to create an open dialogue" about the latter. He also challenged business executives from the two countries to raise bilateral trade by the year 2000 from $5 billion to $20 billion.

This Asian trade tour also involved Hong Kong, Indonesia, and Vietnam. Agreements signed between Canadian and Indonesian companies approached $1 billion. In Vietnam, where Chrétien inaugurated the new Canadian embassy, the ten commercial contracts signed were worth about $110 million. In addition, Canada announced aid disbursements to the two countries: $30 million over five years would support aid projects helping Indonesian women, higher education, and community development; and $16 million over five years in Vietnam would contribute to three cooperative projects.[25]

The success of Jean Chrétien's Asian mission presupposed preparatory contacts and visits by other Canadian officials. Thus, Roy MacLaren had already travelled to China in March-April 1994. In this he was returning the November 1993 visit to Canada by Mrs Wu Yi, China's minister of foreign trade and economic cooperation. During his trip, MacLaren (who was accompanied by representatives from about forty Canadian firms) announced that the Canadian government would make available "financing resources for Canadian exporters attempting to break into the Chinese market."[26] Within weeks, high-level meetings between Canadian and Chinese leaders proliferated. They included André Ouellet's July-August visit to China, when he also went to Hong Kong, Japan, South Asia, and Thailand. Raymond Chan's visits to Asia in August 1994 covered Australia, New Zealand, Malaysia, the Philippines, and Singapore.

In this manner, the Chrétien government was substantiating its conception of Asia-Pacific as a high priority area of Canadian foreign policy. The network of bilateral agreements was expanding, while trade promotion was coupled with parallel or overlapping extra-commercial arrangements. Significant Canadian partners in Asia, besides China, included Japan, South Korea, India, Thailand, and Malaysia.

Japan's obvious importance was confirmed from the outset. Asian tours by Canadian leaders frequently included Tokyo and other major economic centres. From November 1993 to July 1994, seven federal cabinet ministers visited Asia. Ouellet's discussions with Japanese Prime Minister Murayama and Foreign Minister Yohei Kono covered a number of bilateral issues. They explored the opportunities for increased Canadian-Japanese cooperation in the UN, ASEAN, the OECD, and the Canada-Japan 2000 Bilateral Forum. They also discussed cooperation in the fields of nuclear non-proliferation, development and culture.[27] By early 1995 Roy MacLaren could proudly note that, as regards Japan, "we reversed a deficit of $265 million in 1993 and recorded an impressive trade surplus of $1.3 billion."[28]

A special partnership with South Korea was being simultaneously promoted. The new relationship began taking shape during the visits by the Korean foreign affairs minister to Canada in February 1994 and by Roy MacLaren to Korea in April. As the Canadian government explained, the special relationship was being cultivated through the "establishment of a special working group, revitalization of the Canada/Korea Business Council, organization of a high-level South Korean business mission to Canada, creation of an industrial co-operation committee, and regular contacts between the political leaders of the two countries."[29] Within a month, Governor General Hnatyshyn and Agriculture Minister Ralph Goodale visited Seoul to discuss cultural and commercial cooperation. But bilateral Canadian-Korean relations were also explored and enhanced by André Ouellet's visit to South Korea during his own Asian tour of July 1994. This visit was reciprocated when the South Korean minister of trade, industry and energy, Chulsu Kim, came to Ottawa in September to discuss issues pertaining to the working group, including plans to open markets.[30]

Roy MacLaren noted in February 1995: "Few would argue that what we are witnessing is nothing short of a momentous transformation of the world trading system. The myriad of agreements literally breaking out everywhere ensures that our trade policy agenda will be full for years to come." Canadian officials were evidently sharing this perception, so the strategy of aggressive globalism has been pursued in earnest. The fruits are already impressive. As MacLaren reported: "We are on the right course ... we did exceptionally well in 1994. Canadian exports increased by 21 per cent last year, reaching over $219 billion. Our annual trade surplus totalled $17 billion, up almost $8 billion from 1993."[31]

The activism entailed by these results is not confined to trade promotion just as it transcends the boundaries of Asia. For instance, the secretary of state for the Asia-Pacific region, Raymond Chan, travelled several times to Asia early in 1994, heading a Canadian delegation to the second meeting of the International Committee on the Reconstruction of Cambodia in March. Later, he visited Bangladesh, where development and humanitarian aid figured prominently on his agenda.[32]

Within the year, Raymond Chan had returned to the Asia-Pacific region. In early August 1994 he participated in the Dialogue Conference in Australia, where he discussed various issues with the leaders of fifteen South Pacific islands. After the official bilateral visit to Australia, he visited New Zealand where he inaugurated a youth exchange program, and then travelled to Malaysia, Singapore, and the Philippines. In all these countries, he met with government and business leaders to discuss the further development of bilateral ties and the strengthening of economic and academic relations.[33]

Christine Stewart, Mr Chan's counterpart for Latin America and Africa, has proven equally energetic. Early in 1994 she accompanied Roy MacLaren to South Africa where they led a trade mission comprising representatives of Canadian companies from the sectors of manufacturing, technology, and financial services. The same indefatigable

travel logs could be identified in subsequent months, the trips covering issues such as security, peacekeeping, foreign aid, humanitarian
assistance, and concern for human rights. MacLaren's travel to Argentina and Brazil in August 1994 allowed him and the accompanying
group of businessmen to explore investment and joint ventures opportunities, primarily in telecommunications, mining, and transportation.[34]

A tour of Latin America by Jean Chrétien and Roy MacLaren in January 1995 was another confirmation of the Liberal government's commitment to expand Canadian trade with that region. The main
commercial targets of the tour were Argentina, Chile, and Brazil, to
which the Canadian leaders arrived accompanied by some 250 business people representing 195 companies. The contractual fruits of the
mission in Argentina included the signing of $196 million worth of
contracts and agreements-in-principle worth $198 million. In Chile
the signed contracts reached $918 million and the agreements-in-
principle, $846 million. In addition, various bilateral agreements were
signed. They included five academic ones and a $4.35 million agree-
ment between CIDA and the Economic Research Centre for Latin
America. As for Brazil, the thirty-nine contracts and agreements-in-
principle that were signed reached about $602 million, rendering that
country one of Canada's best trade partners in South America.[35]

It should be recalled that Ottawa has committed itself to helping
Chile join NAFTA and regards that country's entry as a test case for the
agreement's success. Here success is conceived in terms of an ample
trade liberalization in the entire hemisphere which, in turn, would
imply containment of the American propensity to dominate the organization. Meanwhile, however, on 29 December 1995 Canada and
Chile agreed to pursue an interim trade agreement, designed to facilitate Chile's accession to NAFTA and to strengthen bilateral trade and
investment. Thus, Canada is now one of the largest foreign investors
in Chile, "with total current and planned investment amounting to
$7 billion in mining, telecommunications, energy distribution, light
manufacturing and other industries."[36]

This emphasis on the Asian-Pacific and Latin American market-
places did not entail any disregard of the trade potential of other
regions. Hardly any corner of the globe was ignored but it would be
tedious to produce here any fastidious details. Suffice it to note the
various visits to Central and Eastern Europe, including Poland, Hungary, and Ukraine, and the abundance of bilateral agreements with
the Russian Federation; André Ouellet's participation in the second
annual Middle East–North Africa Summit, held in Amman, Jordan,
in late October 1995; Prime Minister Chrétien's visit to India and

Pakistan in January 1996; Raymond Chan's May 1995 visit to Sri Lanka (the first by a Canadian minister in twelve years); and the June 1994 signing of a trade treaty with Mongolia.

The Chrétien government has therefore enveloped the globe in a network of bilateral and multilateral trade relations. The reiteration of the current axiom that every $1 billion of exports represents about eleven thousand new jobs should not however be interpreted as implying that the government's vision of Canada is that of a nation of salesmen. To be sure, Roy MacLaren stated to the Canadian Exporters' Association: "We want a Team Canada working every day, coast to coast, and around the world." But he also declared to his audience:

There were times when I felt myself to be among a small, even shrinking, band of idealists. I believed then, as I do now, that free trade was not just a practical necessity but a guiding ideal. Only if trade among nations is free will we maintain the foundations of political and other freedoms.

He then added a proposition reminiscent of the best in the tradition of Canadian internationalism: "I believed then, as I do now, that the free exchange of ideas and capital, the open exchange of goods and services, and the security of agreed rules and common institutions is the basis of civilized intercourse between nations."[37]

THE NEW FACE OF CANADIAN MULTILATERALISM

The forceful energy exhibited by Canadian leaders and officials around the globe since late 1993 was not confined to either trade promotion or mere bilateral relations. Since the goals are set as shared security, shared prosperity, and shared environmentalism, and since the strategy appears to require a synthesis of bilateralism with regionalism and multilateralism, it seems to follow that the erstwhile compartmentalization of diplomatic tactics and means would now be obsolete and ineffectual. Indeed, a Canadian minister visiting an Asian, Latin American, or Eastern European country could be observed to implement an agenda ranging from raising security concerns to environmental issues and from discussing trade liberalization to monitoring CIDA projects.

For instance, the logic of this strategy could well be illustrated by André Ouellet's July 1994 visit to Asia. The Canadian foreign minister would first visit Japan and South Korea before heading the Canadian delegation to the first ASEAN forum on regional security in Thailand. Canada assumed the stance that this initiative is "a conflict prevention instrument which, if adapted to the realities of the region, can provide significant support to the UN." Moreover, Canada proposed the holding of workshops "in which the various countries can share their experience in peacekeeping and other such matters."[38] This regional forum was followed immediately by the ASEAN post-ministerial conference, where Canada, Australia, Japan, New Zealand, the European Union, and the United States joined the six ASEAN countries to discuss "regional and international issues of political and economic significance." Canada raised its concerns about Cambodia and Burma and promised to work to strengthen APEC. After these activities, André Ouellet visited China, where he signed three agreements: a treaty on mutual aid against international crime, an agreement on a $100 million line of credit to promote Chinese imports of Canadian goods, and a letter of intent on environmental cooperation.[39]

For analytic purposes, it makes little difference whether one focuses on multilateral forums or issue-areas, as long as Canada's pragmatic idealism is identified and assessed. Here I propose to extend the discussion on the pre-1993 years by a brief sketch of Canadian internationalism in the major fields of peacekeeping, human rights, ecological concerns, and foreign aid. This sketch will then be supplemented by a concluding survey of complementary issues.

Peacekeeping

Although peacekeeping is the term most commonly used, its meaning has expanded to reflect a concomitant reality in flux. Frequently peacebuilding is employed to express the activity, as in Somalia, Cambodia, and post-1995 Bosnia. In any event, the associated goals of the international community are to prevent conflict from erupting. If, however, preventive diplomacy has failed, that conflict must be contained. Once this is done, the foundations of peace should be built – both metaphorically and literally. Canada's interests in a peaceful world continue to co-exist with the incessant humanitarian impulse to minimize suffering. That is why, in spite of the notorious pressures from some quarters to slide into self-regarding apathy or extreme selectivity, the Chrétien government has responded to every request for UN-sponsored missions. In fact, the foreign affairs minister, Lloyd Axworthy, agreed that Canada should lead the quasi-UN force in Haiti and pay for its contribution.[40]

In addition to participating in all observer missions and blue helmet operations inherited from its predecessors, the Liberal government had to contend with the dramatic deterioration of the civil war in Bosnia. Ottawa reacted to the crisis by inviting parliamentary debates and hoping for consensus before making decisions. In this manner, another Red Book promise was being fulfilled and the country's mood gauged. The government decided to continue its UNPROFOR participation, to go along with the UN/NATO air strikes, and to resist the lifting of the arms embargo in spite of Bosnian and American pressures. Moreover, in September 1994 Canada provided $10 million in humanitarian aid for the former Yugoslavia.

Then in June 1994 Canada responded to the UN's appeals for more troops to address the Rwandan tragedy after the slaughter of thousands of Tutsis at the hands of the Hutu majority. It provided a unit of 350 military communications specialists. Moreover, two Canadian aircraft helped the evacuation of civilians and the delivery of supplies. Estimates suggest that in April–June 1994, nearly two thousand passengers were transported and 730 tonnes of food and materials were delivered.[41]

Peacebuilding in Rwanda continued in July 1994. Canada also responded to new appeals for humanitarian aid, by providing $10 million in funds and offering health and medical services. Illustrating once again the collapse of old conceptual distinctions, the Department of National Defence dispatched a 250-person Canadian team to establish facilities for water purification, and a field ambulance, and to begin rebuilding the airport of the capital, Kigali. In September 1994 Foreign Affairs asked CIDA "to give special attention to refugee repatriation projects and infrastructure reconstruction."[42]

Simultaneously with the Rwanda mission, Canada was involved in the Haitian crisis. In early May 1994 Ottawa refused to consider participation in an invasion of the island. It adopted the UN embargo and thus fifteen Canadian soldiers joined the multinational observer mission at the border with the Dominican Republic. Canada again refused to consent to a military intervention in September 1994. However, when President Aristide's return was announced following the American intervention and the collapse of the totalitarian regime, Canada made available one hundred RCMP officers and six hundred soldiers. As members of the United Nations mission in Haiti, they were to be employed in the rebuilding of the country.

Canada, in addition, hosted a UN meeting on peacekeeping in the spring of 1994. Representatives from twenty-three member states participated in discussions aimed at establishing a long-term strategy to improve peacekeeping operations. As a result of the meeting, three working groups were created. They undertook to explore policy and mandates, military command issues, and the training of peacekeeping personnel. Canada's interest in the work of all three groups is also associated with the recent creation of the Lester B. Pearson Canadian International Peacekeeping Training Centre at Cornwallis, Nova Scotia.

On 26 September 1995, Canada tabled before the United Nations General Assembly the study, *Towards a Rapid Reaction Capability for the United Nations*. André Ouellet and Defence Minister David Collenette sponsored the study, whose goal was to strengthen the UN's capacity to deal with crises promptly and effectively. The result of a year's work, the study utilized the ideas of an international consultative group and drew on Canada's unparalleled peacekeeping experiences. As Ouellet had noted, "A review of several missions over the past five years clearly indicates that a more rapid, coherent response to an emerging crisis could have had a dramatic impact on the evolving situation."[43] The major proposal was the formation of a multi-purpose force of up to five thousand military and civilian personnel capable of rapid deployment under the authority of an operational-level head-quarters. Deploying a peace mission would thus become a matter of a few weeks only. The report called for a more effective partnership be-tween the United Nations and regional organizations in many peace-related operations. It also recommended "a comprehensive approach to peacekeeping, in which military and civilian staffs, drawn from a number of organizations and agencies, some governmental, some inter-governmental, some non-governmental, work to common objec-tives."[44]

Finally, in September 1995 Canada hosted the Conference on Pre-ventive Diplomacy under the auspices of la Francophonie. The Cana-dian proposal to hold such a meeting was prompted by the realization that la Francophonie has lacked the mechanisms to play a conflict prevention role. The Canadian delegates recommended various com-pensatory measures, such as the creation of a ministerial committee to support relevant initiatives and to generate the required political impetus.[45] The logic of this idea also coincided with the Chrétien gov-ernment's emerging conception of multiple partnership among multi-lateral or regional organizations working simultaneously towards the goals of shared security and shared prosperity.

Human Rights

Canada's dilemma concerning China's poor human rights record was mentioned earlier. Idealist purists are justifiably uncomfortable with Team Canada's material success in a country with limited political free-dom. The Chrétien government's solution, however, seems rational. Its approach entails increased access to and influence on China's leaders. It is accompanied by the clear commitment to pressure China in multi-lateral forums where such pressure can be effective. Ottawa is also com-mitted to employing quiet diplomacy on the matter. And there is evidence that human rights were discussed both before and after the

Team Canada visit of November 1994. By mid-February 1996, Chinese officials announced their willingness to let representatives of the UN Commission on Human Rights into China to assess allegations of arbitrary detentions. The announcement occurred during the three-day visit to Beijing by human rights officials of the Canadian government.[46]

Anticipating some criticism in this area, André Ouellet and Roy MacLaren articulated the government's reasoning in their February 1995 letter to the co-chairs of the Special Joint Committee, Senator Allan MacEachen and Jean-Robert Gauthier. They noted that "high profile aid and trade measures may play a role in responding to gross, systematic, and persistent violations of internationally agreed human rights standards." A case-by-case approach seemed to them wiser. Canada's sensitivity to the host of issues covered by the term "human rights" is manifested in the country's controls on the export of military goods "which are among the most restrictive of Western countries." Moreover,

primitive bilateral action in isolation from other countries, however, usually presents the least effective means of achieving results. In the case of trade, it may hurt Canada more than it will change the behaviour of offending governments. Multilateral action, based on international standards and procedures, afford both legitimacy and increased leverage.

The two senior ministers argued that "it is only very rarely the case that promoting human rights and pursuing trade are mutually exclusive objectives. Indeed, trade and growing economic prosperity often nurture a more open society." Ouellet and MacLaren then committed Canada to continue "to lead on human rights issues at the UN, the OSCE, Commonwealth, la Francophonie, and the OAS." For it is these forums that "often provide the most effective means for influencing governments."[47]

This commitment has been honoured by and large. Moreover, as we noted repeatedly above, Canadian officials travelling around the globe have pursued the comprehensive approach of linking trade promotion with security, sustainable development, good governance, and human rights. Therefore, it is arguable that the critics' fixation on China does not justify the deduction that Ottawa is prepared to sell Canada's internationalist soul for new commercial contracts.

The evidence of sustaining the synthesis of pragmatism and idealism includes the Chrétien government's approach to refugees. On 1 November 1994, Immigration Minister Sergio Marchi tabled the new immigration strategy for 1995–2000. While the new plan "will orient immigration more toward Canada's economic needs," the strategy combines pragmatism with compassion: the number of admissible refugees for 1995 was set between 24,000 and 32,000.[48]

In September 1994 Canada participated in the World Conference on Population and Development, held in Cairo. The issues covered by this UN conference included the links between economic and social development, population growth rates, migration, and the environment. Led by Sergio Marchi and Christine Stewart, the Canadian delegation adopted a number of positions premised on human rights. It argued that "basic human rights included a woman's right to decide how many children she should have and what direction her life should take, as well as the right to a job, medical care and education." Canada also announced a $14.9 million contribution to UNICEF for the education of young girls in fifteen African countries.

A year later, Canada participated in the fourth United Nations Women's Conference in Beijing. The Canadian delegation, led by Sheila Firestone, was gratified by many results of the conference where progress was made towards multilateral action for the equality of women. Two particular issues of significance to Canada were the recognition by the Beijing conference of rape as a war crime and of "persecution based on sex differences as grounds to claim refugee status."[49]

It bears repeating that the old classifications of political categories are now collapsing between some domestic and foreign policies. The same is essentially occurring vis-à-vis aid and human rights, peace-keeping and aid, human rights and environmental concerns, or development aid and sustainable development. Thus, for instance, at the borderline between development assistance and promotion of human rights we see Canada allocating $60 million to Bangladesh in September 1995, aimed at creating some fifty thousand jobs for women over the next three years.[50] More generally, as André Ouellet and Roy MacLaren also stated, "Development assistance is a constructive way to address human rights, democracy and governance issues ... Assistance will support such activities as peace and reconciliation initiatives, human rights education, widening access to legal remedies," and helping organizations and individuals to participate "fully and effectively in decision-making in their countries."[51]

The Chrétien government also committed itself to reacting appropriately when gross or persistent violations of human rights were observed. For instance, when the political situation in Myanmar (Burma) deteriorated in February 1995, Canada addressed the ruling junta urging reconciliation with the political opposition. And because of the regime's refusal to restore political legitimacy (by complying with the 1990 election results), Ottawa refuses to establish full bilateral relations with Myanmar.

Similarly, when a military coup overthrew the democratically elected government of Niger, Lloyd Axworthy strongly condemned the action. He also announced a moratorium on new development assistance to Nigeria. And he suspended cooperation with the government until the restoration of civilian rule.[52]

Finally, Lloyd Axworthy, in his 13 February 1996 speech, his first since assuming the Foreign Affairs portfolio, announced Canada's commitment to "take a leadership role on human rights at the United Nations" and to emphasize "Canadian values" in relations with other countries. Axworthy focused in particular on the exploitation of child labour. He announced a $700,000 contribution to the International Labour Organization towards programs that will halt child labour. And he called on human rights activists to collaborate with his department in the development of a "human rights strategy" for Canada. The immediate response has been positive. Indeed, Canadian internationalists have reasons to be optimistic, in view of the new foreign minister's passionate commitment and sophisticated worldview.

Ecological Concerns

Jean Chrétien's Ottawa continued its environmental activism, both in multilateral forums and in its numerous and multi-dimensional bilateral relations. Canada's promotion of sustainable development became one of the central objectives of its foreign policy after October 1993. The country even appointed an ambassador for sustainable development, while its cabinet ministers and officials responsible for foreign affairs keep reiterating the importance of relevant action in view of the global requirement for the "shared custody of the environment."

Among typical illustrations, one could register the Canadian-Russian agreement of 17 December 1993, whereby the two countries agreed to collaborate in establishing a model forest in Siberia. In March 1994, in a meeting of over eighty nations at Geneva, there was renewed agreement to support the Global Environmental Facility, which was proposed at the 1992 Rio summit. Canada announced that, over the following ten years, it will contribute $112 million to the $2 billion fund. The moneys will be used to help developing countries in their ecological efforts. A month later, to signal the authenticity of its commitment, Canada participated in a UN-sponsored conference in Barbados, whose official title was "United Nations World Conference on Sustainable Development for Small Island Developing States."[53] In April 1994 André Ouellet suggested a number of principles for an Arctic policy. He proposed the creation of an Arctic Council for all circumpolar states and Aboriginal peoples. He also announced the

creation of the post of ambassador of circumpolar affairs. And he anticipated further action by Ottawa concerning pollution prevention and
sustainable development in the Arctic as well as the preservation of the
traditional lifestyles of the Aboriginal peoples.

Finally, in addition to insisting on satisfying its environmental
sensitivities in its bilateral relations, Canada participated in the Berlin
Conference on Climate Change. Environment Minister Sheila Copps
represented Canada in this April 1995 conference where progress was
made towards limiting greenhouse-gas emissions. Copps "expressed
deep satisfaction with the results and with the friendliness in the positions of the developed and developing countries."[54]

By far the most dramatic Canadian ecological involvement of these
years was the "Turbot War." As early as January 1994, Fisheries and
Oceans Minister Brian Tobin warned the EU that Canada was contem-
plating unilateral action against the "modern-day pirates." He was
referring to some Europeans overfishing Canadian waters, who were
frequently reflagging their boats in South American countries to bypass
the quota restrictions imposed by the North Atlantic Fisheries Organization (NAFO). While Ottawa was preparing measures (in both the
Justice Department and the Department of National Defence), special
NAFO meetings in February 1994 reassessed earlier quotas and imposed a one-year moratorium on cod fishing. This decision was called
"a victory" by Canada. Brian Tobin then participated in the August
1994 UN Conference on High Seas Fishing. He lobbied on behalf of
Canada to win friends and influence like-minded countries towards
accepting an international convention on controlling fish stocks straddling boundaries in international waters. Canada stressed that "such a
convention would ensure proper management of resources and would
eliminate unilateral controls on the high seas." Canada seemed then to
have won support from some sixty countries.[55]

The turbot crisis, however, came to a head in March 1995, when
Ottawa decided to act unilaterally and board fishing vessels endangering the conservation of the species. On 9 March the Spanish trawler
Estai was intercepted and its captain accused of illegal fishing. Canada
and the European Union (with the marked exception of Britain) were
at loggerheads when Spain demanded the release of the Estai and sent
armed patrol boats to the scene. Negotiations began in Brussels but to
no avail as both sides seemed immovable. In the UN Conference for
the Management of Straddling Fish Stocks, meanwhile, Brian Tobin
described Spanish overfishing as "ecological folly." He insisted on
elevating the dispute to an issue of protecting the global commons.
The Canadian minister's strategy was successful. The United Nations
approved a new convention on straddling and migratory fish stocks

aiming at the protection of those in jeopardy. Canada was a major actor in preparing the convention, assisted by Argentina, Chile, Iceland, Indonesia, New Zealand, Norway, and Peru. Brian Tobin described the day the convention was approved (4 August 1995) a great day for the United Nations and Canada.[56]

Foreign Development Assistance

In his February 1994 budget speech, Paul Martin Jr committed the government to continue "our tradition of strong support for international development assistance." Given, however, that "the fiscal challenge requires additional restraint in spending," the Chrétien government reduced ODA spending by 2 per cent for 1994–5. Spending was to remain at the same level until 1996–7. "International assistance spending will still amount to $2.6 billion annually. That compares favourably to that of other industrialized countries."[57]

Paul Martin's statement is defensible. In its 1995 report, *The Reality of Aid*, an international consortium of aid groups lamented the drop in rich donors' foreign aid, from US$61 billion in 1992 to $56 billion in 1993. Even so, Canada's ranking in terms of aid as a percentage of GNP was seventh – the traditional place of Canada since the Trudeau years. Moreover, noting the general intensification of the pragmatic preoccupation, the report observed that "even countries such as Denmark, proportionally one of the highest aid donors, are moving to link the choice of projects receiving aid to Danish business interests."[58]

In their report, *Canada's Foreign Policy* the Special Joint Committee reaffirmed that "human rights, good governance and democratic development are universal values that should find central expression in Canadian foreign policy, influencing and guiding other areas of policy." Whereas the 1994 level of support for basic human needs was less than 20 per cent of aid, the committee recommended a minimum of 25 per cent. The six program priorities recommended were "basic human needs; human rights, good governance and democratic development; the participation of women; environmental sustainability; private sector development; and public participation."

Pragmatism was therefore already represented by the introduction of private sector development, which could be used to cover Ottawa's support for export promotion. Pragmatism was also served by the committee's suggestion that "Canada's desire to fight global poverty occurs side by side with a crisis of runaway national debt." And it was present in the double prescription that CIDA's mandate and priorities be clarified and that its limited resources be concentrated "in the most effective ways possible."[59]

Overall, then, the parliamentary committee retained a rational and reasonable balance of pragmatism and idealism. Its final recommendations on aid included the proposal "that the government commit itself to stabilizing ODA at the present GNP ratio and seek to make progress towards the 0.7% target when Canada's fiscal situation permits."[60] The government's response accepted the clear majority of the relevant premises and recommendations of the committee. There was, of course, reassertion of the pragmatism implied in Paul Martin's February 1994 budget speech. The government also adopted the private-sector development recommendation; the idea that "the Canadian private sector is an important development partner for CIDA"; that "a major portion of ODA resources should be focused on a limited number of countries"; and that progress should be made "toward the target of 0.7 per cent when Canada's fiscal situation permits."[61] But the Chrétien government also committed itself to an active and effective ODA program "as a vital element of Canadian foreign policy." It accepted the notion of universal values and promised to continue "to lead on human rights issues at the UN, the OSCE, the Commonwealth, la Francophonie and the OAS." And it produced the following statement of purpose: "The purpose of Canada's Official Development Assistance is to support sustainable development in developing countries in order to reduce poverty and to contribute to a more secure, equitable and prosperous world."[62]

The Chrétien government's commitments thus seem to be premised on sophisticated conceptual and causal linkages, including ODA, sustainable development, security, peace, and prosperity. It seems fair to argue that Canada's record in development aid should not be gauged exclusively in terms of ODA ratios and figures. If the internationalist agenda adopted by the Chrétien government aims ultimately at shared security-prosperity-environmental sanity for the purpose of achieving a more satisfied Canada and a more civilized world, then the millions of dollars spent annually by Canada on this agenda should also legitimately count in any assessment of Canadian aid's role in the world.

CONCLUSIONS

Several years after assuming power, the Chrétien government's foreign policy patterns may be identified and assessed. Pragmatism was necessitated by familiar domestic requirements and pressures and by the fluidity of the external environment. This meant that idealist excesses had to be contained. It also implied an emphasis on an aggressive trade globalism intent on improving the domestic socio-economic picture through economic stimulation and job creation. This globalism is already bearing promising fruits. Global trade promotion, however, is not intended as an end in itself. It also seems to be a means towards the implementation of the policies of shared security, shared prosperity, and shared environmentalism. Thus, while the Liberal government encourages global Canadian entrepreneurial motivation, export growth, and investment activism, it also utilizes these opportunities to cultivate a strategic parallelism. This is already clearly demonstrated in the harmonization of bilateralism with regionalism and multilateralism. This harmonization seems to aim at the entrenchment of multiple partnerships with even overlapping mandates and goals to secure solid foreign policy results.

These being central formal properties of the new Canadian diplomacy, its substance represents a revised internationalism. Canadian pragmatic idealism is now being adapted to new domestic and international conditions. Ample evidence exists to verify the proposition that Canadian multilateralism continues to transcend narrow self-interest through its commitments to moderation, mediation, the broad conception of security, and the functional improvements of international and global organizations. Moreover, our evidence has detected the continual visceral Canadian engagement in such areas of the internationalist agenda as peacekeeping and peacebuilding, sustainable development, international law, human rights, and foreign aid. Therefore, it remains quite remarkable that in spite of obvious constraints, Canadian idealism is being confirmed and extended even as it is pragmatically adapted.

To be sure, even this sympathetic interpretation can advance criticism vis-à-vis Ottawa's recent human rights record where more clarity and moral transparency are needed to combat the appearance of excessive commercialization. There can also be reservations regarding the further reductions in the ODA envelope. Precisely because other major donors seem currently stingy; because trade promotion, human rights, and sustainable development are all central pillars of the new foreign aid mandate; and because of the critical role of this issue for Canada's self-definition and role in the world – for all these reasons it is arguable that now is the time for a renewed celebration of Canada's humanitarian impulse. A Canadian fall in the OECD rankings will be unfortunate, particularly because the reversal of the recent tendency to save can be accomplished with small increases in aid volume. Such increases might be derived, for instance, by limiting the excessive Canadian generosity exhibited in some peace-building operations. Similarly, it is easy to conceive of imaginative fund-raising campaigns sponsored by CIDA or groups of non-governmental organizations, whereby Canada's ODA/GNP ratio will improve.

On the other hand, further good news about the Chrétien government's foreign policy record should be stressed. Among other things,
one must note that Canadian multilateralism has been particularly
strengthened, as attested by the numerous proposals and recommendations submitted to the UN, la Francophonie, APEC, and OSCE, and as
noted in Canada's leadership role during the June 1995 G-7 meeting
at Halifax.[63] Second, the Red Book promise of a more independent
Canadian foreign policy towards the United States is also being
successfully met.[64] Third, our discussion of peacekeeping and foreign
aid may suffice to show that the heart of pragmatic idealism remains
intact. Finally, it is equally true that further foreign policy democratization has been accomplished. In addition to the sophistication of the
foreign policy review and its open process, we may also recall the establishment of the annual National Forum on Canada's International
Relations, the frequent debates in the House of Commons in mid-
February 1996, and the decision by Lloyd Axworthy to employ the
Internet for Canadians to make comments and suggestions on foreign
policy matters.[65]

In sum, by early 1996, Canadian internationalism as pragmatic
idealism was alive and well; it was creative, adaptable, consistent, and
coherent.

PART THREE

9 Conclusion: Retrospect and Prospects

RETROSPECT

In our analysis of Canadian foreign policy we have examined the major decisions, actions, motives, concerns, preoccupations, and results of Canada's international performance from 1945 to 1995. What gave coherence to our discussion was the analytic framework of Canadian internationalism, chosen because post-1945 Canadian foreign policy was premised on the policymakers' conscious and sustained decision to combine idealism and pragmatism. In other words, Canadian foreign policy pursued a set of goals which incorporated cosmopolitan values in Canada's best interests. These interests and values together determined or conditioned the ends and means of Canada's foreign policy style and substance.

Specifically, Canada's post-1945 performance has demonstrated authentic and persistent support for multilaterally institutionalized cooperation; moderation in rhetoric and actions; commitment to mediation and communication; caring for and sharing with the less privileged; a broad conception of security, which emphasized economic development and implied non-militarism; and active endorsement of the primacy of justice over power, of ecological sanity, and of the satisfaction of global or human needs. Canada's idealism has been neither utopian nor exclusively other-regarding; hence "pragmatic idealism" captures Canada's pursuit of its enlightened self-interest in harmony with the broad human interests for peace, justice, order, and development.

To reflect the form and content of fifty years of Canadian internationalism the logic of our argument has exhibited the following structure:

1. Canada's interests, principles, and values were clearly articulated by the architects of postwar Canadian foreign policy during the golden age from 1945 to 1957. The internationalists were manifestly enthusiastic about the role that Canada, with other middle powers, could play in the postwar landscape. Security, development, and peace were conceived and defined in terms remarkably reflecting the spirit of the United Nations Charter's statement of Purposes and Principles.[1] Even at the height of the Cold War, this idealist vision, far from being abandoned, was far-sightedly modified. Canada thus distinguished itself by combining its Western credentials with the simultaneous pursuit of the defusion of regional and global crises haunting the two antagonistic camps.

2. The values and interests of the golden age were crystallized in a set of foreign policy objectives that have been consistently respected ever since. Canadians have employed skilfully the legal-moral-political strategies and tactics of multilateralism, functionalism, mediation, and moderation. The golden age legacy was both too authentically Canadian and clearly effective to be altered by succeeding policymaking elites. It derived naturally from the country's political culture with its established emphases on dialogue, compromise, generous caring and responsible sharing, among other things. This political culture was conditioned by Canada's historical, geographic, demographic, and socio-economic idiosyncrasies, which shaped Canada's conception of its interests as imbued with its humane values.

3. While Canada's interests and values helped it contribute to "the betterment of the international community," they also contributed to its internal unity and its prestigious place among states. Thus, the style and substance of Canadian foreign policy have been widely recognized as "generous," "peace-promoting," "principled," and "moral."[2] Such an image, while not an unintended consequence of what we have termed Trudeau's synthesis, has clearly satisfied many of Canada's particular interests and needs, including the one for distinctness.

4. That Canadian pragmatic idealism was an intended overall policy follows not only from the consistent programmatic statements and declarations of Canada's policymakers. It is also manifest in the general coherence among their actions and pronouncements, in the overall consistency of their decisions and their actions, and in the motives behind Canada's objectives. These motives, moreover, have been generally endorsed, cherished, and often celebrated by the Ottawa bureaucracy, the foreign policy practitioners, the activist non-governmental organizations, the media, and Canadian public opinion. After all, these

domestic influences on Canada's foreign policymaking reflect the interests and values of the idealist and pragmatic components of the country's political culture.

5. The effectiveness of Canadian internationalism in action was established by considering the concrete implementation of its avant garde agenda throughout the Cold War, which generated a momentum for principled pragmatism in the areas of arms control and disarmament, peacekeeping and peacemaking, human rights, ecological concerns, and aid to the Third World. In all these fields – which at the end of the Cold War have emerged as central and decisive for the survival and well-being of the planet – Canada's record has ranged from remarkable to honourable. This record becomes more impressive when compared to that of the overwhelming majority of the members of the international community.

6. Finally, Canada's post-1945 international performance deserves to constitute a clear, if rarely appreciated, mirror of Canada's elusive identity. In other words, Canada's foreign policy could not be what it was except for the fact that its *sui generis* interests and values shaped its external behaviour. And because there is a demonstrable affinity or structural resemblance between its widely respected domestic image and its highly recognized external one, it would seem to follow that the country's self-perception should finally catch up with the perception it enjoys in the community of states.

The logic of our argument was sustained by the empirical record. By interpreting this record according to its own demands, we endorsed internationalism as the best framework for the analysis of Canadian foreign policy. Of course, this framework was never meant to function as an analytic straitjacket. Therefore, just as we had to point out occasional discordances between declarations and actions or between actions and results, we could not gloss over some missed opportunities for greater commitment in some fields. Ultimately, however, none of these can be surprising in the real world of fifty years of Canadian foreign policy.

If, then, the validity of the internationalist thesis seems confirmed, the weaknesses of the alternative approaches become now more transparent, for two kinds of reasons. First, our framework necessitated the study of the entire internationalist agenda. Moreover, this framework emerged as the one that corresponds to the professed interests, values, and goals of Canadian foreign policy. Therefore, the major challenges of realism and economic nationalism would have to demonstrate that Ottawa, from 1945 to 1995, has either exhibited sustained hypocrisy or has suffered from profound self-deception. Neither can be demonstrated, given the ample empirical record. At most, arguments could point to occasional discrepancies between foreign policy declarations and actions. Here the internationalist response may be as follows: (a) that some discrepancies were inevitable given the Canadian activism in so many fields over so many years; (b) that many demands on Ottawa regarding, for instance, human rights or foreign aid have simply been unrealistic or excessive; and (c) that the genuinely internationalist counter-evidence seems quite compelling.

Second, the near silence on the internationalist agenda by the alternative approaches justifies scepticism about them. As regards the realist model, the primary sources of its evasion are, first, the *a priori* endorsement of theses and assumptions of limited applicability to Canada; and second, the consequent neglect of the premises that have defined Canada's self-professed internationalism. As for the nationalist school, its major flaw is a fixation on the Canadian-United States relationship from which flow hyperbolic claims about Canada's foreign policy impotence which fly in the face of the impressive activism of Canadian internationalism.

As a parting comment on these alternative approaches we should reiterate that any valid insights they may provide on aspects of the empirical record must, of course, be endorsed. This may serve to moderate some of the celebratory conclusions contained in this book. After all, our reading of Canadian foreign policy never harboured narcissistic delusions of perfect objectivity: it only promised to make the best sense of Canada's foreign relations, in terms of the empirical record, and considering the alternatives.

PROSPECTS

At the best of times, foreign policy predictions are highly risky, may hide wishful thinking, and may also imply intellectual arrogance.[3] Yet it is incumbent on us to distinguish warranted predictions from mere alarmism and to venture some optimistic suggestions on the future of Canadian internationalism, if only because of the pessimism frequently expressed about the internationalist project.

Some pessimism has been aired regarding the recent North-South policies of the like-minded middle powers. These policies pertain primarily to the trade, monetary, and investment decisions of rich internationalist states of the North which, in the 1980s, were perceived as betraying their erstwhile "humane internationalist" commitments. A certain fatigue was detected in their governments' political will to implement policies to combat global poverty by means other than disbursements of aid. Accusations have simultaneously been uttered that countries of the South are often responsible for irrational allocation of resources, corruption, and ineffective economic policies. Northern middle powers are sometimes confronted with serious domestic challenges from both industrialists and trade unionists who favour protectionism of the sectors threatened by the "unfair" competition from low-wage less developed countries' producers. The recent microelectronic revolution, with its managerial and labour implications, can also be expected to cause social dislocation, growth in unemployment figures, and socio-political frustration in the North.[4]

Another form of pessimism concerns the security sphere in the post-euphoria phase of the early post-Cold War era. Whereas the fall of the Berlin Wall, the dissolution of the Soviet Union and of the Warsaw Pact, and the celebration of the United Nations' renaissance marked the years 1989–92, the last few years have witnessed increasing alarmism primarily as a result of the tragedies in the former Yugoslavia, the former Soviet Union, Somalia, and Rwanda. Anxieties have been articulated about "this new, unstable, and often dangerous international environment"; and about "[i]nternal disorder, economic hardship, boundary disputes, and breakaway movements" in the newly independent states. Such concerns led Margaret Doxey to lament: "All this turmoil makes nonsense of any new international order: war is often the prevailing condition."[5]

These concerns could sustain the suspicion that the global security and political-economic environments might experience a retreat from internationalist commitments. The momentous changes in the international political economy over the last decade include the fact that the socialist camp has all but disappeared, and earlier experiments by developing countries with alternative (non-capitalist) strategies for trade and economic development are all but abandoned. In the absence of rhetorical, moral, and economic support from the erstwhile metropolis of socialism, the former non-aligned states resort to the North-dominated international economic institutions, with all that this implies for autonomy of action. The deep and protracted global recession of the early 1990s fuelled gloomy predictions, including suggestions that trade protectionism will reassert itself and that, in the post-Cold War era, the South will be left to its own devices. Finally, it is true that disorder did engulf large sectors of the post-1992 world. Major international organizations, from the United Nations to NATO to the CSCE/OSCE, have not always performed effectively. And after a short hiatus, assertive realist voices can again be heard at least in the congressional corridors of power of the only remaining superpower.

On reflection, however, these features of the pessimistic reading do not suffice to undermine the validity of internationalism. If anything, they form compelling grounds for the mobilization of multilateral

means towards internationalist ends. Moreover, numerous propositions can be advanced in defence of internationalist-multilateralist
optimism.

First, the gloomy economic predictions about the North need not
come true. While the new technological revolution has generated
socio-economic discontents, governments of the North are now learn-
ing to readjust their growth strategies to address the dislocations and
unemployment problems of the early 1990s. Moreover, innovative
thinking is being pursued in various areas related to economic growth
and employment solutions,[6] including proposals for job-sharing, programs for intensified retraining of laid-off employees, novel conceptions of comparative advantage, and even a certain moderation of the
Northern infatuation with consumerism. And as regards obstacles to
freer global trade, the recent G-7 summits, such as those in Tokyo
(1993) and Halifax (1995), as well as the completion of GATT's
Uruguay Round in December 1993, and the promises of the APEC
summits have clearly signalled the willingness of the countries of both
North and South to resist at all costs the protectionist spectre and to
pull the global economy out of its 1990s malaise.

Second, the internationalist perspective may, after all, offer the
wisest answers to the North's economic needs in conjunction with
the needs of the South. In addition to the billions of dollars in development aid provided yearly by the middle powers, these countries can
continue to create strategies to assist the development of the South.
Among these strategies, noteworthy are Bernard Wood's proposals for
the cooperation of Northern and Southern middle powers. Similarly,
there is the model of the "mini-NIEO," whereby a group of developing
countries, members of the Southern Africa Development Coordination Conference or SADCC, will coordinate aid and trade policies with
the Nordic countries. This, as Cranford Pratt has noted, will be "a
living out of a relationship between rich and poor countries that
reflects a sense of global solidarity and is not dominated by considerations of market efficiency."[7] Such a pattern could be multiplied to
create "alliances" among Northern non-middle powers and groups of
Southern states. Such arrangements can aim at the rational allocation
of skills, knowledge, and resources, so that by rationalizing the development of the South, the Northern states can thereby also help themselves. Thus, whether one prefers Cranford Pratt's ethically-premised
set of proposals, or Bernard Wood's liberal internationalism of mutu-
ality of interests,[8] or – as this book has implied throughout – a combination of both sets of premises, pragmatic idealism can inspire novel
and imaginatively articulated strategies for the alleviation of global
poverty and the simultaneous economic growth of the North. Such
new strategies cannot be expected to issue from unilateral (state-

centric) sources; almost by definition the answers must come from internationalist/multilateral arrangements.

Third, the internationalist agenda is far richer than the orthodox money-trade-investment triptych of North-South concerns. What Jim MacNeill has called the alternative agenda amounts to a revolutionary internationalist project, which covers a host of urgent concerns under the umbrella of sustainable development. This is suggested by the following constellation of linkages à la Jim MacNeill, and it appears to be wholeheartedly endorsed by the government of Jean Chrétien:
– Population, human resources, development and environment
– Urbanization and urban development
– Energy, development and environment
– Agriculture, forestry, development and environment
– Industry, development and environment
– International economic relations, development and environment, human rights, security and peace.[9]

In short, the greening of international relations both implies and calls for intensified international cooperation to implement multilaterally the policies of the alternative agenda – namely, the linkages among environment, development, trade, aid, security and peace.

Already the signals suggest that more than the like-minded middle powers are considering the merits of adopting this project. In the aftermath of the influential 1992 Rio conference, there is little hyperbole in saying that a global consciousness is penetrating common sense. Consider the goals of the proliferating UN-sponsored summits since Rio: the 1993 Vienna Conference on Human Rights was followed by the 1994 Cairo Conference on Population and Development and then by the March 1995 Copenhagen World Summit for Social Development and the September 1995 World Women's Conference in Beijing. Regarding the Copenhagen "people's summit," *The Economist* (a bastion of conservative thinking), commented that it was "designed to complement the 1992 earth summit" so as to "fit people, rather overlooked at the Rio meeting, into the newly accepted concept of sustainable development."[10]

At Copenhagen, consistent with its internationalist traditions, the host country – now standing as the world's largest per capita donor of development aid, with 1.02 per cent of GNP – announced the cancellation of the debts of Angola, Bolivia, Ghana, Nicaragua, and Zimbabwe. Contrasting Denmark's record and motives to those of the Republican-controlled US Congress, an American journalist observed:

Denmark stands as proof that there are places in the industrialized world where even rock-ribbed Conservatives are pleased that their governments have big foreign aid programs – and even want them increased. One recent poll, by

Denmark's Vilstrup Research organization, showed that 62 per cent of Danes are happy their country gives as much as it does and that 15 per cent wish it would give more. Even among far-right voters, the pollsters found, Danish foreign assistance is favored by 42 per cent.[11]

To be sure, the costs associated with the global duties inherent in the agenda of sustainable development are high. We know by now, however, that the price of inaction (or of half-hearted action) could well be the destruction of the planet. It follows that only concerted multilateral means can serve the end of a dignified global survival. The internationalist impulse is further stimulated by the emerging consensus among North and South countries. Contradicting the Cassandra-esque scenarios of the sceptics, Australian ambassador Richard Butler, who chaired one of the working groups responsible for the final agreements at the 1995 Copenhagen conference, stated: "political commitments were being made which would have been unthinkable three or four years ago. They reflected changes in the political landscape since the end of the Cold War."[12]

Fourth, it seems indisputable that only multilateralism can promise the effective handling of the security dangers of the 1990s and beyond. Proliferation of weapons of mass destruction (nuclear, biological, chemical), ethnic-religious disputes, massive refugee movements, and the insecurities deriving from socio-economic misery, can cause inter-state crises with regional or global implications. It seems to follow that the community of states will either appeal to the old multilateral organizations – refitted to address the new challenges – or create new international instruments. In both cases more, not less, multilateralism is required. This is so, if only because the remaining alternatives are either inaction or self-serving state-centric action.

Internationalists can receive limited satisfaction from arguing that many of the insecurities of the 1990s are the legacy of the Cold War – which realist thought and practice tolerated and, in extreme cases, cultivated. Similarly, sceptics of multilateralism are unjustified when they harp exclusively on the weaknesses of such organizations as the United Nations. The strengths of the UN are analogous to the empowerment it has received from its members. The reinvigorated organization is only a few years old. Moreover, the manifold demands on it have never been more burdensome. Finally, it is doubly disingenuous to accuse it of inability to cope with the tragedies of Bosnia-Herzegovina, Somalia, or Rwanda: first, because these tragedies were clearly alleviated by the UN's performance, and second, because no defensible alternatives had really been advanced.

Therefore, even if multilateralism did not exist before the end of the Cold War, we would have had to invent it. Today it is commonly agreed that a reinvented United Nations needs strengthening through more funding, bureaucratic restructuring, a more representative Security Council, and a number of new or revamped special agencies to handle human rights, women's issues, refugees, the population crisis, peace-building, and the environment/development nexus. As Tom Keating wrote, "While the UN offers the best prospect for a truly international consensus to deal with problems, its effectiveness, credibility, and legitimacy depend on a number of important reforms."[13] Internationalist thinking seems ideally suited to advance creative proposals for multilateralist reforms regarding the United Nations system, as well as the Organization for Security and Cooperation in Europe and the Atlantic Alliance itself.

Fifth, internationalist arguments to this point have been anchored primarily on a pragmatic conception of the commonality of global interests. But we can also appeal to the normative (idealist) dimension for compelling grounds over and above the rationality of multilateralist efficiency. Throughout this book, we have emphasized the ethical reality of duties beyond borders. We have implied and frequently demonstrated the moral unacceptability of the present state of the world. And we have presented empirical evidence that international organizations, states, groups of states, groups of individuals under non-governmental auspices, and ordinary citizens demonstrate palpably their adoption of the cosmopolitan principles and values contained in pragmatic idealism. Therefore, as more thought and action expand the factual knowledge of the benefits of international cooperation and of the means necessary to implement the internationalist agenda, internationalist optimism will be further justified.[14]

Sixth, we may now turn to the particular case of Canada. Most studies of Canadian foreign policy have not concerned themselves with Canada's established credentials, with the domestic sources of its pragmatic idealism, with the leadership role exercised by Canada in the internationalist/multilateralist field, or with the beneficial consequences for Canada and the world that flow from the country's international performance. Therefore, such studies have downplayed or ignored the importance of pragmatic idealism for Canada's self-definition, for other domestic interests such as trade, economic growth, and internal unity, and for the country's international status and prestige. Because internationalism is no incidental or redundant appendage to Canada's foreign policy style and substance, it follows that the continued commitment to the interests and values of Canada's pragmatic idealism should not be questioned even during hard times. Not only has this policy worked, it is manifestly in Canada's interests to see that it works, as it is obviously required, both morally and pragmatically, by the condition of the world.

Prescriptively, then, it can be suggested that internationalism is the most rational and ethical policy for Canada. This policy will strengthen Canada's *self-definition* as a caring, enlightened, generous, and highly civilized state, and will confirm the vision of Canada as a "mentor state". Canada's continued internationalist vocation will solidify its international *recognition* and prestige. When other middle powers hesitate, Canada will have the opportunity to play a *leadership* role. Such a role does not imply harbouring delusions of grandeur or omnipotence: both the Canadian psyche and the nature of pragmatic idealism contradict such attitudes. Rather, our sense of leadership connotes, first, that some states can be creative models for forward-looking policies with global import, and second, that their example could then be emulated by more than like-minded middle powers.

Finally, it is crucial to stress that only the respect, credibility, and internationalist credentials accumulated by states such as Canada can render them agents of change vis-à-vis aspects of the global malaise. As regards the plights of overpopulation, ecological degradation, violation of human rights, poverty and malnutrition, uneven development, irrational allocation of resources, violence and war, few states can voice authoritatively their internationalist concerns without raising suspicions of ethnocentricity, hypocrisy, or patronizing paternalism. Canada's motives and record, as we have seen, qualify this country for an influential internationalist role in the post-Cold War world.

Notes

CHAPTER 1

1 Holmes, *Life with Uncle: The Canadian-American Relationship*, 112.
2 Peyton Lyon has come close to acknowledging a continuity until 1984. He might, however, disagree with my pragmatic-idealist reading. See his "The Evolution of Canadian Diplomacy since 1945," in Painchaud, ed., *From Mackenzie King to Pierre Trudeau: Forty Years of Canadian Diplomacy, 1945–1985*. Sympathetic to an overall internationalist reading until 1984 is also Hawes, *Principal Power, Middle Power, or Satellite?*
3 For a discussion of cosmopolitan values, see Beitz, *Political Theory and International Relations*; Hoffmann, *Duties Beyond Borders: On the Limits and Possibilities of Ethical International Politics*; and Melakopides, "Ethics and International Relations: A Critique of Cynical Realism," in Haglund and Hawes, eds., *World Politics: Power, Interdependence and Dependence*.
4 "Pragmatic" here denotes "realistic," that is, adaptable to the real world. It also alludes to (but does not endorse) the notion advanced by the American pragmatists, John Dewey, William James, and C.S. Peirce, that "true is what works." In this way we avoid the appearance of a paradox in "realistic idealism."
5 Keohane, "Multilateralism: An Agenda for Research," 731.
6 Postwar Canadian multilateralism as essentially realist has been recently discussed in Keating, *Canada and World Order: The Multilateralist Tradition in Canadian Foreign Policy*.
7 See Melakopides, "Ethics and International Relations."
8 For an introduction to the theory of (political) realism, see below, chapter 2. The most extreme expression of anti-internationalist

vehemence by a Canadian realist is Ranger, "The Canadian Perspective," in Northedge, ed., *The Foreign Policies of the Powers.*

9 Canada, House of Commons, *Debates*, 9 July 1943, 4561. In his speech Mackenzie King introduced the "functional principle."

10 External Affairs, *Statements and Speeches*, no. 47/2, 13 January 1947.

11 Ibid.

12 Lester Pearson, *Words and Occasions*, 68–9.

13 Quoted in Thomson and Swanson, *Canadian Foreign Policy: Options and Perspectives*, 30.

14 Department of External Affairs, *Foreign Policy for Canadians*, 55.

15 Ibid., "International Development," 8–9.

16 Pearson, *Words and Occasions*, 68.

17 *Foreign Policy for Canadians*, "International Development," 9.

18 Ibid., 55.

19 See Crenna, ed., *Pierre Elliott Trudeau: Lifting the Shadow of War*, passim.

20 "Notes for Remarks by the Prime Minister at the Mansion House," ibid., 18–22.

21 See Dobell, *Canada's Search for New Roles: Foreign Policy in the Trudeau Era*, 136.

22 Department of External Affairs, *Canada's International Relations: Response of the Government of Canada to the Report of the Joint Committee of the Senate and the House of Commons*, 86. *Independence and Internationalism* made this statement on p. 137, where it was also stated: "We conclude that Canada's activities abroad should be guided by an approach based on constructive internationalism. This would impart both a vision and a sense of purpose to Canadian foreign policy."

23 Wood, "Canada and Southern Africa: A Return to Middle Power Activism," 285–6.

24 Department of External Affairs and International Trade, *The Disarmament Bulletin* 14 (Fall 1990), 27.

25 McDougall, Introduction, in English and Hillmer, eds., *Making a Difference? Canada's Foreign Policy in a Changing World*, ix–x.

26 More specifically, the Mulroney government's internationalist activism and, at times, even multilateralist leadership will be illustrated in the following areas: peacekeeping, peacemaking, official development assistance, ecological initiatives, arms control and disarmament, immigration openness, support for an enhanced United Nations role, support for the Commonwealth and la Francophonie, defence of human rights, and anti-apartheid commitment.

27 *Canada's Foreign Policy: Principles and Priorities for the Future*, Report of the Special Joint Committee Reviewing Canadian Foreign Policy, November 1994, 1.

28 Canada, Government Statement, February 1995, *Canada in the World*, 1.

29 Ibid., 8.

30 Nossal, *The Politics of Canadian Foreign Policy.* In private correspondence in February 1993, Professor Nossal agreed with my reading of his approach as "refined realist." He also pointed to the reconsideration of his views on middle powers contained in Andrew F. Cooper, Richard A. Higgott, and Kim Richard Nossal, *Relocating Middle Powers: Australia and Canada in a Changing World Order* (Vancouver: UBC Press 1993). I am grateful to Kim Nossal for this exchange.

31 Major representatives of the various strands of this approach can be found in Clarkson, ed., *An Independent Foreign Policy for Canada?*; Lumsden, ed., *Close the 49th Parallel: The Americanization of Canada*; Rotstein and Lax, eds., *Independence and the Canadian Challenge.* Stephen Clarkson's *Canada and the Reagan Challenge* is the most sophisticated recent work in this approach. Finally, notable also is Hurtig, *The Betrayal of Canada.*

32 Tom Axworthy, introduction, in David Crenna, ed., *Pierre Elliott Trudeau, Lifting the Shadow of War*; Axworthy, "To Stand Not So High Perhaps but Always Alone: The Foreign Policy of Pierre Elliott Trudeau," in Axworthy and Trudeau, eds. *Towards a Just Society: The Trudeau Years.*

33 Pratt, ed., "Ethics and Foreign Policy: The Case of Canada's Development Assistance"; and chapters 1 and 2 in Pratt, ed., *Internationalism under Strain: The North-South Policies of Canada, the Netherlands, Norway, and Sweden.* For the latest sceptical work which repeatedly admits Canada's internationalist ODA legacy but laments its post-1990 stress on commercial interests, see Pratt, ed., *Canadian International Development Assistance Policies: An Appraisal.* See also my review of Pratt's volume in *Canadian Journal of Political Science* (March 1995).

34 For rich bibliographical information up to the mid-1980s, see Hawes, *Principal Power, Middle Power, or Satellite?*

35 See Beitz, "Recent International Thought."

36 Myrdal, *Objectivity in Social Research.*

CHAPTER 2

1 Classic formulations of traditional and modern realism can be found in the works of E.H. Carr, Hans Morgenthau, Henry Kissinger, and Kenneth Waltz, among others. While many erstwhile realists have moderated dramatically their stance since the end of the Cold War and the fall of the Soviet Union, the November 1994 American elections and the Republican-dominated new Congress demonstrated that their worldview is still popular in Conservative American circles.

2 Major representatives of recent idealist thought include Richard Falk, Charles Beitz, and Henry Shue. For an important survey of recent idealist literature, see Beitz, "Recent International Thought." J. David Singer may also qualify as an idealist since he wrote: "Specialists in world affairs have a

special responsibility ... to address the major problems confronting the global village ... The human condition is, on balance, morally unacceptable" (see "The Responsibilities of Competence in the Global Village," 245–59).

3 For an excellent introduction to behaviouralism, see Banks, "The Evolution of International Relations Theory," in Banks, ed., *Conflict in World Society*. Robert Keohane has offered a powerful methodological-conceptual critique of realism and neorealism in chapters 1 and 7 of *Neorealism and Its Critics*.

4 The fullest discussion of marxist thought as applied to international politics is Kubalkova and Cruickshank, *Marxism and International Relations*.

5 See Banks, "The Inter-Paradigm Debate," in Light and Groom, eds., *International Relations: A Handbook of Current Theory*. For a recent sophisticated argument on additional insights, see Brown, "Marxism and International Ethics," in Nardin and Mapel, eds., *Traditions of International Ethics*, 225–49.

6 For an introductory discussion of this issue, see my article "Marxological Investigations."

7 Authors in this school have included Karl W. Deutsch, James N. Rosenau, J. David Singer.

8 Banks, "The Evolution of International Relations Theory."

9 See Pentland, "Integration, Interdependence, and Institutions: Approaches to International Order," in Haglund and Hawes, eds., *World Politics: Power, Interdependence and Dependence*. Terminological confusion is frequently caused when scholars object to the classification accorded them by other scholars. See, for instance, Keohane's denial that he should be classified as a neorealist in *Neorealism and Its Critics*, 25, n7. See also Richard Ashley's list, and contrast Keohane's denunciation to that of Gilpin, both in ibid. David Dewitt and John Kirton are two Canadian scholars at the borderline between realism and neorealism.

10 Henry Kissinger, "A New National Partnership," based on his speech at Los Angeles, 24 January 1975; quoted by Keohane and Nye, *Power and Interdependence*, 3.

11 For a parallel summary, see Viotti and Kauppi, *International Relations Theory: Realism, Pluralism, Globalism*, 7–8.

12 The rational actor model is usefully discussed in Brewer, *American Foreign Policy: A Contemporary Introduction*, chapter 2.

13 Rosenau, "Once Again into the Fray: International Relations Confronts the Humanities," 84–5.

14 For an excellent survey of American revisionist and post-revisionist thinking on early post-1945 American foreign policy, see Gaddis, "The Emerging Post-Revisionist Synthesis on the Origins of the Cold War."

15 For the use of these terms, as applied to the United States and the Soviet Union, see Jönnson, *Superpower: Comparing American and Soviet Foreign Policy.*

16 Tucker, *Canadian Foreign Policy: Contemporary Issues and Themes,* 1–2.

17 Notice that, in addition to these states, the like-minded group, which was active in the late 1970s on the North-South dialogue, also included Austria, Belgium, Finland, Ireland and, "on occasion, Great Britain and France." Pratt, "Humane Internationalism: Its Significance and Its Variants," in Pratt, ed., *Internationalism under Strain,* 23. For obvious reasons, the last two states do not belong to *our* like-minded group, because they are generally considered as more powerful than middle powers.

18 Strictly speaking, "celebrated" may be too strong regarding Michael Tucker's book; but it is not inappropriate in connection with Tom Axworthy and Peter Dobell.

19 Doran, *Forgotten Partnership: US-Canada Relations Today,* 164.

20 Axworthy, "Introduction" to *Lifting the Shadow of War.*

21 Cranford Pratt's relevant contribution includes the excellent introduction and conclusion to the anthology on human rights he recently co-authored with Robert Matthews. See *Human Rights in Canadian Foreign Policy.*

22 Supererogation is defined by the Concise Oxford Dictionary as "doing of more than duty requires." For a recent critique of Pratt's position, see my review of Cranford Pratt, ed., *Canadian International Development Assistance Policies: An Appraisal,* in *Canadian Journal of Political Science,* 188–90.

23 Nossal, *The Politics of Canadian Foreign Policy,* 59.

24 Ibid., 81 n64.

25 Ibid., 54, 76.

26 For a discussion of ego role conceptions and alter's role conceptions, as they relate to the superpower status, see Jönsson, *Superpower,* 15ff, which contain related references.

27 John Holmes coined this term in sardonic and clear juxtaposition to brinkmanship, made notorious by US Secretary of State John Foster Dulles.

28 Martin, *The Presidents and the Prime Ministers.*

29 A somewhat pompous way of capturing the methodological proclivities of the present project is to label it "quasi-Lakatosian" or reminiscent of Imre Lakatos's "sophisticated methodological falsificationism." For, as two British scholars summarized Lakatos's proposal on corroborating or abandoning a theory (T), "it is reasonable to abandon T if and only if there is an alternative theory T¹ which explains everything that T explains, and generates predictions not derivable from T, some of which have been confirmed by empirical testing." Russell Keat and John Urry, *Social Theory as Science* (London and Boston: Routledge & Kegan Paul 1982), 49. See Lakatos's argument in "Falsification and the Methodology of Scientific Research Programmes," in I. Lakatos and A. Musgrave, eds., *Criticism and the Growth of Scientific Knowledge* (Cambridge: Cambridge University Press 1970).

CHAPTER 3

1 For the early years of the Department of External Affairs, see Eayrs, "The Origins of Canada's Department of External Affairs."

2 On Canada's declaration of war, see Eayrs, *In Defence of Canada*. Vol. II: *Appeasement and Rearmament*. Vol. III, *Peacemaking and Deterrence* (1972) is invaluable for the period 1943–49.

3 Middlemiss and Sokolsky, *Canadian Defence: Decisions and Determinants,* wrote: During World War II Canada once again contributed out of all proportion to its size. More than in the previous war, Canada was able to exploit its contributions to play an active role in Allied diplomacy and also to reinforce the image of the country as a truly distinct and indeed major international player. With the fall of the Axis powers and the weakening of Britain and France, Canada, physically untouched by the war, had been strengthened relative to other nations by the boost it gave to the development of its industry and resources (p. 16).

4 Canada, House of Commons, *Debates,* 9 July 1943, 4558. On the meaning of "functionalism," see Tucker, *Canadian Foreign Policy,* and Blair Fraser, *The Search for Identity: Canada, 1945–67.*

5 Lester Pearson provided illuminating background information and authoritative judgments on the Canadian delegation's goals, and its life and times, in *Words and Occasions.*

6 See Canada, Department of External Affairs, *Canada and the United Nations, 1945–1975, passim.*

7 Department of External Affairs, *Statements and Speeches,* no. 47/2, 13 January 1947, 3–11.

8 Quoted in Thomson and Swanson, *Canadian Foreign Policy: Options and Perspectives,* 26.

9 For details on the Suez crisis and Pearson's role, see Fraser, *The Search for Identity.*

10 Ronning, in *Canada's Role as a Middle Power,* ed. J. King Gordon, 42.

11 Thomson and Swanson, *Canadian Foreign Policy,* 26.

12 Sanger, ed., *Canadians and the United Nations,* 14.

13 Thomson and Swanson, *Canadian Foreign Policy,* 90. Writing in 1971, these authors added: "Canada has demonstrated an active interest in the activities of UNESCO and UNICEF, in the FAO, which was founded in Quebec City, and in ICAO, which has its headquarters in Montreal."

14 John F. Kennedy's book review of Pearson's *Diplomacy in the Nuclear Age* first appeared in *Saturday Review* and is reprinted in *International Journal,* 66–70.

15 Lyon, "The Evolution of Canadian Diplomacy since 1945," in Painchaud, ed., *From Mackenzie King to Pierre Trudeau: Forty Years of Canadian Diplomacy, 1945–1985,* 16.

16 Doxey in "John Holmes: An Appreciation," *Behind the Headlines,* 6.

17 Lyon, "The Evolution of Canadian Diplomacy," 18.
18 See Gaddis, "Towards a Post-Revisionist Synthesis"; also LaFeber, *America, Russia, and the Cold War, 1945–1984,* 1–73.
19 See Thomson and Swanson, *Canadian Foreign Policy,* ch. 5.
20 Reid, "The Creation of the North Atlantic Alliance, 1948–1949," in Granatstein, ed., *Canadian Foreign Policy,* 158–82.
21 Article 2 reads as follows:
    The Parties will contribute toward the further development of peaceful and friendly international relations by strengthening their free institutions, by bringing about a better understanding of the principles upon which these institutions are founded, and by promoting conditions of stability and well-being. They will seek to eliminate conflict in their international economic policies and will encourage economic collaboration between any or all of them.
    Nato Facts and Figures. Brussels: NATO Information Service (1971), 270.
22 Thomson and Swanson, *Canadian Foreign Policy,* 63.
23 Ibid., 80.
24 Dayal, "The Power of Wisdom," 112.
25 Quoted in Donald Page, "Détente: High Hopes and Disappointing Realities," in Balawyder, ed., *Canadian-Soviet Relations,* 25–6.
26 Quoted in Collins, "Canadian-Soviet Relations during the Cold War," in ibid., 44–5.
27 Ibid., 44.
28 Ibid., 51.
29 Ibid., 53.
30 Lester Pearson gave his own colourful account of the trip in *Mike: The Memoirs of the Right Honourable Lester B. Pearson,* vol. 2, ed. Munro and Inglis, 191–211.
31 Black and Hillman, "Canada and the Soviet Union as Neighbours," in *Nearly Neighbours: Canada and the Soviet Union,* 6.
32 Pearson, *Words and Occasions,* 69.

CHAPTER 4

1 Ranger, "The Canadian Perspective," in Northedge, ed., *The Foreign Policies of the Powers,* 278–83.
2 Lyon, "The Evolution of Canadian Diplomacy since 1945," 22. It should, however, be noted that Lyon's 1968 assessment was far less benign (see below).
3 On NORAD's life and times and on Diefenbaker's defence policy in general, see Middlemiss and Sokolsky, *Canadian Defence: Decisions and Determinants.*
4 Diefenbaker, *One Canada: The Tumultuous Years 1962 to 1967,* chapter 4. Dale Thomson and Roger Swanson themselves extended the argument from NORAD obligation to the United States. They wrote that "the

argument can be made that the Kennedy Administration did not fulfill its obligation with regard to early consultation." *Canadian Foreign Policy: Options and Perspectives*, 28.

5 Quoted in Martin, *The Presidents and the Prime Ministers*, 179.

6 The next day, Arnold Heeney was summoned by the prime minister again. Diefenbaker read him more letters, "all promoting Canadian neutrality." Ibid.

7 For details on the material of this paragraph, see ibid., 180–209.

8 Diefenbaker's somewhat elusive treatment of the Bomarc crisis in his auto-biography seems premised on the claim that the Bomarc system was already becoming obsolete. See *One Canada: The Tumultuous Years 1962 to 1967*, chapters 3 and 4.

9 Lyon, "The Evolution of Canadian Diplomacy," 22. Lyon also noted that "some of Mr. Diefenbaker's more specific difficulties were not entirely of his own making, his problem with the Avro Arrow and the Bomarc, for example, was similar in some respects to Prime Minister Macmillan's prob-lem with the Skybolt, nations with limited means now find it difficult to avoid embarrassment when they undertake major weapons programs" (*Canada in World Affairs*, 530–1).

10 Ibid., 223.

11 Burns, *A Seat at the Table: The Struggle for Disarmament*, 171, quoted in Barrett, "Arms Control and Canada's Security Policy," 739.

12 Lyon, *Canada in World Affairs*, 223–4.

13 Barrett, "Arms Control," 736.

14 Department of External Affairs, *Canada and the United Nations, 1945–1975*, 64.

15 Ibid., 71.

16 General Burns quoted in Barrett, "Arms Control," 736–7.

17 Ibid., 739, n11.

18 Lyon, *Canada in World Affairs*, 224.

19 All editorial quotations in this paragraph are from ibid., 227–8.

20 Blanchette, ed., *Canadian Foreign Policy 1955–1965: Selected Speeches and Documents*, 30.

21 Lloyd, *Canada in World Affairs*, 139–40.

22 Department of External Affairs, *Canada and the United Nations, 1945–1975*, 45.

23 Preston, *Canada in World Affairs*, 267.

24 Lyon, *Canada in World Affairs*, 281–2.

25 Ibid., 283.

26 Keating, *Canada and World Order: The Multilateralist Tradition in Canadian Foreign Policy*, 138–9.

27 For a succinct introduction to the goals, achievements, and problems of these international economic institutions, see Blake and Walters, *The Politics of Global Economic Relations*, esp. chapters 3 and 5.

28 Lloyd, *Canada in World Affairs*, 145–6.
29 The data in this paragraph are from ibid., 146–7.
30 Preston, *Canada in World Affairs*, 235.
31 Ibid., 235–6.
32 Ibid., 228. By now, the Colombo Plan "had drawn in the United States and Japan which, like two of the charter members, the United Kingdom and Canada, were outside the region" (p. 227).
33 Ibid., 229, 231.
34 Lyon, *Canada in World Affairs*, 357.
35 Ibid., 353–4.
36 Ibid., 352. This statement, made during a House of Commons debate in September 1961, was accompanied by one by Paul Martin who said: "I do not believe … Canada need feel it has shirked its responsibility."
37 Ibid., 358.
38 Robinson, *Diefenbaker's World: A Populist in Foreign Affairs*, 4.
39 Ibid., 281.
40 Lloyd, *Canada in World Affairs*, 204–5.
41 Preston, *Canada in World Affairs*, 200.
42 "If expulsion on grounds of internal policy were once introduced, there was no telling where the process could end" (ibid., 206).
43 Ibid., 207.
44 Robinson, *Diefenbaker's World*, 315.
45 Lyon, "The Evolution of Canadian Diplomacy," 22.
46 Robinson, *Diefenbaker's World*, 318.

CHAPTER 5

1 English, *The Worldly Years: The Life of Lester Pearson*, II, 317.
2 Dobell, *Canada's Search for New Roles: Foreign Policy in the Trudeau Era*, 134.
3 Girard, *Canada in World Affairs*, 19.
4 Munro and Inglis, eds., *Mike: The Memoirs of the Right Honourable Lester B. Pearson: III 1957–68*, 106 (hereafter *Mike*, III).
5 John F. Kennedy, "On *Diplomacy in the Nuclear Age*," 67.
6 See Middlemiss and Sokolsky, *Canadian Defence: Decisions and Determinants*, 23.
7 Munro and Inglis, eds., *Mike: The Memoirs of the Right Honourable Lester B. Pearson: II 1948–1957*, 32.
8 Girard, *Canada in World Affairs*, 133–7, is the source of this paragraph's data.
9 Ibid., 131.
10 Dobell, *Canada's Search*, 29; Girard, *Canada in World Affairs*, 259.
11 For details on the 1964 white paper, see Middlemiss and Sokolsky, *Canadian Defence*, 27–30.
12 Blanchette, ed., *Canadian Foreign Policy, 1955–1965*, 143–4.

13 *Mike*, III, 143–4.
14 Girard, *Canada in World Affairs*, 346; Lyon, "The Evolution of Canadian Diplomacy since 1945," in Painchaud, ed., *From Mackenzie King to Pierre Trudeau*, 25.
15 English, *The Worldly Years*, 361.
16 *Mike*, III, 148 (emphasis in original).
17 Ibid., 148–50.
18 English, *The Worldly Years*, 363; Martin, *The Presidents and the Prime Minister*, 2.
19 English, *The Worldly Years*, 371–2.
20 Blanchette, ed., *Canadian Foreign Policy*, 132.
21 Ibid., 133. Sharp made the statement on 17 June 1971.
22 *Mike*, III, 155.
23 English, *The Worldly Years*, 379.
24 *Mike*, III, 158.
25 Quoted in Peers, "Oh Say, Can You See?" in Lumsden, ed., *Close the 49th Parallel*, 136.
26 Blanchette, ed., *Canadian Foreign Policy*, 80.
27 Legault, "Some Aspects of Canadian Diplomacy in the Area of Disarmament and Arms Control," in English and Hillman, *Making a Difference? Canada's Foreign Policy in a Changing World Order*, 170–1.
28 Blanchette, ed., *Canadian Foreign Policy*, 77.
29 Department of External Affairs, *Canada and the United Nations*, 69, 72, 75.
30 Legault and Fortmann, *A Diplomacy of Hope: Canada and Disarmament*, 211.
31 Ibid., 568.
32 Girard, *Canada in World Affairs*, 316–17.
33 Blanchette, ed., *Canadian Foreign Policy*, 43.
34 Ibid., 189.
35 Girard, *Canada in World Affairs*, 326, 327, n109.
36 Ibid., 344 (emphasis in original).
37 Dobell, *Canada's Search for New Roles*, 135.
38 Blanchette, ed., *Canadian Foreign Policy*, 101–2.
39 *Paul Martin Speaks for Canada*, 132.
40 Ibid., 133–4. Barbara Ward was quoted from her inaugural Massey Lecture.
41 Ibid., 134–5.
42 Girard, *Canada in World Affairs*, 145–6.
43 Department of External Affairs, External Aid Office, *Annual Review, 1966–67*, 9.
44 Ibid., 17.
45 Ibid., 19.
46 Girard, *Canada in World Affairs*, 240–2.
47 External Aid Office, *Annual Review, 1966–67*, 5.
48 Ibid., 7, 24.
49 Ibid., 3.

50 See, for instance, his 14 February 1966 speech "Canada and the Common-wealth," in *Paul Martin Speaks for Canada*, 51–8; and his statement to the Senate Committee on External Affairs and National Defence of 4 April 1966 on sanctions to Rhodesia, in Blanchette, ed., *Canadian Foreign Policy*, 160–5.

51 *Mike*, III, 312.

52 Thomson and Swanson, *Canadian Foreign Policy*, 29.

53 *Mike*, III, 305–6.

54 Ibid., 307.

55 Quoted in Blanchette, ed., *Canadian Foreign Policy*, 162; English, *The Worldly Years*, 370.

56 *Mike*, III, 310.

57 English, *The Worldly Years*, 371.

58 Dewitt and Kirton, *Canada as a Principal Power: A Study in Foreign Policy and International Relations*, 67.

59 English, *The Worldly Years*, 302. According to English, the "revelation that, in 1961, French-speaking Quebeckers controlled only 15.4 per cent of the province's manufacturing sector and 47.1 per cent of its economy, even though they were roughly four-fifths of the population of Quebec, embarrassed Liberals like Mike Pearson" (p. 303).

60 *Mike*, III, 279.

61 Ibid.

62 Ibid., 286.

63 Pearson himself seems incapable of fathoming de Gaulle's precise logic. For such an attempt, see English, *The Worldly Years*, 314–45, *passim*.

64 *Mike*, III, 284.

65 English, *The Worldly Years*, 345.

66 Stairs, "Present in Moderation: Lester Pearson and the Craft of Diplomacy." The following quotations are from pp. 145–6. The quotation of John W. Holmes is from *The Better Part of Valour: Essays on Canadian Diplomacy*, vii.

67 The Vancouver speech, "Some Principles of Canadian Foreign Policy" is in *Words and Occasions*, 67–76. Special attention can also be paid to chapter 2 of *Mike*, II, where Pearson wrote *inter alia* that " 'participatory international-ism' to maintain and strengthen world peace was a principal objective of Canada's national policy. We always asked ourselves not only 'What kind of Canada do we want?' but 'What kind of a world do we want?' This world-view was consistent with a proper regard for our own interests" (p. 32).

68 Martin, *Paul Martin Speaks*, 134.

69 English, *Shadow of Heaven: The Life of Lester Pearson*, I, ix.

70 Stairs, "Liberalism, Methodism, and Statecraft: The Secular Life of a Canadian Practitioner," 679–80.

71 Hamilton, "Thoughts on the Chairman," 142.

CHAPTER 6

1 Dewitt and Kirton, *Canada as a Principal Power*, 68–75.

2 Von Riekhoff, "The Impact of Prime Minister Trudeau on Foreign Policy," reprinted in Granatstein, ed., *Canadian Foreign Policy*, 249–61.

3 Granatstein and Bothwell, *Pirouette: Pierre Trudeau and Canadian Foreign Policy*, 378–82.

4 Blanchette, ed., *Canadian Foreign Policy 1966–1976*, 335.

5 Ibid., 337–40.

6 Ibid., 341.

7 Von Riekhoff, "The Impact of Prime Minister Trudeau," 252.

8 Department of External Affairs, *Foreign Policy for Canadians*, 6.

9 Ibid. (emphasis added).

10 Ibid., 10–11.

11 Secretary of State for External Affairs, "Canada–US Relations: Options for the Future," 46.

12 Blanchette, ed., *Canadian Foreign Policy, 1966–1976*, 342, 47, and 48.

13 Ibid., 46.

14 Ibid., 343. This statement was made by Trudeau to the Alberta Liberal Association at Calgary on 12 April 1969.

15 Dobell, *Canada in World Affairs, 1971–73*, 226. The more modest tone was justifiable by the UN's serious problem of financing peacekeeping operations and the sad memory of the expulsion of the UNEF by Egypt's President Nasser in 1967.

16 Department of External Affairs, *Canada and the United Nations*, 37.

17 Blanchette, ed., *Canadian Foreign Policy, 1966–1976*, 345.

18 *Canada and the United Nations*, 115.

19 Thomson and Swanson, *Canadian Foreign Policy*, 70–1.

20 Balawyder, ed., *Canadian-Soviet Relations*, 216.

21 *Statements and Speeches*, 71/16, 1971.

22 McMillan, "Canada's Postwar Economic Relations with the USSR – An Appraisal," in Balawyder, ed., *Canadian-Soviet Relations*, 167.

23 For details, see Ghent, "Cooperation in Science and Technology," in ibid.

24 Among other things, the Soviet Academy of Sciences added a Canadian division to its Institute of the United States in 1973.

25 Black and Hillmer, eds., *Nearly Neighbours: Canada and the Soviet Union from Cold War to Detente and Beyond*, 10.

26 Bromke, "Canada's Relations with the USSR and Eastern Europe," in Painchaud, ed., *From Mackenzie King to Pierre Trudeau*, 306.

27 Ibid., 307.

28 Cf. Middlemiss and Sokolsky, *Canadian Defence: Decisions and Determinants*: "Judged on the basis of major spending decisions, there was clear continuity between the defence policy of the Trudeau government and previous

governments ... Canada had decided to retain all its alliance commitments" (p. 42).

29 A fair and balanced discussion of the free-rider myth is contained in Doran, *Forgotten Partnership: US-Canada Relations Today,* especially pp. 164–71.

30 *Foreign Policy for Canadians,* 37–8.

31 Quoted in Dobell, *Canada's Search for New Roles,* 29.

32 Thomson and Swanson, *Canadian Foreign Policy,* 73.

33 Quoted in ibid.

34 Dobell, *Canada's Search for New Roles,* 34.

35 Tucker, *Canadian Foreign Policy: Contemporary Issues and Themes,* 120–1.

36 *Foreign Policy for Canadians,* 23–4.

37 See Dobell, *Canada's Search for New Roles,* 62, for 1968 statistics.

38 For representative statements of the nationalist critiques see, for instance, Lamsden, ed., *Close the 49th Parallel,* and Rotstein and Lax, eds., *Independence: The Canadian Challenge.*

39 The most sophisticated discussion of Washington's responses is contained in Clarkson, *Canada and the Reagan Challenge.*

40 For an excellent discussion of Bill C-58 and the surrounding bilateral sensitivities, see Meisel, "Escaping Extinction: Cultural Defence of an Undefended Border," in Flaherty and McKercher, eds., *Southern Exposure: Canadian Perspectives on the United States.*

41 Quoted in Munton, "Reagan, Canada, and the Common Environment," 4.

42 Tucker, *Canadian Foreign Policy,* 98.

43 See ibid., 93–101, for a perceptive analysis of the Garrison Diversion crisis and the IJC's role.

44 See Crenna, ed., *Pierre Elliott Trudeau; Lifting the Shadow of War,* 36.

45 Ibid., 27–8.

46 Ibid., 35–6.

47 Von Riekhoff, "The Impact of Prime Minister Trudeau," 255.

48 Legault, "Some Aspects of Canadian Diplomacy," 173.

49 The concept of Canada as a mentor state was introduced by Trudeau in *Federalism and the French Canadians.* It amounted to his vision of Canada as a model for the world.

50 Geoffrey Pearson, "Trudeau Peace Initiative Reflections," 3–6.

51 Quoted in Gwyn and Gwyn, "The Politics of Peace."

52 Von Riekhoff, "The Impact of Prime Minister Trudeau," 256.

53 Quoted in ibid.

54 Environment Canada, *Canada and the Human Environment,* 85–6.

55 *Foreign Policy for Canadians,* 16.

56 Tucker, *Canadian Foreign Policy,* 181.

57 The quotations and information about Canada's activism at the Stockholm conference are derived from Environment Canada, *Conference on the Human Environment,* 10–13.

58 *Canada and the United Nations, 1945–1975*, 117.
59 Von Riekhoff, "The Impact of Prime Minister Trudeau," 256–7.
60 *Foreign Policy for Canadians*, 27.
61 See the important volume edited by Matthews and Pratt, *Human Rights in Canadian Foreign Policy*, especially the essay by Victoria Berry and Allan McChesney, "Human Rights and Foreign Policy-Making."
62 Keenleyside and Taylor, "The Impact of Human Rights Violations on the Conduct of Canadian Foreign Policy," 4.
63 See Howard, "Black Africa and South Africa," in Matthews and Pratt, *Human Rights in Canadian Foreign Policy*, 275–6.
64 Arbour, " 'America's Backyard': Central America," in ibid., 233, 236.
65 Tucker, *Canadian Foreign Policy*, 116–17.
66 *Canada and the United Nations, 1945–1975*, 115.
67 Foster, "The UN Commission on Human Rights," in Matthews and Pratt, *Human Rights in Canadian Foreign Policy*, 93–4.
68 The UN Human Rights Committee was established by the International Covenant on Civil and Political Rights in order to interpret the covenant, to review countries' reports, and to protect individual victims of human rights abuse.
69 Cathal Nolan, "The Human Rights Committee," in Matthews and Pratt, *Human Rights in Canadian Foreign Policy*, 333, n30. Among other grounds for such praise one may mention that in 1979 "Canada submitted by far the largest and most comprehensive report of any nation to date" (p. 104). Nolan added that Canada's relevant record "was singled out by UN officials as a model for other states" (p. 331, n14).
70 Ibid., 110–11.
71 LeBlanc, "Canada at the UN Human Rights Commission," 22.
72 Tucker, *Canadian Foreign Policy*, 114.
73 Quoted in ibid.
74 Blanchette, ed., *Canadian Foreign Policy*, 165.
75 Tucker, *Canadian Foreign Policy*, 115. Mitchell Sharp's statement was made to SCEAND in March 1974.
76 Keenleyside, "Development Assistance," in Matthews and Pratt, *Human Rights in Canadian Foreign Policy*, 199.
77 Dobell, *Canada in World Affairs*, 215.
78 Dobell, *Canada's Search for New Roles*, 124.
79 Such observers include Tom Axworthy, Peter Dobell, Peyton Lyon, and Michael Tucker.
80 *Foreign Policy for Canadians*, "International Development," 8–10.
81 Cosmopolitanism as an ethical model or framework has Kantian origins. It was revived, however, as late as 1979 by Charles R. Beitz, *Political Theory and International Relations*, and by Stanley Hoffmann, *Duties Beyond Borders: On the Limits and Possibilities of Ethical International Politics*.
82 Quoted in von Riekhoff, "The Impact of Prime Minister Trudeau," 257.

83 *Lifting the Shadow of War,* 19–22.

84 Dobell, *Canada's Search for New Roles,* 140.

85 OECD, *Twenty-Five Years of Development Cooperation: A Review,* 334–5. It is notable that by the early 1970s the OPEC countries had also begun being aid donors, outside the OECD framework.

86 Lyon, "Introduction," in Lyon and Ismael, eds., *Canada and the Third World,* xv–xvi.

87 Dobell, *Canada's Search for New Roles,* 138; OECD, *Development Cooperation, 1985,* 227.

88 One of those who exaggerated the review's caution was Peyton Lyon in his article "The Trudeau Doctrine." However, in his essay in Painchaud, ed., *From Mackenzie King to Pierre Trudeau,* he repeatedly recognized Trudeau's successes: "He emerged as one of the most eloquent champions of the underdeveloped Third World, and Canada's development assistance increased significantly during most of his tenure (p. 27)." He noted that "Pierre E. Trudeau had emerged as a widely admired statesman (p. 29)." And in view of the opinion research that he and Brian Tomlin had conducted in 1975–6, Professor Lyon could have added that Canada's international image, after eight years of Trudeauvian leadership, was most flattering. See Lyon and Tomlin, *Canada as an International Actor,* 78ff, esp. Table 5.1, where the five top adjectives attached by the interviewed foreign experts to countries acting "like Canada" were: generous (28%), peace-promoters (11%), internationalist (8%), responsible (6%), and pragmatic (6%).

89 Barry, "Interest Groups and the Foreign Policy Process: The Case of Biafra," in A. Paul Pross, ed., *Pressure Group Behaviour in Canadian Politics,* 142–3.

90 Dobell, *Canada's Search for New Roles,* 128.

91 The figures are from Bromke and Nossal, "Tensions in Canada's Foreign Policy," 346. The "Open Letter to All Canadians" is reprinted in *Lifting the Shadow of War.*

92 *Lifting the Shadow of War,* 50–2.

93 Trudeau's interview with Jack Cahill of the *Toronto Star* (14 May 1983) is reprinted in ibid., 53, where Trudeau noted: "As you know, I have denuclearized Canada in NATO; I have taken away our nuclear role in Europe. With the F-18s I am taking away any need for nuclear weapons to be stationed in Canada. I think I have done more in denuclearizing Canada than people realize."

94 Bothwell and Granatstein, *Pirouette,* xii.

95 Pratt, "Humane Internationalism and Canadian Development Assistance Policies," in Pratt, ed., *Canadian International Development Assistance Policies: An Appraisal,* 340–1.

96 Ibid., 341. Ironically, a senior advisor in CIDA at the time was Escott Reid. His essay "Canada and the Struggle against World Poverty" suggested that "if Canada were to increase its net expenditures on foreign aid to poor countries by 1.8 billion Canadian dollars a year" this would increase the

foreign aid of Western countries by 33 per cent. The sum of $1.8 billion was Canada's "present defence expenditures." Quoted in Dobell, *Canada's Search for New Roles*, 137.

97 See Pratt's concluding chapter and his "Profile" of Canadian ODA, chapter 1, *Canada's International Development*, passim.

98 See my review of Pratt's anthology in *Canadian Journal of Political Science*, 188–90.

99 For instance, in "Ethics and Foreign Policy: The Case of Canada's Development Assistance," 264–301.

100 Von Riekhoff, "The Impact of Prime Minister Trudeau," 250–60.

101 Bothwell and Gananstein, *Pirouette*, 381.

102 See Tom Axworthy's revealing introductory essay, "A Singular Voice: The Foreign Policy of Pierre Elliott Trudeau," in *Lifting the Shadow of War*, xi–xvii.

103 See Stanley Hoffmann's bizarre inclusion of Nixon and Reagan under the liberal internationalist umbrella in "The Crisis of Liberal Internationalism."

104 These terms are found on pp. 378, 379, 381, and 382.

105 The case studies discussed in the second half of the book deal with Canada's immigration, energy, and space policies and its policy towards the Middle East.

106 See their brief survey on pp. 68–75.

107 Dewitt and Kirton, *Canada as a Principal Power*, 75.

CHAPTER 7

1 Department of External Affairs, *Canada's International Relations*, 9, 43.

2 *Independence and Internationalism*, 99; *Canada's International Relations*, 71: "The government affirms that the international promotion of human rights is a fundamental and integral part of Canadian foreign policy."

3 *Independence and Internationalism*, 127; *Canada's International Relations*, 85.

4 *Independence and Internationalism*, 137.

5 *Canada's International Relations*, 89. The response affirmed Canada's commitment to both the United Nations and "the more restricted groups such as the Economic Summit, the Commonwealth and la Francophonie."

6 The most powerful arguments in defence of the FTA can be found in Lipsey, *Evaluating the Free Trade Deal*. The case for the opposition is best represented in Cameron, ed., *The Free Trade Deal*.

7 As Margaret Atwood put it, "The future is like life after death. You can say anything you like about it, because nobody can actually go there and come back and tell us about it." See "The only position they've ever adopted toward us, country to country, has been the missionary position ...," in LaPierre, ed., *If you Love this Country: Facts and Feelings on Free Trade*, 18.

8 Doern and Tomlin, "Was Canada Politically Out-negotiated?" in Charlton and Riddell-Dixon, eds., *Crosscurrents: International Relations in the Post-Cold War Era*. See also Gigantes, *Is the Free Deal Really for You?*

9 For some perceptive, non-alarmist insights on such potential consequences, see Stairs, "Free Trade – Another View."

10 See Middlemiss and Sokolsky, *Canadian Defence: Decisions and Determinants*, 47–8.

11 Department of National Defence, *Challenge and Commitment*, 5–6.

12 *Defence Update*, 4–5.

13 Calder and Furtado, "Canadian Defence Policy in the 1990s: International and Domestic Determinants," 9.

14 Masse, *Canadian Defence Policy*, 31–2.

15 A most eloquent and passionate statement of this can be found in Roche, "Potential Alternative Strategies for Canada," 12, where the former Canadian ambassador for disarmament wrote: "The Canadian government cannot, by itself, stop the arms race, cure world poverty, or protect the global commons, but it can – and it must – take more initiatives to solve these problems. Concerned Canadians must push politicians in this direction."

16 Hollins et al., *The Conquest of War*, 72.

17 Wood, "Peace and Security in the Midst of International Turmoil," 19.

18 Department of External Affairs and International Trade, *The Disarmament Bulletin*, no. 14 (fall 1990), 27.

19 Munton, *Peace and Security in the 1980s: The View of Canadians*, 5, 7.

20 Chapin, "The Canadian Public and Foreign Policy," 14.

21 *International Canada*, February and March 1987, 14.

22 Black and Hillmer, "Canada and the Soviet Union as Neighbours," in Black and Hillmer, eds., *Nearly Neighbours: Canada and the Soviet Union from Cold War to Detente and Beyond*, 12.

23 *International Canada*, December 1988-January 1989, 46.

24 *Maclean's* magazine, 13 November 1989, 45.

25 *Canadian International Relations Chronicle* (hereafter *Chronicle*), October–December 1989, 24–5.

26 *The Disarmament Bulletin* 13 (spring 1990), 4.

27 *Chronicle*, January–March 1991, 13.

28 Ibid., July–September 1991, 13.

29 External Affairs and International Trade, "Task Force on Central and Eastern Europe" (summer 1992), 3, 9.

30 Middlemiss and Sokolsky, *Canadian Defence*, 46.

31 Barrett, "Arms Control and Canada's Security Policy," 739.

32 The negotiations on mutual and balanced force reductions in Europe began at the end of 1973 in the climate of the (short-lived) detente of the early 1970s. They would only come to a conclusion with the end of the Cold War.

33 See CIIPS, *1990 Guide*, 111–16 for Canadian contributions to verification.

34 Ibid., 96.
35 Barbara McDougall signed the Chemical Weapons Convention on behalf of Canada, noting that it was the first "ever both to ban a complete category of weapons of mass destruction and to provide for comprehensive verification." Secretary of State for External Affairs, *Statement*, No. 93/1, 13 January 1993.
36 Legault, "Some Aspects of Canadian Diplomacy in the Area of Disarmament and Arms Control," in English and Hillmer, *Making a Difference*, 179.
37 *The Disarmament Bulletin*, no. 18 (winter 1991/92), 1.
38 Legault and Fortmann, *A Diplomacy of Hope: Canada and Disarmament*, 575–6. They added that, in the future, Canada "can best make her influence felt through the 'peace through law' approach, both for historical and cultural reasons."
39 Boutros Boutros-Ghali, *An Agenda for Peace*, 28.
40 See, for instance, External Affairs Minister Barbara McDougall's statements at the December 1991 Toronto conference on "Has Canada Made a Difference?"
41 See Norton and Weiss, "Superpowers and Peace-Keepers."
42 It should be noted that Canada has also participated in non-UN peacekeeping missions. The most important recent one is Multinational Force and Observers (MFO), created to monitor the implementation of the 1974 Camp David Accord between Israel and Egypt. Canada joined the MFO in 1986, at times with 140 personnel.
43 Boutros-Ghali, *An Agenda for Peace*, 11.
44 Morrison, "Canada's Peace and Security Agenda: A Seminar Report," 12.
45 McDougall, "Introduction," in English and Hillmer, *Making a Difference?*, x.
46 McDougall, Address to the American Society, New York, 17 May 1993; Secretary of State for External Affairs, *Statement*, 93/36, 3.
47 *Chronicle*, January–March 1989, 16; April–June 1989, 15; January–March 1992, 11; Government of Canada, *News Release*, no. 231, 11 December 1992; *Chronicle*, July–September 1991, 10.
48 *Chronicle*, April–June 1992, 18–19; July–September 1992, 16–17.
49 Wirick, "Canada, Peacekeeping, and the United Nations," 95.
50 Dirks, "World Refugees: The Canadian Response," 1.
51 Nolan, in Matthews and Pratt, eds., *Human Rights in Canadian Foreign Policy*, 333.
52 *International Canada*, October and November 1986, 15.
53 *Statements and Speeches*, 24 September 1986, quoted by Nolan, 113.
54 Department of External Affairs, *Communiqué* no. 162, 14 August 1987, 2, 3.
55 Joe Clark to the House of Commons, 2 December 1987, reprinted in Blanchette, ed., *Canadian Foreign Policy, 1977–1992*, 23.
56 Ibid., 25. This was contained in Joe Clark's response to the report by the House of Commons Special Committee on Central America, 26 September 1988.

57 Quoted in ibid., 22, from Mark MacGuigan's speech to the University of Toronto Law Faculty, 31 March 1982.
58 Ibid., 24.
59 Ibid., 25.
60 Brown, "Canada and Southern Africa: Autonomy, Image, and Capacity in Foreign Policy," in Molot and Hampson, eds., *Canada Among Nations*, 223.
61 Nossal, "Cabin'd, Cribb'd, Confin'd?: Canada's Interest in Human Rights," in Matthews and Pratt, eds., *Human Rights in Canadian Foreign Policy*, 57–9.
62 Ibid., 303.
63 Wood, "Canada and Southern Africa: A Return to Middle Power Activism," 285.
64 Ibid., 286.
65 Munton and Shaw, "Apartheid and Canadian Public Opinion," 10–11.
66 DEA *Communiqué*, 14 August 1987, 2.
67 Mahoney, "Human Rights and Canada's Foreign Policy," 589.
68 See World Commission on Environment and Development, *Our Common Future*, 359.
69 MacNeill, "The Greening of International Relations," 15–34.
70 The greenhouse effect denotes that heat is kept from escaping into outer space. It is thus suspected as capable of leading to the rise in the earth's temperature with potentially catastrophic consequences. Put succinctly, "the more greenhouse gases, the more is reradiated and the warmer the planet gets." *Washington Post National Weekly Edition*, 8–14 June 1992, 6.
71 *Chronicle*, January–March 1989, 20.
72 Hampson, "Pollution Across Borders: Canada's International Environmental Agenda," in Molot and Hampson, *Canada among Nations*, 183.
73 Canada's frustrations regarding acid rain originating south of its border were appeased by the signing of the first Canadian-US Air Quality Agreement. It was finalized during George Bush's March 1991 visit to Ottawa. Both sides were committed to reduce sulfur dioxide and nitrogen oxide emissions, among other things. *Chronicle*, January–March 1991, 11.
74 *Chronicle*, January–March 1989, 22.
75 Quoted in Blanchette, ed., *Canadian Foreign Policy*, 123.
76 *Chronicle*, January–March 1989, 20–1.
77 Blanchette, ed., *Canadian Foreign Policy*, 123 (emphasis added).
78 Buxton, "Sustainable Development and the Summit: A Canadian Perspective on Progress," 783, 776.
79 *Chronicle*, April-June 1992, 13–14.
80 Cooper and Fritz, "Bringing the NGOs in: UNCED and Canada's International Environmental Policy," 804–11.
81 For this distinction, see Nossal, *The Politics of Canadian Foreign Policy*, ch. 4. Nossal's scepticism, however, leads him to downplay the role of NGOs in Canadian foreign policymaking.

82 DEA *Communiqué*, 14 August 1987, 2.
83 Canadian International Development Agency, *Report to CIDA: Public Attitudes Toward International Development Assistance*, 12.
84 Ibid., 9.
85 OECD, *Development Cooperation, 1992 Report*, 84.
86 The latest example of anti-CIDA lamentation is Pratt, ed., *Canadian International Development Assistance Policies: an Appraisal.* For a judgment that praises the contributions of David Gillies, Martin Rudner, and Jean-Philippe Thérien, see my review of the Pratt volume in *Canadian Journal of Political Science*, 188–90.
87 OECD, *Development Cooperation, 1992 Report*, 92. The figures for the EC member-states exclude their EEC aid contributions.
88 Clark, "Overseas Development Assistance: The Neo-Conservative Challenge," in Molot and Hampson, eds., *Canada Among Nations, 1989*, 199.
89 See O'Neill and Clark, "Canada and International Development," in Hampson and Maule, eds., *Canada Among Nations, 1992–93*, 226, 230.
90 See *Chronicle*, October–December 1991, for details.
91 O'Neill and Clark, "Canada and International Development," 228, 232.
92 It should be stressed that even the participation in the Gulf War – probably because it attracted dubious popularity – was constantly couched by Ottawa in explicitly UN-premised terms.
93 See *North-South News*. The excerpt is from Joe Clark's speech to the University of Western Ontario, 26 October 1990.

CHAPTER 8

1 Liberal Party of Canada, *Creating Opportunity: The Liberal Plan for Canada*, chs. 1–4, 104–6. The last section of chapter 4 ("Sustainable Development") adopted the notion of Canada's international leadership in this field: "Canada must promote sustainable development around the world. Under a Liberal government, environmental security through sustainable development will be a cornerstone of Canadian foreign policy; we will promote this goal at forums such as UN agencies as well as through bilateral and multilateral aid programs" (p. 70).
2 Ibid., 105–6.
3 Government of Canada, *Canada in the World: Government Statement*, iv; Special Joint Committee of the Senate and the House of Commons Reviewing Canadian Foreign Policy, *Canada's Foreign Policy: Principles and Priorities for the Future.*
4 Ibid., 1, 2.
5 Ibid., 1. The report also noted: "Foreign policy matters to Canadians. They have deep-rooted values that they carry over into the role they want Canada to play – nurturing dialogue and compromise; promoting democracy,

human rights, economic and social justice; caring for the environment; safeguarding peace; and easing poverty."

6 Ibid., 8. Special acknowledgment is deserved by the writers of the report, Albert Breton and John Halstead.

7 Ibid., 8.

8 Ibid., 76. We may recall that one aspect of this strategy was employed most successfully by the Trudeau government at the 1972 Stockholm Conference on the Human Environment.

9 Ibid., 81.

10 Ibid., 81–3. Notable are also the following statements:
It is the Committee's conclusion that it would be undesirable as well as unrealistic for Canada to try to choose between bilateralism, regionalism and multilateralism. We must play in all three games ... Clearly the objective should be to maximize Canada's leverage to protect its independence and its interests, to promote rules-based regimes, and to strengthen the international institutions best suited to provide this framework.

11 Ibid., 61–71.

12 Ibid., 88.

13 *Government Response to the Recommendations of the Special Joint Parliamentary Committee Reviewing Canadian Foreign Policy* (Ottawa: February 1995).

14 *Canada in the World*, i, 9, and 10.

15 *Creating Opportunities*, 105, 23, 24.

16 Alexandroff, "Global Economic Change," in Molot and Riekhoff, eds., *Canada Among Nations, 1994*, 49.

17 *Chronicle*, January–March 1994, 15.

18 During this meeting, the two leaders discussed Canada's revisionist requests but "left it to their trade ministers to continue these negotiations." Ibid., October–December 1993, 15–16.

19 A fee of $1,500 was charged to us fishing vessels passing through Canada's territorial waters. *Chronicle*, April–June 1994, 13.

20 Ibid., July–September 1994, 13, 14; October–December 1994, 14.

21 Ibid., April–June 1994, 13.

22 "Closing Remarks," in Chrétien, ed., *Finding Common Ground*, 245.

23 Quoted in Alexandroff, "Global Economic Change," 44.

24 *Chronicle*, April–June 1994, 21.

25 Ibid., October–December 1994, 23–4.

26 Ibid., January–March 1994, 24.

27 Ibid., July–September 1994, 22: "A joint production agreement for films, television programs and videos signed on July 20 should encourage the development of economic and cultural relations between Canada and Japan."

28 Department of Foreign Affairs and International Trade (DFAIT), *Statement* 95/3.

29 *Chronicle*, January–March 1994, 25.

30 Ibid., July–September 1994, 22.

31 DFAIT, *Statement* 95/13, 22 February 1995.

32 *Chronicle*, January–March 1994, 26.

33 Ibid., July–September 1994, 24.

34 Ibid., 17–18.

35 *Chronicle*, January–March 1995, 15–16. According to *Chronicle*, July–September 1994, 17, "Canada's 1993 exports to Argentina were 23 per cent higher than in 1992, and exports to Brazil rose by 20 per cent; in the same year Canada imported $115 million worth of goods from Argentina and $788 million worth from Brazil."

36 DFAIT, *News Release* 240, 29 December 1995.

37 DFAIT, *Statement* 95/2, 18 January 1995, from an address to the Centre for International Studies and the Centre for International Business, entitled "Canada's Trade Policy for the 21st Century: The Walls of Jericho Fall Down."

38 *Chronicle*, July–September 1994, 23.

39 Ibid. CIDA will "implement projects enabling China to attain the objectives of the United Nations Conference on Environment and Development (UNCED)." These projects will cover energy conservation in buildings, "set standards for environmentally sound industrial production, and establish a sustainable development strategy for the resources of the Tarim Basin."

40 See the *Globe and Mail* editorial of 2 March 1996 for an excellent analysis and endorsement of Lloyd Axworthy's decision.

41 *Chronicle*, April–June 1994, 19–20. The UN mission in Rwanda was led at the time by Canadian Major-General Roméo Dallaire.

42 Ibid., July–September 1994, 20–1. Canadian Major-General Guy Toussignant was appointed commander of the mission after August 1994 when Roméo Dallaire's term ended.

43 DFAIT, *News Release 1*, 4 January 1995.

44 Government of Canada, *Towards a Rapid Reaction Capability for the United Nations*, 66.

45 *Chronicle*, July–September 1995, 9.

46 Mickleburgh, "China Agrees to Let UN Take Look at Rights Issues."

47 Letter attached to *Government Response*, 5–6.

48 *Chronicle*, October–December 1994, 10. The number of all immigrants for 1995 was set at 215,000.

49 Ibid., July–September 1995, 8.

50 Ibid., 16.

51 Letter by Ouellet and MacLaren, 5.

52 Department of Foreign Affairs and International Trade, *News Release 12*, 28 January 1996.

53 Canada was represented by the environmental ambassador, John Fraser, and parliamentary secretary to the minister of the environment, Clifford Lincoln. *News Release 82*, 25 April 1994.

54 *Chronicle*, April–June 1995, 7–8.
55 Ibid., July–September 1994, 12.
56 Ibid., July–September 1995, 8.
57 Martin, *Budget Speech*, 15.
58 Knox, "Rich Nations Failing Poor, Report Says."
59 *Canada's Foreign Policy*, 47, 50, 57.
60 Ibid., 58.
61 *Government Response*, 62, 67, and 71.
62 Ibid., 58.
63 See *Chronicle*, April–June 1995, 8–9, and chairman's statement and final news release of the Halifax Summit, 15–17 June 1995.
64 An impressionistic indicator is the limited space recently occupied by this bilateral relationship in the *Chronicle*. At most, one and a half pages are devoted to it, out of a typical length of eighteen pages per issue.
65 See Sallot, "Canada Casts Net for Input on Haiti." Although the immediate stimulus was provided by the Canadian plans for renewed peacekeeping in Haiti, Lloyd Axworthy "intends to use the Internet regularly, but it will not replace more traditional sorts of consultations, such as public forums, parliamentary hearings and face-to-face meetings."

CHAPTER 9

1 Chapter I of the United Nations Charter is entitled "Purposes and Principles." Article 1 sets out these "Purposes" as going beyond the maintenance of international peace and security, to include the development of "friendly relations among nations" and the strengthening of "universal peace"; the achievement of international cooperation in solving economic, social, cultural and humanitarian problems; the encouragement of respect for human rights and "for fundamental freedoms for all without distinction as to race, sex, language, or religion"; and the harmonization of the actions of nations "in the attainment of these common ends."
2 These were the leading epithets attached to Canada by the respondents to Peyton Lyon and Brian Tomlin's relevant research. See *Canada as an International Actor*, 83.
3 This might well have been one reason why Marshall McLuhan once quipped that he did not mind predicting, as long as what he predicted had already occurred!
4 For a sophisticated survey of relevant grounds, see Pratt, ed., *Middle Power Internationalism: The North-South Dimension*. For an analysis of the nature and possible global consequences of the micro-electronic revolution, see Kaplinsky, "Technological Revolution and the Restructuring of Trade Production," in ibid.

5 Doxey, "New States, New Problems in the Post-Cold War World," 19, 18 and 16. See also Stanley Hoffmann's recent argument on "the realm of chaos" (regarding "disintegrating states") and the "confused" responses of what he terms "liberal internationalism," in "The Crisis of Liberal Internationalism."

6 See, for instance, the editorial of *The Economist*, "Where will the jobs come from?" as reprinted in the *Globe and Mail*, 25 May 1993. It predicted that future new jobs will "share two important features": first, many of them "will require more education and skills than the jobs they replace"; and second, "fewer workers will have full-time, permanent jobs." *The Economist* concluded that tomorrow's workers "will have to be more adaptable, but their employment prospects should be brighter. A challenging rather than dispiriting message."

7 Pratt, *Middle Power Internationalism*, 160.

8 See Wood, "Towards North-South Middle Power Coalitions," in ibid.

9 MacNeill, "The Greening of International Relations," 14.

10 *The Economist*, 4 March 1995, 46.

11 Walsh, "us, Denmark Worlds Apart in How They View Foreign Aid."

12 United Nations, Press Release DH 1847, 9 March 1995.

13 Keating, "The Future of Multilateralism," 12.

14 For an earlier discussion of these arguments see Constantine Melakopides, "Ethics and International Relations: A Critique of Cynical Realism," in Haglund and Hawes, eds., *World Politics: Power, Interdependence and Dependence*. David Gillies, reporting on the 1993 Vienna Conference on Human Rights, wrote: "Over 1,000 NGOs were in Vienna. They came from all points of the compass and represented every conceivable cause. This convincing expression of a *growing international civil society* was itself one of the major achievements of the world conference." See "Vienna and After: The United Nations Human Rights Agenda," 28 (emphasis added). For further evidence on the underlying universalism of the values of international NGOs, see Cooper, "Questions of Sovereignty: Canada and the Widening International Agenda." *Behind the Headlines*.

Bibliography

Alexandroff, Alan S. "Global Economic Change: Fashioning Our Own Way." In *Canada Among Nations, 1994: A Part of the Peace*, ed. Maureen Appel Molot and Harald von Riekhoff. Ottawa: Carleton University Press 1994.

Arbour, Frances. " 'America's Backyard': Central America." In *Human Rights in Canadian Foreign Policy*, ed. Robert O. Matthews and Cranford Pratt. Kingston and Montreal: McGill-Queen's University Press 1988.

Axworthy, Tom. "A Singular Voice: The Foreign Policy of Pierre Elliott Trudeau." In *Pierre Elliott Trudeau: Lifting the Shadow of War*, ed. David C. Crenna. Edmonton: Hurtig Publishers 1987.

– "To Stand Not So High Perhaps But Always Alone: The Foreign Policy of Pierre Elliott Trudeau." In *Towards a Just Society: The Trudeau Years*, ed. Tom Axworthy and Pierre E. Trudeau. Markham, Ont.: Viking 1990.

Balawyder, Aloysius, ed. *Canada-Soviet Relations, 1939–1980*. Oakville, Ont.: Mosaic Press 1981.

Banks, Michael. "The Evolution of International Relations Theory." In *Conflict in World Society*, ed. Michael Banks. Brighton: Wheatsheaf Books 1984.

– "The Inter-Paradigm Debate." In *International Relations: A Handbook of Current Theory*, ed. M. Light and A.J.R. Groom. London: Frances Pinter 1985.

Barrett, John. "Arms Control and Canada's Security Policy." *International Journal* 42:4 (autumn 1987).

Beitz, Charles. *Political Theory and International Relations*. Princeton: Princeton University Press 1979.

– "Recent International Thought." *International Journal* 43:2 (spring 1988).

Black, J.L. and Norman Hillmer. "Canada and the Soviet Union as Neighbours." In *Nearly Neighbours: Canada and the Soviet Union from Cold War to Detente and Beyond*, ed. J.L. Black and Norman Hillmer. Kingston, Ont.: R.P. Frye 1989.

Blake, David H. and Robert S. Walters. *The Politics of Global Economic Relations.* Englewood Cliffs, NJ: Prentice-Hall 1987.

Blanchette, Arthur E., ed. *Canadian Foreign Policy, 1955–1965: Selected Speeches and Documents.* Toronto: McClelland and Stewart 1977.

– *Canadian Foreign Policy, 1966–1976: Selected Speeches and Documents.* Ottawa: The Carleton Library 118, 1980.

– *Canadian Foreign Policy, 1972–1992: Selected Speeches and Documents.* Ottawa: Carleton University Press 1994.

Bothwell, Robert and J.L. Granatstein. *Pirouette: Pierre Trudeau and Canadian Foreign Policy.* Toronto: University of Toronto Press 1990.

Boutros-Ghali, Boutros. *An Agenda for Peace: Preventive Diplomacy, Peacemaking and Peacekeeping.* New York: UN Department of Public Information 1992.

– "A New Departure on Development." *Foreign Policy 98* (autumn 1995).

Brewer, Thomas L. *American Foreign Policy: A Contemporary Introduction.* 2nd ed. Englewood Cliffs, NJ: Prentice-Hall 1986.

Bromke, Adam. "Canada's Relations with the USSR and Eastern Europe." In *From Mackenzie King to Pierre Trudeau: Forty Years of Canadian Diplomacy, 1945–1985*, ed. Paul Painchaud. Québec: Les Presses de l'Université Laval 1989.

– and Kim Richard Nossal. "Tensions in Canada's Foreign Policy." *Foreign Affairs* 62:2 (winter 1983–4).

Brown, Chris. "Canada and Southern Africa: Autonomy, Image and Capacity in Foreign Policy." In *Canada Among Nations, 1989: The Challenge of Change*, ed. Maureen Appel Molot and Fen Osler Hampson. Ottawa: Carleton University Press 1990.

Brown, Chris. "Marxism and International Ethics." In *Traditions of International Ethics*, ed. Terry Nardin and David R. Mapel. Cambridge and New York: Cambridge University Press 1992.

Burns, E.L.M. *A Seat at the Table: The Struggle for Disarmament.* Toronto: Clarke, Irwin 1972.

Buxton, G.V. "Sustainable Development and the Summit: A Canadian Perspective on Progress." *International Journal* 42:3 (autumn 1992).

Calder, Kenneth J. and Francis Furtado. "Canadian Defence Policy in the 1990s: International and Domestic Determinants." *Canadian Defence Quarterly* (August 1991).

Canada. House of Commons. *Debates.* 9 July 1943.

– Department of External Affairs. *Statements and Speeches.* No. 47/2, 13 Jan. 1947.

– External Aid Office. *Annual Review, 1966–67.*

– *Foreign Policy for Canadians.* Ottawa: Queen's Printer 1970.

– *Canada and the United Nations, 1945–1975.* Ottawa: Supply and Services Canada 1977.

– *Competitiveness and Security: Directions of Canada's International Relations.* Ottawa: Supply and Services Canada 1985.

- *Canada's International Relations: Response of the Government of Canada to the Report of the Joint Committee of the Senate and the House of Commons.* Ottawa: Supply and Services Canada 1986.
- Report of the Special Joint Committee of the Senate and House of Commons on Canada's International Relations. *Independence and Internationalism.* Ottawa: Supply and Services Canada 1986.
- External Affairs and International Trade. "Task Force on Central and Eastern Europe" (summer 1992).
- *Canada's Foreign Policy: Principles and Priorities for the Future.* Report of the Special Joint Committee Reviewing Canadian Foreign Policy. Ottawa: Parliamentary Publications Directorate, November 1994.
Government of Canada. *Canada in the World: Government Statement.* Ottawa: DFAIT, February 1995.
- *Towards a Rapid Reaction Capability for the United Nations: Report of the Government of Canada.* Ottawa, September 1995.
- Department of National Defence. *Challenge and Commitment: A Defence Policy for Canada.* Ottawa: Supply and Services Canada 1987.
- Defence Update. Ottawa: Department of National Defence, March 1988.
- Environment Canada. *Canada and the Human Environment.* Ottawa: Information Canada 1972.
- *Conference on the Human Environment.* Ottawa: Information Canada 1972.
Canadian International Development Agency. *Report to CIDA: Public Attitudes Toward International Development Assistance, 1990.* Ottawa: Supply and Services Canada 1990.
Canadian Institute for International Peace and Security. *1990 Guide to Canadian Policies on Arms Control, Disarmament, Defence and Conflict Resolution.* Ottawa: CIIPS October 1990.
- *Peace and Security.*
Canadian International Relations Chronicle.
Chapin, P.H. "The Canadian Public and Foreign Policy." *International Perspectives* (January-February 1986).
Chrétien, Jean. "Closing Remarks." In *Finding Common Ground.* Hull, Québec: Voyageur Publishing 1992.
Clark, Robert E. "Overseas Development Assistance: The Neo-Conservative Challenge." In *Canada Among Nations, 1989: The Challenge of Change,* ed. Maureen Appel Molot and Fen Osler Hampson. Ottawa: Carleton University Press 1990.
Clarkson, Stephen, ed. *An Independent Foreign Policy for Canada?* Toronto: McClelland and Stewart 1968.
- *Canada and the Reagan Challenge.* Toronto: Lorimer 1982.
Collins, Larry. "Canadian-Soviet Relations during the Cold War." In *Canadian-Soviet Relations, 1939–1980.* Oakville, Ont.: Mosaic Press 1981.

Cooper, Andrew Fenton and J.-Stefan Fritz. "Bringing the NGOs in: UNCED and Canada's International Environmental Policy." *International Journal* 47:3 (autumn 1992).

– "Questions of Sovereignty: Canada and the Widening International Agenda." *Behind the Headlines* 50:3 (spring 1993).

Crenna, C. David, ed. *Pierre Elliott Trudeau: Lifting the Shadow of War.* Edmonton: Hurtig Publishers 1987.

Dayal, Rajeshwar. "The Power of Wisdom." *International Journal* 29:1 (1973–4).

Dewitt, David and John Kirton. *Canada as a Principal Power: A Study in Foreign Policy and International Relations.* Toronto: John Wiley & Sons 1983.

Diefenbaker, John G. *One Canada: The Tumultuous Years 1962 to 1967.* Toronto: Macmillan of Canada 1977.

Dirks, Gerald E. "World Refugees: The Canadian Response." *Behind the Headlines.* Toronto: CIIA 45:5 (June 1988).

The Disarmament Bulletin.

Dobell, Peter C. *Canada's Search for New Roles: Foreign Policy in the Trudeau Era.* London: Oxford University Press 1972.

– *Canada in World Affairs, 1971–73.* Toronto: Canadian Institute of International Affairs 1985.

Doran, Charles. *Forgotten Partnership: US–Canada Relations Today.* Toronto: Fitzhenry & Whiteside 1984.

Doxey, Margaret. "John Holmes: An Appreciation." *Behind the Headlines* 46:1 (1988).

– "New States, New Problems in the Post-Cold War World." *Behind the Headlines* 51:1 (autumn 1993).

Eayrs, James. "The Origins of Canada's Department of External Affairs." *Canadian Journal of Economics and Political Science* 25:2 (1959).

– *In Defence of Canada.* Vol. II: *Appeasement and Rearmament,* and Vol. III: *Peacemaking and Deterrence.* Toronto: University of Toronto Press 1965 and 1972.

English, John. *Shadow of Heaven: The Life of Lester Pearson – Volume One: 1887–1948.* Toronto: Lester and Orpen Dennys 1989.

– *The Worldly Years: The Life of Lester Pearson: II, 1949–1972.* Toronto and New York: Alfred A. Knopf Canada 1992.

Foster, John W. "The UN Commission on Human Rights." In *Human Rights in Canadian Foreign Policy,* ed. Robert O. Matthews and Cranford Pratt. Kingston and Montreal: McGill-Queen's University Press 1988.

Fraser, Blair. *The Search for Identity: Canada, 1945–67.* Garden City, NY: Doubleday and Co. 1967.

Gaddis, J.L. "The Emerging Post-Revisionist Synthesis on the Origins of the Cold War." *Diplomatic History* 7:3 (1983).

Ghent, Jocelyn M. "Cooperation in Science and Technology." In *Canadian-Soviet Relations, 1939–1980.* Oakville, Ont.: Mosaic Press 1981.

Gilles, David. "Vienna and After: The United Nations Human Rights Agenda." *Behind the Headlines* 51:1 (autumn 1993).

Girard, Charlotte S.M. *Canada in World Affairs, 1963–1965.* Toronto: Canadian Institute of International Affairs 1980.

Gordon, J. King, ed. *Canada's Role as a Middle Power.* Toronto: Canadian Institute of International Affairs 1966.

Granatstein, J.L. *Canadian Foreign Policy: Historical Readings.* Toronto: Copp Clark Pitman 1986.

Gwyn, Richard and Sandra Gwyn. "The Politics of Peace." *Saturday Night,* May 1984.

Hamilton, Edward K. "Thoughts on the Chairman." *International Journal* 29:1 (1973–4).

Hampson, Fen Osler. "Pollution Across Borders: Canada's International Environmental Agenda." In *Canada Among Nations, 1989.* Ottawa: Carleton University Press 1990.

Hawes, Michael K. *Principal Power, Middle Power, or Satellite?* Toronto: York Research Program in Strategic Studies 1984.

Hoffmann, Stanley. "The Crisis of Liberal Internationalism." *Foreign Policy* 98 (autumn 1995).

– *Duties Beyond Borders: On the Limits and Possibilities of Ethical International Politics.* Syracuse: Syracuse University Press 1981.

Hollins, Harry et al. *The Conquest of War.* Boulder: Westview Press 1989.

Holmes, John W. *Life with Uncle: the Canadian-American Relationship.* Toronto: University of Toronto Press 1981.

– *The Better Part of Valour: Essays on Canadian Diplomacy.* Toronto 1970.

Howard, Rhoda E. "Black Africa and South Africa." In *Human Rights in Canadian Foreign Policy,* ed. Robert O. Matthews and Cranford Pratt. Kingston and Montreal: McGill-Queen's University Press 1988.

Hurtig, Mel. *The Betrayal of Canada.* Toronto: Stoddard 1991.

Jönsson, Christer. *Superpower: Comparing American and Soviet Foreign Policy.* London: Frances Pinter 1984.

Keating, Tom. *Canada and World Order: The Multilateralist Tradition in Canadian Foreign Policy.* Toronto: McClelland and Stewart 1993.

– "The Future of Multilateralism." *Behind the Headlines* 51:1 (autumn 1993).

Keenleyside, T.A. "Development Assistance." In *Human Rights in Canadian Foreign Policy,* ed. Robert O. Matthews and Cranford Pratt. Kingston and Montreal: McGill-Queen's University Press 1988.

– and Patricia Taylor. "The Impact of Human Rights Violations on the Conduct of Canadian Foreign Policy: A Contemporary Dilemma." *Behind the Headlines* 42:2 (November 1984).

Keohane, Robert and Joseph Nye, Jr. *Power and Interdependence.* 2nd ed. Glenview, Ill.: Scott, Foresman/Little, Brown 1989.

Keohane, Robert. *Neorealism and Its Critics*. New York: Columbia University Press 1986.

– "Multilateralism: An Agenda for Research." *International Journal* 45:3 (1990).

Kennedy, John F. "On Diplomacy in the Nuclear Age." *International Journal* 29:1 (1973–4). Special Issue, "Lester Pearson's Diplomacy."

Knox, Paul. "Rich Nations Failing Poor, Report Says." *Globe and Mail*, 14 June 1995.

Kubalkova, V. and A.A. Cruickshank. *Marxism and International Relations*. Oxford: Clarendon Press 1985.

Lafeber, Walter. *America, Russia, and the Cold War, 1945–1984*. 5th ed. New York: Alfred A. Knopf 1985.

Langille, Howard Peter. *Changing the Guard: Canada's Defence in a World of Transition*. Toronto: University of Toronto Press 1990.

LaPierre, Laurier, ed. *If You Love this Country: Facts and Feelings on Free Trade*. Toronto: McClelland and Stewart 1987.

LeBlank, Philippe. "Canada at the UN Human Rights Commission." *International Perspectives* (September-October 1985).

Legault, Albert. "Some Aspects of Canadian Diplomacy in the Area of Disarmament and Arms Control, 1945–1988." In *Making a Difference? Canada's Foreign Policy in a Changing World*, ed. John English and Norman Hillmer. Toronto: Lester Publishing 1992.

– and Michel Fortmann. *A Diplomacy of Hope: Canada and Disarmament, 1945–1988*. Montreal and Kingston: McGill-Queen's University Press 1992.

Liberal Party of Canada. *Creating Opportunity: The Liberal Plan for Canada*. Ottawa: Liberal Party of Canada 1993.

Lloyd, Trevor. *Canada in World Affairs, 1957–1959*. Toronto: Oxford University Press 1968.

Lyon, Peyton. *Canada in World Affairs, 1961 to 1963*. Toronto: Oxford University Press 1968.

– "Introduction." In *Canada and the Third World*, ed. Peyton Lyon and Tareq Ismael. Toronto: Macmillan 1976.

– and Brian Tomlin. *Canada as an International Actor*. Toronto: Macmillan 1979.

– "The Evolution of Canadian Diplomacy since 1945." In *From Mackenzie King to Pierre Trudeau: Forty Years of Canadian Diplomacy, 1945–1985*, ed. Paul Painchaud. Québec: Les Presses de l'Université Laval 1989.

Lumsden, Ian, ed. *Close the 49th Parallel: The Americanization of Canada*. Toronto: University of Toronto Press 1970.

Mahoney, Kathleen E. "Human Rights and Canadian Foreign Policy." *International Journal* 47:3 (summer 1992).

MacNeil, Jim. "The Greening of International Relations." *International Journal* 45:1 (winter 1989–90).

Martin, Lawrence. *The Presidents and the Prime Ministers: Washington and Ottawa Face to Face: The Myth of Bilateral Bliss, 1867–1982*. Toronto: Paperjacks 1983.

Martin, Paul. *Paul Martin Speaks for Canada: A Selection of Speeches on Foreign Policy, 1964–67.* Toronto and Montreal: McClelland and Stewart 1967.

Martin, Paul Jr. *The Budget Speech.* Ottawa: Department of Finance, 22 February 1994.

Masse, Marcel. *Canadian Defence Policy.* Ottawa: Department of National Defence, April 1992.

Matthews, Robert O. and Cranford Pratt, eds. *Human Rights in Canadian Foreign Policy.* Kingston and Montreal: McGill-Queen's University Press 1988.

McDougall, Barbara. "Introduction." In *Making a Difference? Canada's Foreign Policy in a Changing World,* ed. John English and Norman Hillmer. Toronto: Lester Publishing 1992.

McMillan, Carl H. "Canada's Postwar Economic Relations with the USSR – An Appraisal." In *Canadian-Soviet Relations, 1939–1980,* ed. Aloysius Balawyder. Oakville, Ont.: Mosaic Press 1981.

Meisel, John. "Escaping Extinction: Cultural Defence of an Undefended Border." In *Southern Exposure: Canadian Perspectives on the United States,* ed. D.H. Flaherty and W.R. McKercher. Toronto: McGraw-Hill Ryerson 1986.

Melakopides, Constantine. "Marxological Investigations." *Queen's Quarterly* 89:1 (1982).

– "Ethics and International Relations: A Critique of Cynical Realism." In *World Politics: Power, Interdependence and Dependence,* ed. David Haglund and Michael Hawes. Toronto: Harcourt Brace Jovanovich Canada 1990.

– Review of *Canadian International Development Assistance Policies: An Appraisal,* ed. Cranford Pratt. In *Canadian Journal of Political Science* 28:1 (March 1995).

Mickleburgh, Rod. "China Agrees to Let UN Take Look at Rights Issues." *Globe and Mail,* 16 February 1996.

Middlemiss, D.W. and Joel Sokolsky. *Canadian Defence: Decisions and Determinants.* Toronto: Harcourt Brace Jovanovich Canada 1989.

Morrison, Alex. "Canada's Peace and Security Agenda: A Seminar Report." *Disarmament Bulletin* 21 (summer 1993).

– "Canada and Peacekeeping: A Time for Reanalysis?" In *Canada's International Security Policy,* ed. David Dewitt and David Leyton-Brown. Scarborough: Prentice-Hall Canada 1995.

Munton, Don. "Reagan, Canada, and the Common Environment." *International Perspectives* (May-June 1982).

– *Peace and Security in the 1980s: The View of Canadians.* Ottawa: Canadian Institute of International Peace and Security 1988.

– and Timothy M. Shaw. "Apartheid and Canadian Public Opinion." *International Perspectives* (September-October 1987).

Munro, John A. and Alex Inglis, ed. *Mike: The Memoirs of the Right Honourable Lester B. Pearson.* Toronto: University of Toronto Press 1973.

– *Mike: The Memoirs of the Right Honourable Lester B. Pearson. III. 1957–68.* Toronto: University of Toronto Press 1975.

Myrdal, Gunnar. *Objectivity in Social Research.* London: Dudworthy 1970.

Nolan, Cathal. "The Human Rights Committee." In *Human Rights in Canadian Foreign Policy,* ed. R.O. Matthews and Cranford Pratt. Kingston and Montreal: McGill-Queen's University Press 1988.

North-South Institute. *North-South News.*

Norton, Augustus R. and Thomas G. Weiss. "Superpowers and Peacekeepers." *Survival* 32:3 (May-June 1990).

Nossal, Kim Richard. *The Politics of Canadian Foreign Policy.* 2nd ed. Scarborough: Prentice-Hall 1989.

– "Cabin'd, Cribb'd, Confin'd?: Canada's Interest in Human Rights." In *Human Rights in Canadian Foreign Policy,* ed. R.O. Matthews and C. Pratt. Kingston and Montreal: McGill-Queen's University Press 1988.

O'Neill, Maureen and Andrew Clark. "Canada and International Development." In *Canada Among Nations, 1992–93: A New World Order?,* ed. F.O. Hampson and Christopher Maule. Ottawa: Carleton University Press 1992.

Organization for Economic Cooperation and Development. *Twenty-Five Years of Development Cooperation: A Review.* Paris: OECD November 1985.

– *Development Cooperation, 1985.* Paris: OECD 1985.

– *Development Cooperation, 1992 Report.* Paris: OECD December 1992.

Peacekeeping and International Relations 22:2 (March/April 1993).

Pearson, Geoffrey. "Trudeau Peace Initiative Reflections." *International Perspectives* (March/April 1985).

Pearson, Lester B. *Words and Occasions.* Toronto: University of Toronto Press 1970.

Peers, Frank. "Oh Say, Can You See?" In *Close the 49th Parallel: The Americanization of Canada,* ed. Ian Lumsden. Toronto: University of Toronto Press 1970.

Pentland, Charles. "Integration, Interdependence, and Institutions: Approaches to International Order." In *World Politics: Power, Interdependence and Dependence,* ed. D.G. Haglund and M.K. Hawes. Toronto: Harcourt Brace Jovanovich Canada 1990.

Pratt, Cranford. "Ethics and Foreign Policy: The Case of Canada's Development Assistance." *International Journal* 43:2 (spring 1988).

– ed. *Internationalism under Strain: The North-South Policies of Canada, the Netherlands, Norway, and Sweden.* Toronto: University of Toronto Press 1989.

– ed. *Middle Power Internationalism: The North-South Dimension.* Kingston and Montreal: McGill-Queen's University Press 1990.

– ed. *Canadian International Development Assistance Policies: An Appraisal.* Montreal and Kingston: McGill-Queen's University Press 1994.

Preston, Richard. *Canada in World Affairs, 1959 to 1961.* Toronto: Oxford University Press 1965.

Ranger, Robin. "The Canadian Perspective." In *The Foreign Policies of the Powers,* ed. F.S. Northedge. 2nd ed. London: Faber & Faber 1974.

Reid, Escott. "Canada and the Struggle Against World Poverty." *International Journal* 25:1 (winter 1969–70).

– "The Creation of the North Atlantic Alliance, 1948–1949." In *Canadian Foreign Policy: Historical Readings*, ed. J.L. Granatstein. Toronto: Copp Clark Pitman 1986.

– *Radical Mandarin*. Toronto: University of Toronto Press 1989.

Robinson, H. Basil. *Diefenbaker's World: A Populist in Foreign Affairs*. Toronto and Buffalo: University of Toronto Press 1989.

Roche, Douglas. "Potential Alternative Strategies for Canada." *Financial Post*, 7 November 1989.

Rosenau, Pauline. "Once Again into the Fray: International Relations Confronts the Humanities." *Millenium* 19:1 (1990).

Rotstein, Abraham and G. Lax, ed. *Independence and the Canadian Challenge*. Toronto: Committee for an Independent Canada 1972.

Sallot, Jeff. "Canada Casts Net for Input on Haiti." *Globe and Mail*, 13 February 1996.

– "Axworthy Vows to Push Rights, 'Canadian Values'." *Globe and Mail*, 14 February 1996.

Sanger, Clyde, ed. *Canadians and the United Nations*. Ottawa: Department of External Affairs 1988.

Secretary of State for External Affairs. "Canada–US Relations: Options for the Future." *International Perspectives*, Special Issue (autumn 1972).

Singer, J. David. "The Responsibilities of Competence in the Global Village." *International Studies Quarterly* 29 (September 1985).

Stairs, Denis. "Present in Moderation: Lester Pearson and the Craft of Diplomacy." *International Journal* 29:1 (1973–4).

– "Free Trade – Another View." *International Perspectives* (May/June 1987).

– "Liberalism, Methodism, and Statecraft: The Secular Life of a Canadian Practitioner." *International Journal* 49:2 (1994).

Thomson, Dale C. and Roger F. Swanson. *Canadian Foreign Policy: Options and Perspectives*. Toronto: McGraw-Hill Ryerson 1971.

Tucker, Michael. *Canadian Foreign Policy: Contemporary Issues and Themes*. Toronto: McGraw-Hill Ryerson 1980.

Viotti, Paul R. and Mark V. Kauppi. *International Relations Theory: Realism, Pluralism, Globalism*. 2nd ed. New York: Macmillan 1993.

Von Riekhoff, Harald. "The Impact of Prime Minister Trudeau on Foreign Policy." *International Journal* 33:2 (spring 1978).

Walsh, Mary Williams. "US, Denmark Worlds Apart in How They View Foreign Aid." *Los Angeles Times*, 12 March 1995.

Wirick, Gregory. "Canada, Peacekeeping and the United Nations." In *Canada Among Nations, 1992–93: A New World Order?* ed. F.O. Hampson and C. Maule. Ottawa: Carleton University Press 1992.

Wood, Bernard. "Canada and Southern Africa: A Return to Middle Power Activism." *The Round Table* 315 (1990).

– "Towards North-South Middle Power Coalitions." In *Middle Power Internationalism: The North-South Dimension*, ed. Cranford Pratt. Kingston and Montreal: McGill-Queen's University Press 1990.

– "Peace and Security in the Midst of International Turmoil." *Peace and Security* 5:2 (summer 1990).

World Commission on Environment and Development. *Our Common Future*. Oxford: Oxford University Press 1987.

Index

Aboriginal peoples, 182–3
Aeroflot, 96
Afghanistan, 94, 149
Africa, 77, 79
Agenda 21, 158
Agenda for Peace, An, 146
Air Canada, 83
Alcan, 99
Altruism, 17
Amchitka, Alaska, 98
Amin, Idi, 110, 111, 115
Amnesty International, 111
Andropov, Yuri, 121
Anti-Americanism, 55, 65, 93
Anti-apartheid, 53, 151–4
Anti-militarism, 125
Anti-nuclearism, 65, 105
Anti-racism, 53, 64, 80–2, 84, 114, 152
Arctic, 97, 130
Arctic Council, 182
Arctic policy, 182
Arctic Waters Pollution Prevention Act, 97
Argentina, 113, 172, 175, 184
Arms control and disarmament, 4, 56–8, 73, 103–6, 141–3; central to "in-

ternationalist agenda," 4; Diefenbaker's record, 56–8; Mulroney's record, 141–3; Trudeau's peace initiative, 105–6; Trudeau's record, 103–6; Trudeau's "suffocation strategy," 103, 121. *See also* Burns, Gen. E.L.M.; Green, Howard; Legault, Albert
Aristide, Jean-Bertrand, 178
ASEAN, 176, 177
Asia Pacific Economic Cooperation (APEC), 187
Atomic Energy of Canada Limited (AECL), 172
Australia, 14, 45, 64, 104, 119, 161, 173, 174, 177
Auto Pact, 70
Axworthy, Lloyd, 177, 182, 187
Axworthy, Thomas, 16, 27–8, 125, 127

Balfour Declaration (1926), 37
Baltic states, 140
Bangladesh, 174, 181

Barbados, 182
Barrett, John, 141
Basel Convention, 157
Beaulne, Yvon, 113
Behaviouralism, 20–1, 23–4
Belgium, 119
Berger, Earl, 60
Berlin blockade (1948–9), 48, 50
Biafra, 120–1, 122
Bill C-58, 10
Bolivia, 197
Bomarc missiles, 55–6, 68
Bosnia-Herzegovina, 177, 198
Bothwell, Robert, 123, 126
Boutros-Ghali, Boutros, 144, 146
Brazil, 155, 172, 175
Bretton Woods Conference, 38, 41–2
Brezhnev, Leonid, 93
British-Canadian Protestant tradition, 85
Bromke, Adam, 95
Brundtland, Gro Harlem, 109
Brundtland Commission, 155

Bulgaria, 68, 156
Burns, Gen. E.L.M., 41, 74, 75, 141
Bush, George, 10
Butler, Richard, 198
Butterworth, Walt, 72

Cambodia, 76, 145, 148, 177
Canada in the World, 11, 168
Canada's Foreign Policy, 166, 184
Canada's International Relations, 129
Canada's status: as a power, 28–30; as bridge-builder, 60; as front-line state, 154; as helpful fixer, 43; as honest broker, 43, 60; as linchpin of the English-speaking world, 38; as middle power, 29–30; as satellite, 154; as top-tier nation, 14
Canadian Arms Control and Disarmament Agency, 136
Canadian distinctness, 50, 99, 167, 192
Canadian Film Development Corporation, 101
Canadian identity, 4, 14, 46, 89, 90, 106, 132, 144; served by pragmatic idealism, 4, 186, 199, 200
Canadian Institute of International Peace and Security, 136
Canadian International Development Agency (CIDA), 89, 118, 120, 160–2, 175, 176, 178, 184–5, 186
Canadian internationalism, 3–14, 15, 17, 26–32; defined, 13; St Laurent on, 6–7; synthesis of idealism and pragmatism, 22
Canadian Jewish Congress, 118

Canadian nationalists, 15, 31, 193–4
Canadian national unity, 8, 82, 90, 117
Canadian political culture, 3–4, 13, 192. *See also* Canadian values, Cosmopolitanism, Canadian public opinion
Canadian public opinion, 137–8, 163; on Central America, 150; on East-West relations, 137; on foreign aid, 150, 160; on human rights, 150; on international security, 137; on South Africa, 153–4; on Third World poverty, 137
Canadian Radio-Television and Telecommunications Commission, 101
Canadian realists, 31, 193–4
Canadian values, 3, 4–5, 11–12, 29, 84, 132, 153, 191, 199; McDougall on, 10; St Laurent on, 6; Trudeau and, 90, 106–7, 116–20, 122–7
CANDU, 79, 104, 172
Caribbean states, 77, 79, 80
Carter, Jimmy, 102, 110
Central African Republic, 113
Ceylon, 45, 64, 79
Challenge and Commitment, 134
Chan, Raymond, 171, 173, 174, 176
Chapin, P.H., 137
Charest, Jean, 159
Chateauguay, 135
Chicago Tribune, 101
Chile, 113, 172, 184
China, Peoples Republic of, 32, 68, 88, 105; and human rights, 32, 172, 179–80; recognition of, 89; trade with, 172–3
Chisholm, Brock, 41
Chrétien, Jean, 94, 98, 170,

171, 175–6, 197; and ecological concerns, 182–4; and foreign aid, 184–5; on globalization, 171; and globalized Canadian trade, 171–6; and human rights, 179–82; and peacekeeping, 177–9; on protectionism, 171; and relations with US, 169–71
Churchill, Winston, 38, 43
Clark, Joe, 94, 136–7, 139, 143, 150, 163; endorsed cooperative security, 10; tutored in Pearsonian internationalism, 9–10
Climate change, 157–8
Clinton administration, 169–70
Collective defence, 43, 96; and containment, 123. *See also* NATO
Collective security, 20, 31, 43. *See also* Common (cooperative) security
Collenette, David, 179
Collins, Larry, 48
Colombo Plan, 45–6, 78, 79
Columbia River Treaty, 67, 68, 69
Common (cooperative) security, 10, 136–7
Commonwealth, 13, 40, 45–6, 63–5, 73, 79–81, 116, 167, 180. *See also* Anti-racism, Colombo Plan, South Africa
Conference on Security and Cooperation in Europe (CSCE/OSCE), 13, 31, 166, 180, 185, 187
Congo, 59, 76, 78
Constructive internationalism, 10, 128, 162–3; endorsed by DEA, 131
Contadora Plan, 150, 151
Containment, 47–8
Contras, 151
Cooper, Andrew Fenton, 159

Cooperative federalism, 82
Copps, Sheila, 183
Cosmopolitanism, 5, 11–12, 26–7, 32, 99, 107, 214 n81; and Trudeau's values, 99, 107, 117, 118, 125
Costa Rica, 145, 172
Counterweights, 44, 73, 102, 144
Creating Opportunities (the Red Book), 164
Cruise missile, 120, 122, 170
Cuba, 68, 143
Cynicism, 122–3
Cyprus, 70, 76
Czechoslovakia, 26, 68, 93, 143

Davidson, George, 41
Dayal, Rajeshwar, 45
Defence Production Sharing Arrangements, 68
Defence Update, 134–5
De Gaulle, Charles, 82–4
De-ideologized trade, Canada's commitment to, 47, 53, 68, 94, 95, 96, 125
Denmark, 13, 76, 119, 161, 184, 197–8
Denuclearization of Canada, 96; 215 n93
Detente, 13, 88, 93, 95
Development Assistance Committee (DAC), 119
Dewitt, David, 14–15, 29, 82, 126
Diefenbaker, John G., 52–65; and anti-racism, 64; and arms control and disarmament, 56–8; and Arrow affair, 54–5; and Bomarc crisis, 54–5; and Commonwealth, 60, 62, 63–5; and Cuban missile crisis, 54, 56, 60; and European Common Market, 63; and External Aid Office, 61; and foreign aid, 60–3; and Kennedy,

53–6, 65; and peacekeeping, 58–69; and World Food Program, 63
Dirks, Gerald E., 149
Dobell, Peter, 15, 27, 66, 77, 92, 118, 127
Dominican Republic, 178
Doran, Charles,
Doxey, Margaret, 43, 195

Ecological concerns, 106–10, 125, 154–60, 182–4. *See also* UN Conference on Environment and Development; UN Conference on the Human Environment
Economist, 61, 197
EH-101 helicopter, 169
Eighteen-Nation Disarmament Committee (ENDC), 73–4, 75
Eisenhower, Dwight D., 40
El Salvador, 113, 145, 151
English, John, 66, 73, 85
Environmental Protection Agency (EPA), 102
Equatorial Guinea, 113
Esquipulas Agreement, 145
Estai, 183
Euromissiles, 96, 105, 121
European Union, 177, 183
Export Development Corporation, 111
External Aid Office, 78

Financial Post, 58
Finland, 76, 161
Firestone, Sheila, 181
First World War, 37
Foreign Investment Review Agency (FIRA), 100
Foster, John W., 113
Fredericton Gleaner, 58
Free Trade Agreement (FTA), 131–3, 169
Foreign aid: 4, 8, 11, 197–8; Chrétien and, 184–5; Diefenbaker and, 60–3; Mulroney and, 160–2; NGOs and, 120, 186; Pearson and, 77–80;

tied aid, criticism of, 119, 122, 124; Trudeau and, 116–20, 122–4. *See also* Canadian public opinion, on foreign aid
Foreign Policy for Canadians, 89–91, 92, 95, 96, 107, 110, 117, 118, 119, 124
Francophonie, 78, 167, 179, 180, 187
Fritz, J.-Stefan, 159
Functionalism, 29, 38, 43, 57, 74–5, 81, 84, 159, 166
Functional principle, 38

Garrison Diversion Project, 102
Gauthier, Jean-Robert, 180
General Agreement on Tariffs and Trade (GATT), 31, 130–1, 162, 169
Germany, 37–8, 44, 84, 119, 161
Georgia, 140
Ghana, 80, 197
Girard, Charlotte, 68, 76
Global Environmental Facility, 182
Global ethic, Trudeau's emphasis on, 9, 28
Goodale, Ralph, 174
Gorbachev, Mikhail, 134, 136, 138, 139, 142, 145
Gordon, Walter, 47, 67
Granatstein, Jack, 123, 126
Greco-Judeo-Christian ethic, 8
Greece, 70, 76
Green, Howard, 53, 56–8, 60, 62, 65, 75
Greenhouse effect, 156
Gromyko, Andrei, 93, 95
Guatemala, 111, 113, 145, 151
Gulf War (1991), 135
Guyana, 80

Habitat Conference, 109
Hague Declaration (on climate change), 157–8
Haiti, 161, 177, 178

Hamilton, Edward K., 86
Hammarskjold, Dag, 59
Hazardous wastes, 157
Head, Ivan, 116
Heath, Edward, 116
Heeney, Arnold, 55, 86
Helsinki Final Act, 110
Hnatyshyn, Ray, 174
Hobbesian conception of human nature, 21–2
Holmes, John, 3, 4, 43, 85
Honduras, 145, 151
Hong Kong, 172, 173
Human betterment, Canada's commitment to, 9, 13, 90
Humane internationalism, 28, 123
Human Rights, 4, 110–16, 148–54; China's record, 32, 172, 179–80; and Chrétien government, 179–82; and Diefenbaker, 64–5; and Mulroney governments, 148–54; as part of internationalist agenda, 4, 10, 179–82; and South Africa, 151–4; and Trudeau, 99, 110–16
Humphrey, John, 112, 115
Hungary, 26, 49, 175

Iceland, 184
Idealism, 3, 4, 19–22, 31; orthodox, 17; major strengths, 21–2; major weaknesses, 22. See also Cosmopolitanism, Pragmatic Idealism
Idealist agenda, 4, 10; downplayed by nationalists and realists, 31–2
Idealist impulse, 15, 16
Ignatieff, George, 141
Independence and Internationalism, 9 , 129, 140
India, 61, 64, 79, 104, 148, 175
Indian nuclear explosion, 126
Indochina, 76

Indonesia, 64, 155, 162, 172, 173, 184
Intermediate-Range Nuclear Forces Treaty (1987), 134, 145
International Atomic Energy Agency, 61
International Bank for Reconstruction and Development (World Bank), 42, 60, 161
International Court of Justice, 158
International Development Research Centre, 89, 118
International ethics, 21
Internationalism, 3, 25–8. See also Canadian Internationalism
International Joint Commission (IJC), 101–2
International Journal, 124
International Labour Organization, 182
International Monetary Fund (IMF), 42, 60
International Perspectives, 105–6
Interventionism, 26
Iran-Iraq War, 141
Iraq, 141, 143
Isolationism, 25, 124
Israel, 145
Italy, 44, 119

Jamaica, 80
Japan, 60, 100, 119, 155, 161, 173, 176, 177
Johnson, Lyndon B., 69–73

Kashmir, 76
Kaunda, Kenneth, 116, 154
Keating, Tom, 16, 60, 199
Keenleyside, Hugh, 41, 86
Kennedy, Howard, 41
Kennedy, John F., 42, 53, 54, 55–6, 67
Kenya, 80, 155
Keohane, Robert, 21
Khrushchev, Nikita, 40, 49
Kim, Chulsu, 174

King, William Lyon Mackenzie, 6, 37–8, 45, 124
Kirton, John, 14–15, 29, 82, 126
Kissinger, Henry, 24
Kono, Yohei, 173
Korean Airlines 747, shooting of, 96, 105
Korean armistice, 41, 43
Korean War, 41, 48
Kosygin, Alexei, 93, 94
Kurdish people, 141

Laos, 76, 92
Latvia, 139, 140
Lebanon, 59
Legault, Albert, 74, 142, 143
Lewis, Stephen, 149–50
Lithuania, 139, 140
Lloyd, Trevor, 61
Lockean conception of human nature, 22
Lonetree Reservoir Dam, 102
Lyon, Peyton, 16, 27, 53, 58, 62, 127; on Diefenbaker, 65; on golden age internationalists, 42–3; on Howard Green, 56–7, 58; on Trudeau's aid record, 119, 120

McDougall, Barbara, 10–11, 146, 147
MacEachen, Allan, 95, 111
MacGuigan, Mark, 150
MacKenzie, Lewis, 148
MacLaren, Roy, 169, 170, 171–6, 180, 181
Maclean's, 75
MacNeill, Jim, 109, 155, 197
Macquarrie, Heath, 59
Mahoney, Kathleen E., 154
Malaya, 64, 79
Malaysia, 79, 173, 174
Mandela, Nelson, 154
Manhattan, 97, 107, 108
Marchi, Sergio, 180, 181
Martin, Lawrence, 30, 71
Martin, Paul, Jr, 184

Martin, Paul, Sr, 7, 42–3, 62–3, 67, 69, 71–2, 77, 129; on arms control and disarmament, 73, 74; on the Commonwealth, 80; implied pragmatic idealism, 77, 85

Marxism, 23

Masse, Marcel, 135

Matthews, Robert, 152

Mentor state, 9, 105, 117, 124, 200

Mexico, 169

Middlemiss, Dan, 140

Middlepowermanship, 13, 50, 56

Mill, John Stuart, 125

Mitterand, François, 122

Mongolia, 176

Montreal Protocol, 156–7

Montreal Star, 58

Moran, Herbert O., 61

Morrison, Alex, 146–7

Mozambique, 115

Multilateralism, 3, 5, 88, 166, 167, 176–85, 198

Murdoch, R.W., 76

Myanmar (Burma), 181

Myrdal, Gunnar, 18

Namibia, 145, 147

Namibia Contact Group, 126

Nansen medal, 149

National Audubon Society, 101

National Energy Policy (NEP), 100

National Forum on Canada's International Relations, 165, 187

National interest, 5; Trudeau's conception of, 92

Nehru, Jawaharlal, 45, 64

Netherlands, 14, 76, 119

New Global Environmental Facility, 159

New York Times, 98

New Zealand, 14, 45, 64, 76, 104, 161, 173, 174, 177, 184

Nicaragua, 145, 151, 197

Niger, 182

Nigeria, 80

Nigerian civil war, 120–1

Nixon, Richard, 98, 101, 125

Nolan, Cathal, 113–14, 149

Non-Proliferation of Nuclear Weapons Treaty, 74

North American Air Defence Command (NORAD), 69, 88, 91–2, 96, 133–4, 135; and Distant Early Warning (DEW) line, 133; and North Warning System (NWS), 133

North Atlantic Fisheries Organization (NAFO), 183

North Atlantic Treaty Organization (NATO), 13, 30, 31, 43–5, 69, 83–4, 91; Mulroney's attitudes towards, 133–4, 135; Pearson's relations with, 43–5; Trudeau's vicissitudes with, 88, 91–3, 96, 121, 122

Northern Inland Waters Act, 107

North Vietnam, 70–2

Northwest Passage, 97

Norway, 14, 76, 119, 155, 161, 184

Nossal, Kim Richard, 14, 28–9, 152

Novak, Michael, 113

Nyerere, Julius, 116

Oka, 135

Organization of African Unity, 121

Organization of American States, 180

Ottawa Declaration (1989), 157

Ouellet, André, 170, 171, 173, 175, 179, 180, 181, 182

Our Common Future, 155

Outer Space Treaty, 75

Ozone depletion, 156–7

Pacific Rim, 100, 169

Pakistan, 45, 61, 64, 79, 176

Palestine, 76

Paris Peace Conference, 37

PAXSAT, 142

Peacebuilding, 146, 164, 177

Peacekeeping: 4, 11, 40, 58–9, 66, 69–70, 75; Canadian vocation in, 144; Chrétien era, 177–9; Mulroney era, 144–8; Pearson and, 75–7. *See also* UNFICYP, UNPROFOR

Peacemaking, 146

Pearson, Geoffrey, 105–6

Pearson, Lester B., 4, 7, 8, 40, 42, 44, 45–6, 47, 52, 62–3, 90; Nobel Peace Prize, 40; operational code, 84–6; as PM, 66–86; values of, 84; visit to the USSR, 49–51

"Pearsonalities," 53, 65

Peru, 184

Pham Van Dong, 72

Philippines, 173

Pitfield, Michael, 141

Pluralism, 24–5

Poland, 68, 95, 148, 175

Polish crisis (1981), 95

Portuguese colonialism, 115

Positivism, 21, 32; of realism, 21

Post-modernism, 25

Post-revisionism, 26

Pragmatic idealism, 3–17, 22, 29, 31, 191; adaptability of, 52; affirmed by Mulroney-Clark, 138; in Chrétien's foreign policy review, 166; defining features, 17, 29; and enlightened self-interest, 78, 89; implied by Pearson, 7; moral dimension of, 77–8; and Trudeau's internationalism, 120–7

Pragmatism, 3, 4, 5, 17, 201 n4; St Laurent's, 6–7; Trudeau's, 99–100, 118
Pravda, 49, 95
Pratt, Cranford, 16, 28, 123, 124, 152, 196
Preston, Richard, 59, 62
Preventive diplomacy, 146, 164, 177

Quebec, 66, 82–4
Quebec separatism, 121

Rasminski, Louis, 42
Reader's Digest, 68
Reagan, Ronald, 10, 95, 101, 122, 125–6, 134, 154
Realism, 5, 14, 19–22; determinism and positivism of, 21; ethical poverty of, 5; imported to study of Canadian foreign policy, 14; major strengths, 20; major weaknesses, 20–1
Realpolitik, 4, 17, 20, 30, 117
Red Book, 164, 165, 167, 169, 171, 187
Reid, Escott, 4, 41–2, 44, 48, 86
Revisionists, 26
Rhodesia, 81, 115, 116
Riddell, Walter, 86
Rikhye, Indar, 76
Robertson, Norman, 42
Robinson, Basil H., 65
Roche, Douglas, 141
Ronning, Chester, 41, 71–2, 86
Rostow, Walt, 55
Royal Commission on Bilingualism and Biculturalism, 82
Russian Federation, 175
Rwanda, 178, 195, 198

St Laurent, Louis, 4, 6, 8, 39–40, 43, 85, 90, 129; and Gray Lecture, 6–7,

39–40, 77
San Francisco Conference, 4, 27, 38–9
Sarajevo, 148
Sauvé, Jeanne, 102
Schmidt, Helmut, 122
Schultz, George, 99
Seaborn, Blair, 72
Second World War, 37–8
Sharp, Mitchell, 68, 72, 93, 115
Shevardnadze, Eduard, 149
Siberia, 182
Singapore, 64, 173, 174
Smith, Arnold, 81
Smith, Sidney, 56
Sokolsky, Joel, 140
Somalia, 146, 164, 177, 195, 198
South Africa, 32, 62, 64–5, 110, 111, 115, 133, 153–4, 174
South African Reserve Bank, 152
South Asia, 77, 173
Southeast Asia, 77
Southern Africa, 81, 114, 115
South Korea, 173, 174, 176
South Vietnam, 79
Sri Lanka, 176
Stairs, Denis, 85
Stalin, Joseph, 40, 43
Statute of Westminster (1931), 37
Stewart, Christine, 171, 174, 181
Stockholm Declaration (1972), 108
Strategic Defence Initiative (SDI), 137
Strong, Maurice, 89, 108, 109, 118, 155, 158
Suez crisis, 40
Supererogation, 28, 123
Sustainable development, 155, 156, 172, 181, 182, 185, 197
Swanson, Roger F., 15, 45, 80, 98
Sweden, 14, 76, 119
Syria, 59, 145

Tanzania, 80
Team Canada, 172, 176, 179–80
Temple University World Peace Award, 70–1
Thailand, 173, 176
Thatcher, Margaret, 152, 154
Third Option, 100
Thomson, Dale C., 15, 45, 80, 98
Thurow, Lester C., 171
Time, 68
Tito, Josip Broz, 93
Tlatelolco, Treaty of, 75
Tobin, Brian, 183–4
Tomlin, Brian, 16, 223 n2
Toronto Star, 122
Toronto Telegram, 58
Trinidad and Tobago, 80, 172
Trudeau, Pierre E., 87–127, 151; ethic of, 103; and global ethic, 103, 107, 118, 125; his synthesis, 89, 114, 116–17, 192
Truman, Harry, S., 40, 43
Tucker, Michael, 15, 27, 99, 11–12, 125, 127
Turbot War, 183
Turkey, 70, 76

Uganda, 80, 113, 115
Ukraine, 140, 175
Union of Soviet Socialist Republics (USSR): Afghanistan invasion by, 94–5; Canada-Russia hockey series, 94; Canada-USSR General Exchanges Agreement, 94; and early Mulroney security perceptions, 133–5; Mulroney's visit, 139; Pearson's visit, 49–51; Polish crisis, 95; Soviet threat, 96 SS-20s, 105; trade with Canada, 68, 95, 138–9; Trudeau's visit, 93–4
United Kingdom, 37, 38, 40, 45–6, 63–4, 81, 119,